BRITISH SHII...............JS

VOLUME 1 : NO...,rH-EAST COAST

by NORMAN L. MIDDLEMISS

SHIELD PUBLICATIONS LTD.
NEWCASTLE-UPON-TYNE
GREAT BRITAIN

ISBN 1 871128 10 2 9

© First Edition   October,1993: N. L. Middlemiss

British Library Cataloguing-in-Publication Data.
A Catalogue Record is available from the British Library

Published by Shield Publications Ltd.
7, Verne Road, North Shields, NE29 7LP.
Printed by Smith Settle, Ilkley Road, Otley.

Cover illustration is a painting of the Austin & Pickersgill Ltd shipyard
by Arthur McNulty

The 'SD14' BELLOC ready for launch on 10th May,1979 at the Southwick yard
of Austin & Pickersgill Ltd.   (Author).

CONTENTS

The Wallsend Yard of Swan Hunter Shipbuilders Ltd in October,1988 with cable-layer SIR ERIC SHARP ready for launch, a Type 23 frigate building under cover, and two patrol boats undergoing repair (centre). (Author).

INTRODUCTION

This major historical study in three Volumes of all British shipbuilding yards that have built ships during the last hundred years is intended for wide readership. The shipyard welder or painter as well as shipbuilding management will find much of interest here as to achievements, and it will also appeal to seafarers and shiplovers. Since this is the first comprehensive British shipyard study to be published, it is wise at the outset to state what this series attempts to do and what it does not do :-

1. On a historical basis, information is given by river or area sector of the ownership and development of each shipyard, and a full analysis of every type of ship built and for which customers. The British shipbuilding industry was centred on or near sources of coal, iron and steel, with Figure 2 giving comparative percentages for the North East Coast, Clydeside, Belfast, Merseyside and Barrow. It can be clearly seen that the bulk of output came from the first two areas, and this series is thus split into three Volumes :-

Volume I   North-East Coast
Volume II   Clydeside
Volume III   Belfast, Merseyside, Barrow and other Areas.

2. The last shipbuilding yard on the North-East Coast, Swan Hunter Shipbuilders Ltd at Wallsend, recently went into receivership and has been put up for sale to any interested buyer at home or overseas. Indeed there are only two yards left in the United Kingdom capable of building large merchant ships, one on the Clyde and the other at Belfast and both are Norwegian-owned. Thus for the British shipbuilding industry it is very much a case of all 'water under the bridge' and the reasons for the decline from complete supremacy of 81.7% of world market in 1893 to nil in 1993, while deeply interesting, are now largely academic. However it can be quite clearly seen from Figure 1 that the years from 1950 to 1970 were those of crucial decline compared to world competition. United Kingdom output fell in those years from well over 40% to a mere 6% of world output. This dramatic decline in twenty years was not underestimated when noted in the Transactions of the North-East Coast Institution of Engineers and Shipbuilders: **'Shipbuilding provides an instance of spectacular industrial failure; no other British industry declined so rapidly from such a strong position in 1950'**. Shipbuilding employment excluding shiprepairing and marine engineering fell by half from 130,000 in 1950 to 65,000 in 1970.

3. The series is written by an independent author with no axe to grind on British shipbuilding, and who has written a dozen books on maritime subjects. He comes from a family whose forebears on both sides of the family worked in British shipyards, and the author himself has worked in a British shipyard. The motive of the author in writing this series is purely to document a proud and great British industry. Now is the time to document while everything is still fresh in the memory of a major industry, whose size on the North East Coast can be gauged from the list of closure dates at the end of this introduction. However, this series of books makes no comment on British shipbuilding practice either from the management point of view, or from the workers and their trades unions point of view.

4. A work covering such a large and comprehensive subject as British shipbuilding has to be selective in nature when analysing yard lists. Omissions there most certainly will be, but these will hopefully be few in number, and the author invites constructive comment of a major nature or new research from all readers. Abbreviations are few e.g. brake horse power is b.h.p.; deadweight carrying capacity of a ship is d.w.t.; and gross registered tonnage g.r.t. is a measure of the volume of a ship, which is normally identified by gross tonnage/year of build after the name e.g. 9261/69.

The author wishes to acknowledge the invaluable help and information given by John B. Hill, Alan Tennent, George Scott, Eric Kirk, Adrian Osler and the staff of Tyne & Wear Archives, Barbara Jones and the staff of Lloyd's Register of Shipping, the staff of Newcastle City Libraries, Sunderland Museum, Cleveland Archives and The National Maritime Museum. Thanks are due for the courtesy of the various sources for their kind permission to reproduce photographs, illustrations and yard plans, and these are credited alongside the illustrations.

Norman L. Middlemiss

Newcastle-upon-Tyne

August,1993

FIGURE 1.

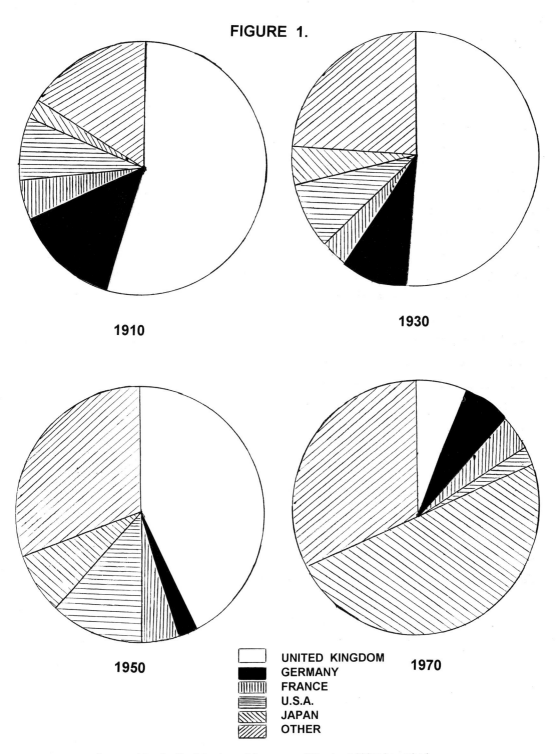

1910

1930

1950

1970

UNITED KINGDOM
GERMANY
FRANCE
U.S.A.
JAPAN
OTHER

Source: Lloyd's Register Annual Summary of Merchant Ships Launched.

FIGURE 2.

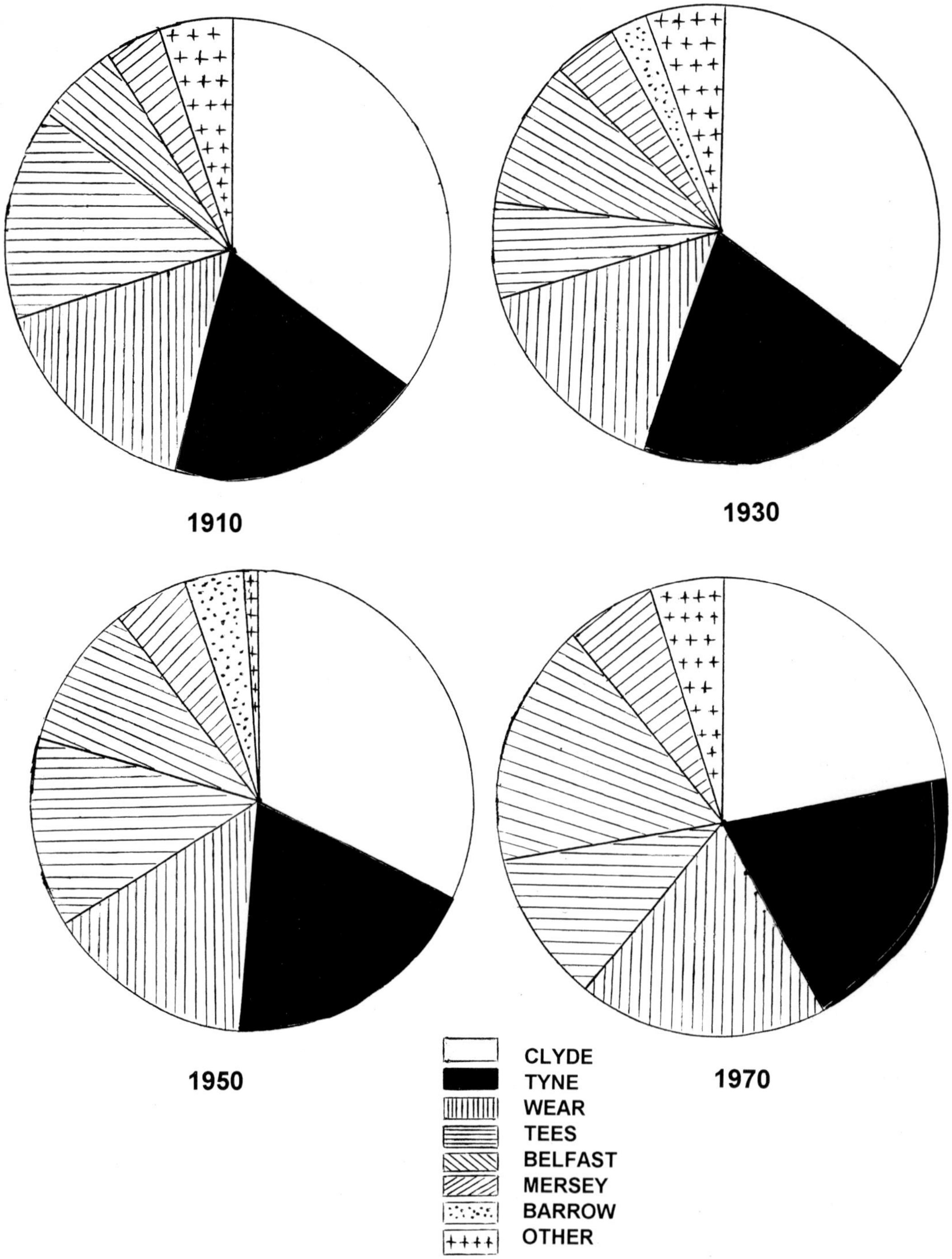

1910

1930

1950

CLYDE
TYNE
WEAR
TEES
BELFAST
MERSEY
BARROW
OTHER

1970

Source: Lloyd's Register Annual Summary of Merchant Ships Launched.

CLOSURE DATES OF NORTH-EAST COAST SHIPBUILDING YARDS

1909 Robert Craggs & Sons, Middlesbrough
1909 Smith's Dock Co. Ltd, North Shields (became shiprepairer only)
1918 Armstrong Elswick yard
1921 Newcastle Shipbuilding Co. Ltd, Hebburn
1922 J.T. Eltringham, Howdon
1922 W. Harkess & Son Ltd, Middlesbrough
1923 J. & D. Morris, Pelaw Main
1923 Sir Raylton Dixon & Co. Ltd, Middlesbrough
1924 Hepple & Co., South Shields
1924 Irvine's Shipbuilding & Dry Docks Co. Ltd, Hartlepool
1925 Ropner Shipbuilding & Repairing Co. Ltd, Stockton (reopened 1930/31)
1925 Richardson, Duck & Co. Ltd, Stockton
1925 Osbourne, Graham & Co., Sunderland
1925 Wood, Skinner, Gateshead
1926 Sunderland Shipbuilding Co. Ltd, Sunderland
1927 John Blumer & Co., Sunderland
1929 Charles Rennoldson, South Shields
1929 J. P. Rennoldson & Sons, South Shields
1930 Craig, Taylor & Co. Ltd, Thornaby
1930 Armstrong Low Walker yard (re-opened 1943/48)
1930 W. Gray EGIS yard, Sunderland
1930 Northumberland Shipbuilding Co. Ltd, Howdon
1931 W. Dobson & Co. Ltd, Walker
1931 Robert Thompson & Sons Ltd, Southwick
1931 Swan, Hunter & Wigham Richardson Ltd, Southwick (re-opened 1943/47)
1933 Sir John Priestman & Co. Ltd, Sunderland
1933 Tyne Iron Shipbuilding Co. Ltd, Willington Quay
1933 Palmer yards at Jarrow and Hebburn
1960 John Crown & Sons Ltd, Sunderland
1961 W. Gray & Co. Ltd, Hartlepool
1964 Wear Dockyard formerly S.P. Austin & Son
1964 Short Brothers, Sunderland
1964 T. Mitchison Ltd, Gateshead
1966 Blyth Shipbuilding & Dry Docks Co. Ltd
1974 Ryton Marine Ltd, Wallsend
1977 Readhead yard at South Shields
1978 Bartram yard at Sunderland
1979 Furness yard at Haverton Hill
1979 J. L. Thompson North Sands yard at Sunderland
1981 Hawthorn, Leslie yard at Hebburn
1983 Clelands yard at Willington Quay
1985 Laing Deptford yard at Sunderland
1985 High Walker Naval Yard
1987 Smith's Dock Co. Ltd, Middlesbrough
1988 Doxford Pallion yard and Austin & Pickersgill yard at Southwick
1988 Neptune Yard of Swan Hunter Shipbuilders Ltd
1993 Swan Hunter Shipbuilders Ltd, Wallsend (in receivership)

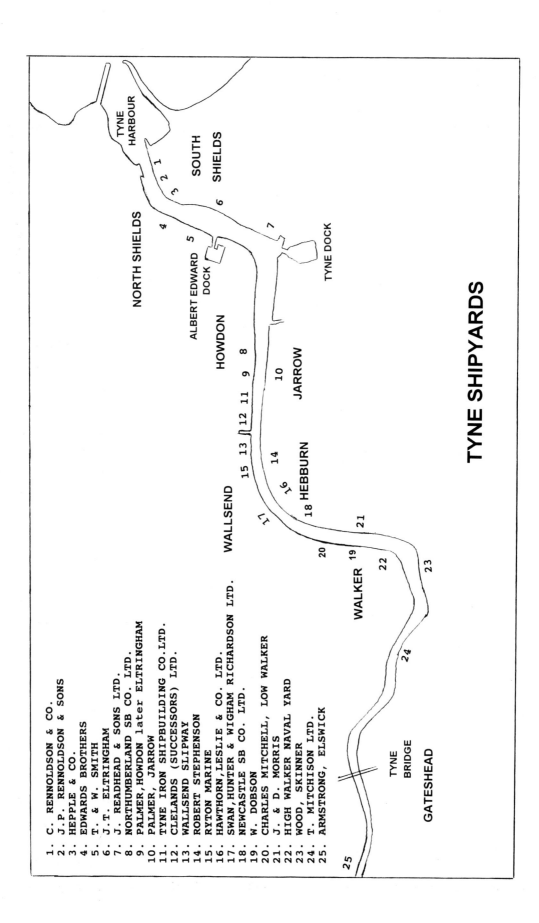

TYNE SHIPYARDS

1. C. RENNOLDSON & CO.
2. J.P. RENNOLDSON & SONS
3. HEPPLE & CO.
4. EDWARDS BROTHERS
5. T. & W. SMITH
6. J.T. ELTRINGHAM
7. J. READHEAD & SONS LTD.
8. NORTHUMBERLAND SB CO. LTD.
9. PALMER, HOWDON later ELTRINGHAM
10. PALMER, JARROW
11. TYNE IRON SHIPBUILDING CO.LTD.
12. CLELANDS (SUCCESSORS) LTD.
13. WALLSEND SLIPWAY
14. ROBERT STEPHENSON
15. RYTON MARINE
16. HAWTHORN, LESLIE & CO. LTD.
17. SWAN, HUNTER & WIGHAM RICHARDSON LTD.
18. NEWCASTLE SB CO. LTD.
19. W. DOBSON
20. CHARLES MITCHELL, LOW WALKER
21. J. & D. MORRIS
22. HIGH WALKER NAVAL YARD
23. WOOD, SKINNER
24. T. MITCHISON LTD.
25. ARMSTRONG, ELSWICK

TYNE HARBOUR

NORTH SHIELDS

SOUTH SHIELDS

ALBERT EDWARD DOCK

TYNE DOCK

HOWDON

WALLSEND

JARROW

HEBBURN

WALKER

TYNE BRIDGE

GATESHEAD

SWAN, HUNTER & WIGHAM RICHARDSON LTD.

This huge shipbuilding company was formed at Wallsend in 1903 from an amalgamation of the Wallsend yard of Charles S. Swan & Hunter and the Neptune yard of Wigham Richardson & Company. The intervening property of the Tyne Ship & Pontoon Company was also purchased at the same time to give a continuous river frontage. The history of the two founding yards is given starting with C.S. Swan & Hunter :-

Charles Mitchell (See Armstrong,Mitchell & Co. Ltd) purchased a 6.5 acre site at Wallsend in 1873 to take up excess orders from his Low Walker yard. His yard manager from Low Walker, John Coulson, and his brother-in-law, Richard Cooke, were put in charge. The yard was to the east of that of Schlesinger,Davis and produced 13 ships before failing financially on the last contract in 1874. Charles Mitchell then put the yard in the hands of his brother-in-law Charles Sheriton Swan (born 1831), one of six sons and five daughters of William and Ann Swan of West Farm, Walker. Charles S. Swan and his younger brother Henry F. Swan (born 1842) had both been trained by Mitchell at his Low Walker yad and then had lived and worked at St. Petersburg at intervals between 1862 and 1870 on a Mitchell contract to build five Russian warships. The Swan brothers were two of the initial directors of the Wallsend Slipway Company, set-up by Mitchell in 1871.

The Wallsend yard prospered under Charles S. Swan with some 30 small tramps and colliers completed for local owners such as William Milburn: *Fernwood* 1851/77, *Teddington* 2016/80, *Darlington* 1990/81 together with tugs,launches and barges. By 1878 he was making arrangements with George B. Hunter of Austin & Hunter at Sunderland with much shipbuilding experience on the Clyde and Wear, to join him. However tragedy struck in April,1879 when Charles S. Swan fell overboard from a Channel steamer while returning from the Continent with his wife. It was left to his wife to continue as a partner with George B. Hunter, who took over as Managing Director in 1880.

The technical and managerial expertise of George B. Hunter soon saw the yard prosper in the boom years of the early 1880s from an initial workforce of 600 men and a 270 feet river frontage. The original West Yard of 6.5 acres with three berths was expanded in 1883 by the purchase of 16 acres of adjacent land for the East Yard. Seven acres of this latter were developed as a well-equipped fitting-out berth with the workforce of both yards totalling nearly 900 men. In the first three years to 1883 some 40 iron steamers up to 2500 grt in size were built, while even in the subsequent slump in the mid-1880s production was maintained at four to seven ships. Eleven ships were completed in 1889, and in 1893 seven ships of 31,088 grt made the yard the top Tyneside builder for the first time. Notable ships of this time were *Venus* 1067/90 for Bergen Line which started her Newcastle to Bergen regular sailings in June,1893; the first two steel ships built at Wallsend - sisters *Burrumbeet* and *Corongamite* both 2420/85, and *Elingamite* 2585/87 for the cargo/passenger trades of Huddart,Parker & Company of Melbourne. The *Elingamite* had also been designed for use as an Admiralty transport and auxiliary armed cruiser. The last sailing ships built at the yard were the three-masted barque *Flottbek* 1988/91 for Knohr & Burchard, and the four-masted barque *Milton Stuart* 3177/92 for the Milton Stuart Shipping Company of London. However tramps of around 3000 dwt for owners such as Bowring, Burrell, Raeburn & Verel and Galbraith, Pembroke and Deutsche Dampf. Rherei of Germany formed the bulk of the yard's production around 1890 together with small passenger steamers for tropical rivers. Tramps were also completed for other German, Danish, Spanish, Chilian, Greek, Norwegian, Italian, French, Austro-Hungarian and Australian owners.

The first refrigerated steamer built at the yard was *Maori* of 2711 grt in 1890 for the New Zealand frozen-meat trade of Shaw,Savill & Albion Ltd, and the larger refrigerated steamer *Westmeath* 6237/93 for the New Zealand trade was the first of a number of such ships of this size completed throughout the 1890s. The first tanker completed at the yard was *Circassian Prince* of 3220 dwt in 1889 for Prince Line of North Shields owned by James Knott. The larger tanker *Mexican Prince* of 4330 dwt followed in September,1893 for the same company, who had also had several dry-cargo ships built at the yard. Other tankers followed for Bowring with *Lucifer* 3823/99, *Mira* 3700/01 but the latter was completed for Bessler,Waechter & Company of London with Stephens, Sutton & Stephens of Newcastle as managers, and *Petroleum* 4586/03 for the Admiralty, and *Goldmouth* 7446/03 of 10000 dwt for Marcus Samuel's Shell oil company.

In 1893 the yard was head of the river for the first time with an output of 31,088 tons of ships, and In 1895 the partnership became a limited liability company by which time the total acreage of the West and East yards had risen to 23 acres with three berths in each yard. In 1897 the recently defunct yard of Schlesinger,Davis to the West of C.S. Swan & Hunter Ltd was purchased for the exclusive construction of floating dry-docks. Older style pontoon docks had been built for the Tyne Pontoon & Dry Docks (1894), Smiths Dock Co. Ltd, North Shields (1896). The first steel self-docking floating gravity dock was built at Wallsend in 1897 for the Spanish Government with a specified lift of 11,000 tons and was built,launched and towed to Havana within 11 months. Larger docks were built for Cardiff and Stettin in 1898, and a 17,000 tons lift dock was towed to Bermuda in

1901. Docks were also supplied to the Riasan Uralsk Railway Company in Russia in 1901 and to the Japanese Government in 1902.

Liner shipowners also well patronised the yards, especially Cunard Line, which purchased a liner on the stocks ordered by Sir Christopher Furness, and had her completed as *Ultonia* of 1898. The purpose-built *Ivernia* of 1900 had accomodation for 200 first-class passengers and 1700 third-class passengers, and an updated sister *Carpathia* was launched in August,1902. She was powered by two sets of quadruple expansion steam engines developing 9000 indicated horse power driving twin propellers at 15 knots. The slipway had to be extended to accomodate this Cunard pair, and the eastern end of the Roman Wall was discovered while making the excavations. A full list of passenger liners and passenger carrying cargo-liners completed by the yard at this time is now given:-

ULTONIA	8056/98	Cunard Line
IVERNIA	13800/00	"
CARPATHIA	13555/03	"
POLITICIAN	7380/99	T. & J. Harrison
TACTICIAN	7280/00	"
PATRICIAN	7878/01	"
MILWAUKEE	7317/97	Elder,Dempster
MONARCH	7295/97	"
MOUNT ROYAL	7044/98	"
LAKE MANITOBA	8851/01	"
LAKE MICHIGAN	7000/02	"
MAORI	2711/90	Shaw,Savill & Albion
KUMARA	6034/99	"
CORCOVADO	4568/96	Pacific Steam Nav.
SORATA	4581/97	"
SAINT ANDREW	6606/99	Saint Line
CONSUELO	6026/00	Thomas Wilson
SANTA FE	4384/02	Hamburg-Sud Amerika
DACIA	3470/00	Hamburg-Amerika-Pacific
MACEDONIA	4343/00	"
AMERICA MARU	6070/98	Toyo Kisen K.K.
PRINCESS VICTORIA	1592/03	Grand Trunk Railway

The other constituent of the merger in 1903 was the Neptune Yard of Wigham Richardson Ltd. This yard had been opened in 1860 on the site of the former John Coutts and Miller & Ravenhill yards which had completed the first iron paddle steamer built on the Tyne - *Prince Albert* of 1842 - as well as *Chuson* 700/51 for P & O, and *Tyne* 1600/54 for Royal Mail Steam Packet Company but then had failed financially. John Wigham Richardson was the son of a well-known Newcastle Quaker family whose views on pacificism were equally well-known and thus the yard

Three Cunard liners: IVERNIA of 1900 (top), CARPATHIA of 1903 (middle) and MAURETANIA of 1907 (bottom), the latter in her cruising colours in the 1930s.

(Cunard Archives, University of Liverpool, F.W. Hawks)

never tendered for Admiralty contracts until after the 1903 merger. At the age of 23 years he bought the four acre yard in 1860 with three berths and a workforce of 200 men, and he brought in a manager from Stirling - Charles J. Denham Christie with good knowledge of ship design and construction - who later became a partner. The first ship built at the Neptune Yard was the Solent paddle ferry *Victoria*, with sailing ships being built in the 1860s as well as *Isabella* in 1862, a shallow-draught paddle-steamer sent via inland navigation to Kiev, and *Ruhr* of 1865 and *Lillibelt* of 1872 for carrying coal trains and a precursor of later rail ferries. By 1872 marine engines had been added to the yard products not only for ships building at the yard but for other yards along the length of the Tyne. By the early 1870s ships of 1500 - 2000 grt were being built and customers included the local William Milburn , and Tyne Steam Shipping Company, as well as Norwegian, French, Italian and German companies.

Larger passenger ships were also built at the Neptune Yard such as the Norwegian *Nordland* in 1865 and *America* in 1875, a paddle steamer 250 feet long with accomodation for 80 first class passengers and a larger number of third class passengers. The four-masted twin-funnelled *Alfonso XII* was completed in 1888 for the Compania Transatlantica of Barcelona of 408 feet overall length with accomodation for 150 first class passengers, 50 second-class, 40 third-class as well as 800 soldiers, and was an outstanding ship and attained 15 knots on trials. The first refrigerated ship built at the yard was *Hornby Grange* 2473/89, which was also the first owned ship for her owners, Houlder Brothers. More land was acquired and the Neptune yard now covered 18 acres with a river frontage of 1100 feet. A dozen cargo-liners were built for the Hansa company of Germany between 1895 and 1901, and the yard completed *Persia* of 5895 grt in April,1903 shortly before the merger for Lloyd Triestino. The directors of Wigham Richardson Ltd at this time were John Wigham Richardson (Chairman), his son Philip, Charles J.D. Christie and his son John Denham Christie, John Tweedy and the founder's second son George B. Wigham Richardson, who had started at the yard in 1896.

One of the reasons for the merger of the yards in June,1903 was a preliminary contract for a new express Transatlantic liner for Cunard which was making heavy demands on the capital and resources of C.S. Swan & Hunter Ltd. A start had been made in 1902 on reorganising the site of the former Schlesinger,Davis yard by laying out two new and larger building berths of 750 feet in length and capable of building the liner. These were the famous gantry crane berths, a Tyneside landmark for over 60 years, which were roofed with glass as had been done to the two smaller berths in the East Yard in 1895, and fitted with seven electric gantry cranes. New machine tools for punching,planing, countersinking etc. further modernised the yard.

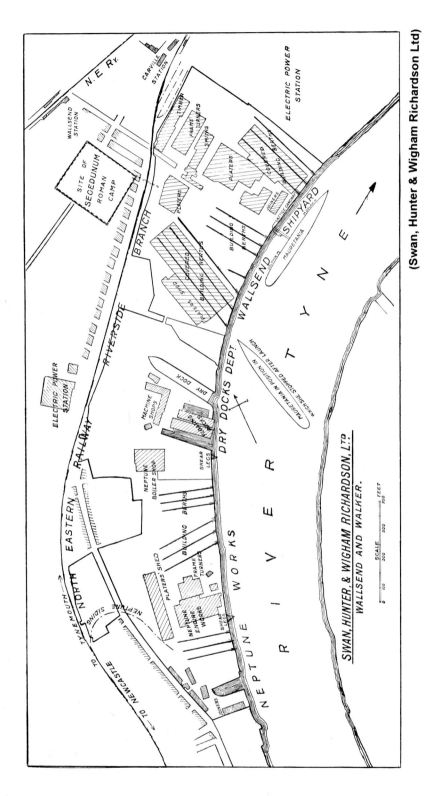

(Swan, Hunter & Wigham Richardson Ltd)

WALLSEND AND NEPTUNE YARDS IN 1906

MAURETANIA on her berth under the famous gantry cranes (above) showing her four massive propellers, and at her launch on 20th September,1906.
(Swan Hunter Shipbuilders Ltd)

Wallsend Slipway & Engineering Co. Ltd was taken over in 1903 to build the huge boilers and turbines for MAURETANIA (below). (Swan Hunter Shipbuilders Ltd)

Cunard had reached agreement in 1903 with the British Government over the guns and mountings to be fitted to two express liners in times of war in return for an annual subsidy of £150,000 and a loan of £2.6M for their construction. Sir William H. White was a Director of the yard and formerly Director of Naval Construction for the Navy, and he was largely instrumental in bringing one of the orders to Tyneside. The actual contracts for *Mauretania* and her sister *Lusitania*, which was built by the John Brown shipyard on the Clyde, were signed in 1904. The keel of *Mauretania* was laid at Wallsend in August,1904 and she was launched two years later on 20th September,1906 by Lady Anne Emily Innes Kerr, Duchess of Roxburghe. She was 790 feet in length with a beam of 88 feet and a gross tonnage of 31938 tons and was designed to carry over 2000 passengers, and after fitting-out left on her maiden voyage on 16th November,1907. She subsequently captured the Blue Riband for the fastest crossing of the Atlantic and held it for a further 22 years. The specifications of the new liner *Mauretania* called for revolutionary steam turbines to be the main propulsion to give a service speed of 26 knots and as a consequence a majority holding in the Wallsend Slipway & Engineering Co. Ltd with the necessary turbine expertise had been taken in 1903.

The Wallsend Slipway Company had been established in 1871 by Charles Mitchell and named after two 300 feet slipways for the sole purpose of repairing ships. In 1873 compound marine engines were first made, later triple and quadruple expansion steam reciprocating engines were built. Under Managing Director William Boyd the 'Engineering' was added to the company name in 1878, and a new boiler making shop was erected in 1881 and was further extended in 1904 to accomodate the gigantic boilers of the *Mauretania*. At the time of the take-over all types of boiler including cylindrical, locomotive and water-tube - the latter particularly useful for warships - were manufactured. The company were pioneeers in turbine machinery at the turn of the century, and constructed all four turbines of 70,000 s.h.p. for the *Mauretania*. Their first oil engine was fitted to *Abelia* owned by Marcus Samuel in 1915. A dry-dock of 540 feet length built in 1897 extended the size of vessels that could be repaired.

The amalgamated company in 1903 now covered nearly 80 acres with an unbroken river frontage of 4000 feet. After the merger George B. Hunter continued as Chairman, a position he held until 1928, with other directors including his son George Ernest Hunter, Charles S. Swan (whose father had been drowned in 1879) together with his son. The output of the two yards was now combined, and included two banana boats completed for Elders & Fyffes in 1904, *Matina* and *Manistee* both of 3868 grt, as well as the yacht *Albion* 1116/04 for Sir George Newnes. Six cargo-liners for the Hansa company of Germany were completed between 1904 and 1907, and further cargo-liners were built at this time for the Indo-China Steamship Co. Ltd *Kut Sang* 4895/05; Hamburg-Sud *Santa Cruz* 4924/05; Glen Line *Glenearn* 4460/05; Khedivail Mail S.S. *Osmanieh* 4041/06 with accomodation for 213 passengers; Union S.S. of New Zealand *Waihora* 4637/07, Shaw,Savill & Albion *Arawa* 9371/07; Prince Line *Ocean Prince* 5101/07; Chargeurs Reunis *Malte* 8351/07 and *Ceylan* 8352/07 and C.G.T. of France with *Guyane* and *Cacique* both 2896/07, and the Great Central Railway Company's *Immingham* 2009/06 with accomodation for 393 passengers and propelled by triple-screw turbine machinery.

　　Tanker sizes increased from 10000 dwt in 1903 to 15500 dwt in March,1913 when *San Fraterno* was launched by Lady Bowring as the largest tanker in the world at that time. Other tankers completed before World War I were :-

CHEYENNE	4987/08	Anglo-American Oil Company
HERMIONE	5200/08	Bowring
TRINCULO	5203/08	Bowring
EL LOBO	4800/08	Bowring
SAN ANTONIO	5250/09	Eagle Oil
DANUBIAN	5064/09	Lane & Macandrew
BRITISH SUN	5564/09	J.N. Pew
CONCH	5620/09	Anglo-Saxon/Shell
PATELLA	5617/09	Anglo-Saxon/Shell
RANELLA	5590/12	Anglo-Saxon/Shell
MITRA	5592/12	Anglo-Saxon/Shell
NATICA	5579/12	Anglo-Saxon/Shell
EBURNA	4739/13	Anglo-Saxon/Shell
CORDELIA	6533/12	Bowring
ROSALIND	6535/13	Bowring
ELSINORE	6542/13	Bowring
EL TORO	5958/13	Bowring
EL ZORRO	5989/14	Bowring
SAN DUNSTANO	6220/12	Eagle Oil
SAN EDUARDO	6225/12	Eagle Oil
SAN SILVESTRE	6233/13	Eagle Oil
SAN TIRSO	6236/13	Eagle Oil
SAN FRATERNO	9587/13	Eagle Oil
SAN GREGORIO	9594/13	Eagle Oil
SAN LORENZO	9607/14	Eagle Oil

　　A new design of train and passenger ferry was completed for the Swedish Government in 1909 as the twin-funnelled *Drottning Victoria* for service between Sweden and Germany. She had excellent accomodation for 96 first-class and 44 third-class passengers in addition to her train carrying facilities. The Grand Trunk Pacific Railway Company of Canada had a similar-sized ferry built by the yard in the same year, *Prince Rupert* 3379/09, and followed by a larger ferry two years later - *Princess Alice* 5099/11 for Canadian Pacific Railway.

Swan, Hunter & Wigham Richardson Ltd were also tramp owners at this time, as main shareholders of the Hopemount Shipping Co. Ltd set-up on 21st June, 1904 with a subscribed capital of £12,000 with the objective of trading 'speculation' ships built by the yard. *Hopemount* 3300/05 had been completed for this company and managed for them by Stamp, Mann & Company of Newcastle. She cost £35,954 to build and a bank mortgage of £23,712 was taken out to provide the majority of her construction capital. She was of 5000 dwt and a conventional 'three-island' tramp with five holds of which no. 3 hold was the cross-bunker hold between bridge and engineer accomodation. The centre island was extended to include no. 4 hatch and no. 5 hatch was in the aft well-deck. After a lean time in the recession from 1906 to 1910, she made her greatest trading profit in 1910/11 of £8711.

Two liners were completed for Cunard in 1911: *Laconia* 18099/11 and *Ascania* 9111/11. The latter had been launched as *Gerona* on 6th March, 1911 for Cairn Line of Steamships Ltd, Newcastle. However their passenger services and goodwill on the Newcastle - Leith - Canada route and three liners were sold to Cunard while she was still fitting out. The other two liners had also been built at the yard: *Tortona* 7997/09 which became *Ausonia*, and *Cairnrona* ex *Consuelo* 6026/00 which became *Albania*. Ellerman and Bucknall Lines also expanded with the delivery of new cargo-liners from the yard:-

CITY OF COLOMBO	5987/09	KIOTO	6181/10
CITY OF POONA	7466/11	SALDANHA	4594/11
CITY OF LAHORE	6875/11	KANDAHAR	6415/13
CITY OF BRISTOL	6741/11		

City of Lahore having accomodation for 106 passengers and *City of Poona* for 144 passengers. *Goldenfels* 7486/11 was completed for Hansa Line of Germany, and *Koursk* 5792/11 for the Russian Volunteer Fleet Association, the latter with accomodation for no fewer than 1214 passengers. Two fine cargo-liners were also completed during 1912 for the Hamburg-Amerika Line with accomodation for 72 passengers: *Emil L. Boas* 5998/12 and *Karl Schurz* 5990/12.

In 1912 Barclay, Curle & Co. Ltd at Whiteinch on the North bank of the Clyde was taken over with a good reputation for building cargo-liners, and three directors from Wallsend then sat on their Board. The Elderslie Dockyard at Scotstoun on the Clyde with a 500 feet dry-dock was purchased in May, 1912 - the dock having been built a few years earlier for John Shearer & Sons Ltd. A new four-berth yard was opened under the Swan, Hunter & Wigham Richardson Ltd name at Southwick on the Wear in 1912 (See Wear yards) to take up excess orders for tramps, colliers and Great Lakes steamers.

The largest floating dock to date was completed in 1912 for the Admiralty with a 33,000 ton lift for use at Portsmouth Dockyard. The yard was the world leader in floating gravity docks, having completed pontoons and docks of all sizes for customers far and near:-   S.P. Austin's Wear Dockyard (1903), Natal Government(1903), Peruvian Government (1908), Trinidad Dock & Engineering Co. Ltd (1907), Wilton Fijenoord, Rotterdam(1907), Nigerian Protectorate,Lagos (1908), Fraserburgh Harbour (1908), Para Construction Company,Amazon (1908), Penarth Pontoon & Slipway (1909) and the Suez Canal Company in 1914.

The magnificent Spanish liner *Reina Victoria-Eugenia* of 9726 grt was completed for Cia Transatlantica in 1913. She was 498 feet in length with accomodation for 200 first-class, 46 alternate first and second, 100 second-class, 80 third-class and 1642 emigrants. She was fitted with reciprocating engines and exhaust turbines on separate shafts. A total of eight cargo-liners with passenger accomodation was completed during 1913/14 for the British India Steam Navigation Co. Ltd:- *Varela,Varsova,Vita* of 4644 grt;   *Mongara,Morvada* of 8205 grt; and *Karoa,Karapara,Karagola* of 7009 grt. The 'V' class having accomodation for 56 cabin passengers and also for Indian deck passengers, and the 'M' and 'K' class for 45 first-class and 64 second-class passengers as well as many Indian deck passengers.

During World War I some 55 warships with a total displacement of 100,000 tons were built and included the cruisers *Comus* of 1914 and *Coventry* of 1918, 28 torpedo boat destroyers, the monitor *Roberts* in 1915, and 20 sloops and some submarines. Merchant construction totalled 290,588 grt and included passenger liners,cargo-liners, refrigerated vessels, ice-breakers, tankers, cable ships and three floating docks. The Cunard liner *Aurania* 13936/17 could carry 2022 passengers but was unfortunately lost after being torpedoed and damaged on 4th February, 1918 when 15 miles NW of Inishtrahull by UB67 while on a voyage from Liverpool to New York in ballast. She was taken in tow but stranded near Tobermory on the Isle of Mull and was wrecked. Two fine cargo-liners for the New Zealand trade were completed: *Northumberland* 12160/15 for Federal Steam Navigation, and *Armagh* 12159/17 for Union Steamship Company of New Zealand. Other customers included The Clan Line Steamers Ltd with *Clan Ross* of 5897 grt completed in November,1914, with tankers *British Admiral* 6842/17 and *British Empress* 6847/17 for the British Tanker Co. Ltd, *Mytilus* 5716/16 *Oliva* 5694/16 for Anglo-Saxon/Shell, *Terek* for Lane & Macandrew, *Elmol* and *Elderol* for the Admiralty. The Shipping Controller took control of some 18 'WAR' standard cargo ships, consisting of 10 'A'

BRITISH PETROL of 1925 (above) and SOLEN of 1922 (below). (A.Duncan & Solomon)

and 'B' tramps of 8300 dwt, one of which was completed as an 'AO' tanker, five 'Z' tankers of 8800 dwt, one 'N' type which was the first of 34 to be completed by British yards as *War Climax* on 28th September,1918, and one 'C1' coaster. The last of these 'Z' tankers was completed as the engines-aft *War Krishna* in November,1919 the only one of its type to be engines-aft, and the yard was fully occupied completing the 'B' types until early 1920 with the last two completing as *Belgian* for F. Leyland and *Kidderpore* for P & O.

One large liner for Italy had lain unfinished on the stocks throughout the war since being laid down in January,1914. The ship was to be named *Giulio Cesare* and had been ordered by Navigazione Generale Italiana of Genoa for service to South America. Admiralty plans to complete her as a seaplane carrier or trooper came to nought, and this large liner of 22576 grt was launched on 7th February,1920 and completed in March,1922. She could carry 2350 passengers of which the 244 first-class had de-luxe staterooms which featured private baths, showers and oak parquet flooring, and tiled luxury bathrooms. The 306 second-class and 1800 third-class passengers had cabins and public rooms comparable with first-class on other liners. Her geared turbines by Wallsend Slipway propelled four screws at nearly 20 knots on trials.   Five other passenger liners were completed by the yard in the early 1920s: two for Cunard - *Laconia* 19679/22 and the replacement *Aurania* 13984/24 for a liner of the same name lost during the war, with *Laconia* towed to Rotterdam for final fitting-out because of labour problems; and *Meduana* 10070/22 and *Mosella* 10249/23 for Cie Sud Atlantique of France; and *Cuba* 11337/23 for Cie Generale Transatlantique,France. This last owner also had the smaller Mediterranean passenger liner *Gamorciere* 4713/21 built by the yard. *Meduana* capsized while fitting-out after a fire and blocked the slipways for a while.

After World War I the company extended its control of, or interest in the North of Ireland Shipbuilding Co. Ltd, Londonderry; shipbuilders Philip & Son Ltd, Dartmouth; the North British Engine Works (1922) Ltd, Glasgow and Stobcross Boiler Works,Glasgow; and iron and steel works in Glasgow and shiprepairers at Swansea. The company then had the capability of producing many sets of steam turbines, Bauer-Wach exhaust turbines and triple expansion steam reciprocating engines both on the Clyde and at the Neptune Engine Works on the Tyne. Later both engine builders were to produce many sets of diesel and oil engines. The Sunderland salvage company of Lindsay, Swan Hunter - an associate company of Swan,Hunter & Wigham Richardson Ltd - salvaged both halves of the new Newcastle tramp *Linerton* from South Shields beach in 1920, as well as undertaking salvage work in the West Indies. Major customers of the yards for cargo-liners

Two liners built in the inter-war years, the Italian GIULIO CESARE of 1922 (above) and the Polish SOBIESKI of 1939 (below).   (A. Duncan)

The twin-screw motorship SOBIESKI had accomodation for 44 first-class, 250 third-class and 850 emigrants and her service speed between Italy and New York after the war was 17 knots. She was of 11030 grt and also had some refrigerated capacity. Her sister CHROBRY completed at the same time in 1939 unfortunately became a war loss.

during the 1920s were Ellerman Lines, and British India Line, owned by P & O, whose ships were :-

CITY OF PARIS	10839/22	MODASA	9070/21
CITY OF CANTERBURY	8431/23	KHANDALLA	7013/23
CITY OF MANDALAY	7049/24	KOLA	1537/24
CITY OF LYONS	7062/26	SANTHIA	7754/25
CITY OF OXFORD	2788/26	JUNA	2190/27
CITY OF ROUBAIX	7108/28	KISTNA	1466/24
		SIRDHANA	7745/25

City of Paris had accomodation for 349 passengers and *City of Canterbury* for 178 passengers. Commonwealth & Dominion Line, which became Port Line in 1936, also ordered five cargo-liners and renewed a link with one of the four constituent fleets, the local William Milburn, who had ships built at both the Neptune and Wallsend yards in the 1880s. *Port Hobart* 7448/25 was a steamer but *Port Huon* 8432/27 , *Port Gisborne* 8390/27, *Port Alma* 8400/28 and *Port Fairy* 8337/28 marked the switch to motor ships for their owners. Two French cargo-liners for Soc. Generale de Transportes Maritimes *Mendoza* 8534/20 and *Alsina* 8600/21 had passenger accomodation and geared turbines for their Far East trades. French Line (Compagnie Generale Transatlantique) took delivery of a smaller cargo-liner *President Dal Piaz* 4866/29. Holland Lloyd's *Montferland* 6742/21 had refrigerated spaces in her 'tween decks, while *Kutsang* 5847/22 of Indo-China S.N. Co. Ltd was a war replacement for a vessel of the same name built by the yard. Orders for a pair of motor-driven cargo-liners were placed by Silver Line, *Silverpine* and *Silverlarch* both 5122/24, and Shaw,Savill & Albion Ltd *Coptic* 10629/28 and *Zealandic* 11300/28. The latter pair were powered by twin 6-cylinder 2SCSA Sulzer oil engines by Wallsend Slipway & Engineering Co. Ltd, while the Doxford-type oil engines of the former pair were in the 'three-quarters aft' position. T. & J. Harrison Ltd ordered a passenger cargo-liner for their West Indies service from London, which was completed in 1925 as *Inanda* with accomodation for 80 first-class passengers. The intermediate Greek passenger liner *Patris II* of 3840/26 was completed for the Byron Steamship Co. Ltd, and the similar Australian *Mernoo* 2517/26 for the Melbourne Steamship Co. Ltd. A major factor in the yards survival in the 1920s was the completion of 50 Great Lakes grain-carrying steamers, with Glen Line ordering six of these engines-aft bridge-forward ships of 2000 grt with names beginning *'Glen'* for their feeder services. The local Tyne-Tees Shipping Co. Ltd had the coastal passenger ships *Hadrian* 1857/23 and *Alnwick* 1857/29 completed at the Neptune Yard.

The twin-funnelled French liner *Campana* was completed in 1929 for Soc. Generale de Transportes Maritimes with accomodation for a total of 1305 passengers. She was of 10816 grt and 528 feet length and turbine-powered to twin propellers. The year 1929 also two high-class passenger ferries completed for Swedish Lloyd *Britannia* and *Suecia* both of 4631 grt. They were single-screw turbine steamers with accomodation for 201 first-class and 40 second-class passengers on the London to Gothenburg service. Over 50 tankers were completed by the yards during the years 1919 to 1931, with the largest being *San Florentino* of 18000 dwt in 1919 and *Pan Scandia* of 14750 dwt in 1931:-

Ship	Tonnage/Year	Owner
SAN FLORENTINO	12842/19	Eagle Oil
BRITISH VISCOUNT	6895/21	British Tanker Co. Ltd
BRITISH GRENADIER	6857/22	"
BRITISH GUNNER	6894/22	"
BRITISH SCOUT	1507/22	"
BRITISH FUSILIER	6943/23	"
BRITISH HUSSAR	6944/23	"
BRITISH MOTORIST	6891/24	"
BRITISH PETROL	6891/25	"
BRITISH GOVERNOR	6840/26	"
BRITISH COLONY	6917/27	"
BRITISH UNION	6987/27	"
BRITISH DOMINION	6983/28	"
BRITISH PLUCK	1025/28	"
BRITISH THRIFT	695/28	"
SPIRILA	5695/22	Anglo-Saxon/Shell
SAXICAVA	5693/22	"
SCALARIA	5683/21	"
SOLEN	5693/22	"
ARNUS	4184/22	Soc.Gen.des Transportes,France
HOPEMOUNT	7434/29	Hopemount Shpg. Co. Ltd
CORDELIA	8190/30	Bowring S.S. Co. Ltd
CAPULET	8190/30	"
ATHELKING	9557/26	Athel Line
OILPIONEER	5666/28	British Oil Shpg. Co. Ltd
OILRELIANCE	5666/29	"
OILSHIPPER	5225/27	"
OILTRADER	5550/28	"
FRONTENAC	7350/28	A/S Baltimore,Oslo
SVENOR	7616/31	Samuel Ugelstad,Oslo
FILEFJELL	7615/30	Olsen & Ugelstad,Oslo
JENNY	4705/28	A/S Olusfart,Oslo
SYDHAV	7536/29	Skibs A/S Sydhav,Oslo
MARATHON	7209/30	Halle & Patersen,Norway
NORE	7618/30	Rasmussen,Norway
EGERO	7589/29	Skjebreds A/S,Norway

The Norwegian whale factory ship VIKINGEN at her launch at Wallsend in September,1929 (above) and the Jubilee floating dock, built in two sections at Wallsend, leaving the Tyne on 17th July,1931 for a 12,000 mile voyage to Wellington (NZ) towed by two Dutch tugs.

(Swan, Hunter & Wigham Richardson Ltd)

HAVBOR	7614/30 Havbor A/S,Norway
MORGENEN	7092/30 Tank Transport A/S,Norway
SVEVE	6313/31 A/SD/SAtlantic(Jebsen),Norway
JOHN P.PEDERSEN	6127/30 A/SHavtank(H. Staubo),Norway
NORBRIS	7618/30 J. Rasmussen,Norway
BELLO	6124/30 Berg Torgersen A/S,Norway
GERMANIC	6320/30 Walter Cockerline,Hull
PAN ARUBA	9231/30 Leif Hoegh A/S,Norway
PAN NORWAY	9231/30 "
PAN SCANDIA	9900/31 Leif Hoegh A/S,Norway
PAN EUROPE	9468/31 "
PAN BOLIVAR	9434/31 "
SOUTH AFRICA	9234/30 "
SINGU	4927/31 Burmah Oil	93
CARDITA 2	8237/31 Anglo-Saxon/Shell
CARDIUM 2	8236/31 "

The twin-funnelled whale factory ship *Vikingen* 14526/30 was completed for the Viking Whaling Co. Ltd., and was overhauled at the Wallsend Dry Docks at the end of each whaling season throughout the 1930s, usually in company with the whale factory ships *Sir James Clark Ross* and *C.A. Larsen*. Tramps built on speculation included *Neptunian* 5125/25 and *Titanian* 4880/25 for companies associated with the yard, and the car carrier *Seatrain* 7624/28 was completed for Overseas Railway Inc of the U.S.A. and was a fore-runner of the huge slab-sided car carriers of the present day. Floating dock sizes rose to 55,000 tons lift with ones for Singapore Docks and the Admiralty, and smaller ones for Lagos Dock (1924), Falkland Islands (1929), Bengal Docks,Calcutta(1929), Wellington Jubilee Dock (1931) and caissons for Devonport Docks in 1927.

The depression years of 1930/32 saw the yards completing existing orders for Norwegian tanker owners as well as three destoyers *Codrington,Brilliant* and *Bulldog* and three sloops *Folkestone,Scarborough* and *Hindustan* for the Admiralty. The passenger and cargo-liner *El Kantara* 5213/32 for Cie Nav de Mixte of France was a valuable order, as was the Norwegian cargo ship *Fjordheim* 4114/30 for Nils Rogenaes, the Chinese train ferry *Changkiang* 2362/32, the Norwegian fruiter *Crawford Ellis* 2161/30 for H. Staubo. Four small cargo ships of 2000 grt were completed leaving only the Stephenson Clarke collier *Sir Russell* 1548/33 and a cargo-liner for Commonwealth and Dominion Line on the order book. This was launched on 2nd October,1933 and completed as *Port Chalmers* of 8535 grt in December,1933 and the only other completions during 1933 were six small orders for craft such as oil barges for Dominion Oil of Canada and the Egyptian Government. The small coaster *Peter G. Campbell*, launched on 13th April,1933 at the yard for Newcastle owners, was significant as she was the first all-welded ship

UMGENI of 1938 (above), and HOPERANGE of 1939 (below) (L. Dunn & T. Rayner)

from the yard. The total tonnage launched from the Tyne as a whole during 1933 amounted to only 11,033 grt with almost every shipyard worker laid idle. The reason why the yard was able to keep going albeit at much reduced capacity when most other Tyne yards were closed was its ability to build every type of ship.

Orders during 1934 for three twin-screw turbine-driven car ferries for the Southern Railway Company kept some of the workforce of the Neptune Yard busy during that year completing them as *Hampton Ferry, Shepperton Ferry* and *Twickenham Ferry*. The Admiralty building programme of orders for two destroyers *Esk* and *Express* and the Australian cruiser *Sydney* kept the yards busy during 1934/35. Two small cargo-liners for China Merchants S.N. Co. Ltd, *Hai Yuan* and *Hai Li,* both 3363/34, were followed by the launch on 4th April,1935 of the Australian coastal liner *Duntroon* 10346/35 with accomodation for 366 passengers for the Melbourne Steamship Co. Ltd and two coasters for Polish Steamship Line, *Puck* and *Hel,* both 1065 grt, were completed in early 1935.

Three cargo-liners were completed later in 1935, *Umtata* of 8141 grt for Bullard,King; *Explorer* of 6295 grt for T. & J. Harrison; and *Port Townsville* of 8661 grt for Port Line and were to lead to further orders from these owners. *Umtali* 8135/36 and *Umgeni* 8180/38 had splendid accomodation for over 100 passengers on their South African run, while *Inkosi* 6618/38 had passenger accomodation for 60 passengers on the West Indies run, and the Port Line cargo-liners *Port Halifax* 5820/37 and fully-refrigerated *Port Jackson* 9687/37 kept within the statutory 12 passenger limit which meant that a doctor was not needed.

The renewed demand for oil brought the tanker building programme back into its stride with the following tankers :-

		GRT
ANCYLUS	8017/35	Anglo-Saxon/Shell
SAN ALVARO	7385/35	Eagle Oil
BRITISH FAME	8206/36	British Tanker Co.
BRITISH ENDURANCE	8406/36	"
BRITISH DILIGENCE	8408/37	"
BRITISH RESOLUTION	8421/37	"
BRITISH TENACITY	8439/39	"
BRITISH INFLUENCE	8431/39	"
ELONA	6192/36	Anglo-Saxon/Shell
MACTRA	6193/36	"
SEPIA	6214/36	"
MATADIAN	4275/36	United Africa Co.
YENANGYAUNG	5447/37	Burmah Oil
REGENT LION	9551/37	Bowring
REGENT PANTHER	9565/37	"
REGENT TIGER	10177/38	"
ABBEYDALE	8299/38	Admiralty

A view of the Wallsend dry-docks in the early 1930s, showing PORT PIRIE and
THEMISTOCLES.
(Swan Hunter & Wigham Richardson Ltd).

The quadruple screw passenger motor vessel DOMINION MONARCH of 1939 in war time
colours.
(Shaw,Savill & Albion Co. Ltd).

ARNDALE	8296/39	Admiralty 192
THIARA	10364/39	Anglo-Saxon/Shell
TORINIA	10364/39	"

The largest were the last two for Shell at 15260 dwt, while the Bowring trio could carry 14540 tons of petrol. Tramps were again ordered by customers such as Helmer Staubo of Oslo: *Hav* 5062/39, and seven were also built and completed for the Hopemount Shipping Co. Ltd, over 90% owned by Swan,Hunter & Wigham Richardson Ltd: *Hopestar,Hopecastle,Hopecrown,Hopepeak,Hoperange, Hoperidge* and *Hopetarn*. These were ideal as grain carriers as they had steel, centre-line bulkheads in their six holds, and plenty of portable, wooden grain boards and trunks for their 9700 ton cargo. They had four-cylinder Doxford-type opposed piston oil engines constructed at the Neptune Works, except for *Hopestar* which was experimentally turbine-powered.

The Admiralty continued to build up their strength from 1936 with six destroyers completed over the next three years: *Hunter,Hyperion,Janus, Khartoum,Somali* and *Tartar*, and with the abandonment of Treaty limitations on battleship size ordered one of 30,000 tons displacement in 1937. Two fine liners featured in the building programme before the outbreak of World War II. A flagship was completed for Shaw,Savill and Albion Co. Ltd for a new service to Australia and New Zealand via the Cape. She was launched as *Dominion Monarch* of 27155 grt at Wallsend on 27th July,1938 and was completed in January,1939 and sailed on her maiden voyage to Wellington on 17th February,1939. She was powered by four Doxford oil engines linked to four propellers, and at times kept up over 20 knots on her maiden voyage, which took 24 days to complete. She carried 517 first-class passengers as a one-class ship and a full load of 16,400 tons of cargo was loaded at London with the passengers embarking at Southampton. Ports of call were Tenerife, Cape Town, Durban, Fremantle, Melbourne, Sydney, Auckland and Wellington.

The other liner was completed for Polish Ocean Lines as a sister for their *Chrobry* of 1939. She was launched as *Sobieski* of 11030 grt as a twin-screw motor-ship and was completed during 1939 with accomodation for 44 first-class, 250 third-class and 850 emigrants. Her service speed to New York was 17 knots and she had some refrigerated cargo capacity. Three passenger cargo-liners were completed at this time for British India with accomodation for 130 cabin-class passengers and 2000 Indian deck passengers:- *Amra* 8314 grt of November,1938 followed by *Aska* of August,1939 followed by *Aronda* launched in August,1940, all powered by six steam turbines driving twin screws.

Extensive orders for private owners were in hand on the outbreak of war in September,1939 and some 55 ships were completed for private owners up to early,1946 under Government licence. Ellerman Lines including Ellerman Wilson Line, and Port Line featured greatly for cargo-liners:-

CITY OF BRISTOL	8424/43	PORT NAPIER	9847/40
CITY OF MADRAS	8582/45	PORT PHILLIP	9947/42
CITY OF LONDON	8434/46	PORT MACQUARIE	9072/44
CITY OF POONA	9962/46	PORT VICTOR	12411/42
PANDORIAN	3146/41	PORT SYDNEY	9847/43
ARIOSTO	2176/40	PORT PIRIE	10561/46
ANGELO	2199/40	PORT NAPIER	11384/47
BASSANO	4986/46	PORT LINCOLN	7258/46
TASSO	1648/45		
VOLO	1797/46		

Port Napier was requisitioned by the Admiralty and completed as a minelayer to carry 500 mines for barrage work, and *Port Sydney* was completed as the escort carrier *Vindex* in December,1943 with a flight deck of 495 feet length and complement of 18 aeroplanes. She survived the war and was reconditioned by the yard between August,1948 and June,1949 when she re-emerged as *Port Vindex*. *Umtata* of 7288 grt was completed in January,1944 for Bullard,King with accomodation for over 100 passengers.

A total of 17 tankers were completed by the yard during the war and up to early 1946 with seven for British Tanker Co. Ltd, two for Anglo-Saxon/Shell, one for Trinidad Leaseholds Ltd - *Regent Hawk* 8169/45, one for United Africa Co. Ltd *Congonian* 6082/42, with four standard *'Ocean'* class of 12000 dwt with another completed as the gantry landing ship *Ennerdale*, and the Fast Fleet Oiler *Olna* 12667/45. Four *'Empire'* tramps were ordered by the Government of which two went to the Belgian Government for operation as well as *Baltyk* for Polish Ocean Lines 7001/42. Two *'MAC'* aircraft carriers were completed: *Empire Maccabe* 9249/43 and *Empire Macmahon* 8856/43, three ferries took *'Empire'* names as well as two coastal tankers. Two cable ships, *Ariel* (1939) and *Iris* (1940) and a number of Bosphorus ferries for the Turkish Government completed the mercantile production.

In June,1941 King George VI and H.M. The Queen made a morale-boosting tour of the Neptune yard and other Tyneside yards. Warship construction was enormous and included the battleship *Anson* of June,1942 and ordered in 1937, four cruisers *Mauritius* (1940), *Newfoundland*(1941), *Gambia* (1942) and *Superb* (1943), 30 destroyers and destoyer escorts including 16 of the *'Hunt'* class. The aircraft carrier *Vengeance* of 1945, the incomplete aircraft carrier *Leviathan* and numerous smaller craft were also built. At the end of hostilities the combined yards covered 80 acres with a river frontage of 4000 feet, and seventeen building berths up to 1000 feet, and three dry-docks.

The Neptune Yard continued its long tradition of building cable ships when it completed the cable-layer *Monarch* of 8052 grt in February, 1946 for the Postmaster-General. The first cable ship to be built by the Neptune Yard had been *Colonia* (1902) followed by *Cambria* (1904), whose first job had been to lay a Northern direct telegraph line between Europe and America, *Telconia* (1909), *All America* (1921), *Marie Louise Mckay* (1922), *John W. Mckay* (1922), *Dominia* (1926), *Ariel* (1939), *Iris* (1940), *Bullfrog* (1944) and *St. Margarets* (1944). *Monarch* became famous in 1955/56 when she laid the first Transatlantic telephone cable between Oban and Newfoundland. The weight of this cable and repeaters was so great that *Monarch* had to make three loadings on her massive drums to complete the task. By that time the yard had also completed the cable ships *Edward Wilshaw* (1948) and *Recorder* (1954) for Cable and Wireless Ltd to make a total of twenty five cable layers built.

The Yards got into their stride in 1946 by resuming tanker production, and this was to be a major feature of the production until they amalgamated with the other yards on the river in 1968. Indeed over 60 tankers were completed out of 180 ships built by the company over this period, or numerically one-third. The Shell 'supertanker' *Velutina* was launched in 1950 by Princess Margaret at the Wallsend yard, which also launched the much larger 'supertankers' *Solen, Narica* and *Nacella* for Shell in the 1960s. The following deadweight table shows clearly the escalating sizes of tankers:-

BRITISH CAUTION	12250/46	British Tanker Co. Ltd
BRITISH EARL	12250/46	"
BRITISH ARDOUR	12250/49	"
BRITISH UNION	12250/50	"
BRITISH VISCOUNT	12250/51	"
BRITISH FAME	16800/49	"
BRITISH FREEDOM	16800/50	"
BRITISH SPLENDOUR	16800/50	"
BRITISH SPORTSMAN	16800/51	"
BRITISH PATROL	16800/54	"
HELICINA	18100/46	Anglo-Saxon/Shell
LEMBULUS	9600/48	"
HYALINA	18090/48	"
PALUDINA	9600/49	"
VELUTINA	28220/50	"
VELLETIA	28106/52	"
HELIX	18000/53	"
HELCION	18000/54	"

DWT

HELDIA	18150/55	Anglo-Saxon/Shell
HELISOMA	18220/56	"
PUNTA MEDANOS	10000/50	Argentine Fleet Oiler
STALAND	13580/49	Helmer Staubo, Norway
DAGLAND	13000/52	John P Pedersen, Norway
BUESTEN	15000/51	Raffen & Loenechen, Norway
STAVIK	13530/51	A/S Havtank, Norway
WILHELM JEBSEN	18160/53	Jebsen, Norway
BURMAH SAPPHIRE	8460/53	Burmah Oil 193
SCOTTISH LION	16310/52	Scottish Tanker Co. Ltd 213
SCOTTISH EAGLE	15710/52	"
HOPEMOUNT 3	19000/53	Hopemount Shpg. Co. Ltd 125
BORDER SENTINEL	15968/55	Lowland Tanker Co. Ltd 189
STANCLOUD	18750/58	Stanhope Shpg. Co. Ltd 132
TIDEREACH	20000/54	Admiralty Oiler 192
BRITISH BULLDOG	30000/51	British Tanker Co. Ltd
BRITISH MERCHANT 2	31750/54	"
BRITISH VALOUR 2	35250/57	"
BRITISH ARCHITECT 2	36046/58	"
BRITISH AVIATOR	37232/59	"
BRITISH DESTINY 2	44900/59	"
OCTAVIAN	30000/54	Hilmar Reksten, Norway
LLANISHEN 3	34300/58	Evan Thomas Radcliffe 70
ELLORA 3	37140/59	British India S.N. 42
ELLENGA 2	37140/60	British India SN 42
EL LOBO 2	18640/59	Bowring 76
BORDER PELE	19610/61	Lowland Tanker Co. Ltd 189
BORDER CASTLE	19610/61	"
ABADESA	21500/62	Furness-Houlder Argentine Lines
BRITISH HAZEL	20462/64	British Tanker Co. Ltd
OLEANDER	30000/65	Admiralty Oiler 192
STALAND	50340/62	Helmer Staubo, Norway
SOLEN 2	71250/61	Anglo-Saxon/Shell
TALAMBA 2	53800/64	British India S.N. 42
OTTAWA	89036/65	Trident Tankers (P & O) 355
CLEMENTINE CHURCHILL	97500/66	Hilmar Reksten, Bergen
SIR WINSTON CHURCHILL	97500/66	"
BRITISH ARGOSY	112800/66	British Tanker Co. Ltd
NARICA	115030/67	Deutsche Shell
NACELLA	117270/68	"
TEXACO WESTMINSTER	102500/68	Texaco

In the early post-war years French owners ordered one liner for South American service and five passenger cargo-liners for Mediterranean and other services. *Provence* of 15889 grt was launched in August, 1950 at the Neptune Yard for Soc. General Transportes Maritimes (SGTM) as a replacement for their *Campana* built at the Neptune Yard in 1929. She was the tenth ship completed for

Shaw,Savill cargo-liner GOTHIC of 1948 carrying H. M. The Queen on her tour of Australia and New Zealand in 1953/54; and the French liner PROVENCE of 1951.
(Furness Withy Group & L. Dunn)

SGTM when she ran trials with her geared turbines giving 19 knots in early 1951, and she sailed on her maiden voyage on 30th March,1951 from Marseilles to Rio de Janeiro and Buenos Aires via Barcelona and Lisbon. She had accomodation for 139 first-class, 113 tourist-class and 1052 third-class passengers. SGTM had also taken delivery in 1948 of the passenger cargo-liner *Sidi del Abbes* of 5226 grt which had accomodation for 95 first-class, 226 tourist-class and 573 third-class passengers, and she had an exact sister *President de Cazalet* in the Cie de Navigation Mixte fleet built by the yard in 1948. The Mixte company also ordered *Djebel Dira* 4180/48 from the yard with accomodation for 56 first-class, 100 tourist-class and 430 third-class passengers, and was turbine-propelled as were her compatriots. Two more cargo-liners of high standard were completed for the Chargeurs Reunis fleet: *Brazza* and *Foucauld*, both 9095/48 and twin-screw motorships with accomodation for 103 first-class, 78 second-class and 400 third-class passengers.

Companhia Nacional de Navegacao,Lisbon took delivery of the twin-screw passenger and cargo-liner *Mocambique* of 12976 grt in 1949 for their service between Portugal and Angola and Mozambique. She had been launched at the Neptune Yard on 1st December,1948 and had accomodation for 93 first-class, 141 second-class and 102 third-class passengers and could also carry 9243 tons of cargo. The first-class entrance hall featured an overlay marquetry panel of the world over the staircase to enable passengers to trace the course of the ship, and they could also enjoy the verandah cafe, music room, smoking room and de-luxe suites. Her twin Doxford-type oil engines constructed by the yard gave her a service speed of 18 knots.

Norwegian America Line took delivery of their new Transatlantic liner *Bergensfjord* in May,1956, having been launched by Princess Astrid of Norway in July,1955. She featured an all-welded aluminium superstructure for lightness and was one of the first liners to make use of this metal. She could carry 730 tourist class, 125 first-class passengers in Scandinavian style and her public rooms featured tapestries, paintings, mosaics and glass-panelled walls. Her twin Stork oil engines gave her a service speed of 20 knots, but she was also designed to cruise in winter and later became a single-class liner. Princess Astrid had travelled to the launching from Norway on *Leda* 6670/53 of Bergen Line, which she had also launched at the yard on 3rd September,1952. *Leda* began her twice-weekly run to Stavanger and Bergen from the Tyne in April,1953 and could carry 119 first-class and 384 tourist-class passengers, and was powered by two sets of steam turbines by Wallsend Slipway to give a service speed of 22 knots. The competitor of Bergen Line, Swedish Lloyd, had previously taken delivery of *Patricia* 6644/51 from the Neptune yard for their Gothenburg to London service.

CLAN FRASER seen afloat in the Tyne after her launch on 27th July,1961 (Clansman); and ILESHA PALM of 1961. (L. Dunn).

The fine Portuguese liner *Principe Perfeito* of 19393 grt was delivered by the Neptune Yard in 1961. She was the largest Neptune ship when launched in September, 1960 for Cia Nacional of Lisbon, and her Parsons turbines built at Wallsend propelled her at 20 knots on a regular run between Lisbon and Beira with accomodation for 1000 passengers and 200 troops. She could also carry 8600 tons of cargo and was sold for cruising in 1976. The major customers of the yards for cargo-liners during this period were Palm Line and Ellerman Lines :-

BADAGRY PALM	5042/56	CITY OF BROOKLYN	7557/49
BAMENDA PALM	5042/56	CITY OF COVENTRY	7568/49
ELMINA PALM	5505/57	CITY OF GUILDFORD	4945/57
ENUGU PALM	5141/58	CITY OF LANCASTER	4950/58
KATSINA PALM	6012/58	MERCIAN	1517/48
KANO PALM	6012/58	MARENGO	4981/47
IBADAN PALM	5799/59	RIALTO	5005/49
IKEJA PALM	5816/61	LEO	1792/47
ILESHA PALM	5816/61	VOLO	1797/46
ILORIN PALM	5442/60		
LOBITO PALM	5923/60		
LAGOS PALM	5927/61		

with *Ilorin Palm* launched 17 weeks ahead of schedule in 1960, and she was fitted with one of the last Swan,Hunter-built Doxford oil engines, as the Neptune engine works ceased production shortly afterwards. British India Line and Clan Line were other good customers:-

SIRDHANA	8608/47	CLAN FERGUSSON	9292/61
DWARKA	4851/47	CLAN FORBES	9240/61
CHAKDINA	7267/51	CLAN FRASER	9292/61
CHAKRATA	7265/51	CLAN FARQUHARSON	9240/62
CHILKA	7087/50	CLAN FINLAY	9077/62
CHINDWARA	7525/50		

Dwarka was powered by Doxford oil engines and had accomodation for 50 passengers in cabins as well as many Indian deck passengers on her regular run into the Persian Gulf, and *Sirdhana* had accomodation for 83 passengers in cabins. Port Line took delivery of four refrigerated cargo-liners for their Australian meat trade *Port Brisbane* 11942/49, *Port Townsville* 8651/51, *Port Sydney* 9992/55 and *Port New Plymouth* 13925/60; while Shaw,Savill & Albion took delivery of three cargo-liners for their New Zealand trade *Gothic* 15911/48, *Megantic* 12226/62 and *Medic* 12220/63. *Gothic* had spacious accomodation for 85 first-class passengers in 53 cabins of which 36 were single-berth, while 23 had the luxury of their own private

Supertankers **SOLEN** of 1961 (top), **TEXACO WESTMINSTER** of 1968 (middle), and **EVERETT F. WELLS** of 1977 (bottom). (T. Rayner, Shields Gazette, British Shipbuilders Ltd)

bathroom. The public rooms were of a high enough standard for the ship to act as a temporary Royal Yacht for a tour of Australia and New Zealand. She arrived at Jamaica on 21st November, 1953 to embark the Royal party and went through the Panama Canal to visit Suva, Tonga, Auckland, Wellington, Bluff, Sydney, Hobart, Melbourne, Townsville, Cairns , Mackay, Adelaide, Fremantle, Cocos Islands, Colombo and Aden, where H.M. The Queen disembarked on 28th April, 1954.

Cargo-liner customers also included Cunard Line, who took delivery of *Assyria* 8683/50 for Transatlantic services, with Scindia Line of India taking *Jaljawahar* 8489/48 with accomodation for 100 passengers. Black Star Line of Ghana took delivery during 1964/65 of three cargo-liners: *Korle Lagoon, Sakumo Lagoon* and *Benya River*, Nigerian National Line took delivery of two during 1962/63: *Nnamdi Azikiwe* and *Ahmadu Bello*. *Eastern Trader* 8950/59 was completed for the Far Eastern services of the Indo-China Steam Navigation Co. Ltd, and two express passenger and cargo-liners were completed in 1965 for Union-Castle Mail Co. Ltd: *Good Hope Castle* and *Southampton Castle* both of 10538 grt, the latter launched by Princess Alexandra. Their required service speeds were high at 23 knots to replace two passenger liners on the weekly South African schedule and they were fitted with powerful oil engines by Wallsend Slipway. These super cargo-liners had much of their cargo spaces refrigerated and they could carry 11034 tons of cargo.

The car ferries *Gaelic Ferry* 3316/63 and *Europic Ferry* 4190/67 were completed for the U.K. coastal services of the Atlantic Steam Navigation Co. Ltd, while *Dover* 3602/65 was completed for the Dover to Dunkirk route and *St. George* 7356/68 for the Harwich to Hook of Holland services of British Rail. *Dover* returned to the Tyne at the end of her career, and is currently moored directly underneath the Tyne Bridge at Gateshead as a leisure ship, while *St. George* operates out of Fort Lauderdale, Florida as *Scandinavian Dawn* on day cruises. Tramps also featured in the building lists with Buries Markes Ltd taking *La Hacienda* 6008/53, Stephens Sutton Ltd *Reaveley* 6072/56 and *Riseley* 6424/57 - the latter being one of the first British tramps to have both bridge and engines aft. Five of 13000 dwt were completed for Greek owners between 1954 and 1957: *Capetan Kostis, Capetan Carras, Capetan Psarros, Michael C* and *Polyxene C.*

The light aircraft carrier *Albion* was completed in 1954, having lain incomplete since being launched at the yard in 1947, and she was later converted into a commando carrier. The cruiser *Lion* had also lain incomplete since the war, and was completed in 1959/60 with four 6-inch guns as main armament. She and her two sisters, *Blake* and *Tiger*, completed on the Clyde, were the last Royal Navy cruisers. The destroyer *Daring* (1952) was followed by the County Class guided missile destroyers *London* (1963) and *Norfolk* (1970), which both had Royal sponsors - the Duchess of Gloucester launching *London* on 7th December,1961 and the Duchess of Norfolk launching *Norfolk* on 16th November,1967. These were followed by the Type 82 missile destroyer *Bristol* , launched on 30th June,1969 and completed at the end of 1972 as the only one of its kind. Frigates *Falmouth* (1961), *Galatea* (1963), oilers *Tidereach* (1954) and *Oleander* (1965), air stores ships *Lyness, Stromness* and *Tarbartness* of 1966/67 completed the naval programme of this period. The three air stores ships were later sold to the U.S. Navy.

E. John Hunter, grandson of the founder, was appointed Chairman in May,1957. He had been educated at Oundle, then served a year as an apprentice at Wallsend shipyard before going up to Cambridge and subsequently to Durham University. He then spent two years in the drawing and design offices of Wallsend shipyard followed by a brief period at the North British Engine Works and Elderslie dry-dock on the Clyde. In 1939 he was appointed Assistant Manager of the Wallsend Dry Docks Department, becoming General Manager in 1943 and a director of Swan,Hunter & Wigham Richardson Ltd in 1945. Sir John Hunter succeeded John W. Elliott who had held the position of Chairman of the company since 1949, and after leading the Group through the 1960s and 1970s he died in retirement in 1983 at the age of 71 years. His younger brother Robert Hunter was appointed Manager of the Wallsend Dry Docks Department in succession to his elder brother in 1957. He had also been educated at Oundle and joined Wallsend shipyard as an apprentice in 1934 and saw active service in many theatres of war for the Royal Navy during World War II with the rank of Lt.-Commander. He then entered Wallsend Dry Docks Department as Assistant General Manager, becoming General Manager in 1955. There were also descendants of the Swan and Wigham Richardson families on the Board at this time in S.C. Swan and George Wigham Richardson, as well as Peter Denham Christie, whose grandfather had been the first manager of the Neptune yard and whose father John Denham Christie had died in October,1950.

Sir E. John Hunter became Chairman of a much larger Group in July,1966 when Swan,Hunter & Wigham Richardson Ltd merged with the Tees yard of Smiths Dock Co. Ltd to form Associated Shipbuilders Ltd - a meaningless name which was quickly changed to Swan Hunter Group Ltd by November of that year. The rationalisation of Tyneside shipbuilding into a regional group in line with the recommendations of the Geddes Report saw the five yards on the river: Wallsend, Neptune, Hawthorn Leslie, Walker Naval Yard and Readhead shipyards merged into Swan Hunter & Tyne Shipbuilders Ltd effective from 1st January,1968. In October,1968 the Furness Yard on the Tees joined the new massive consortium of

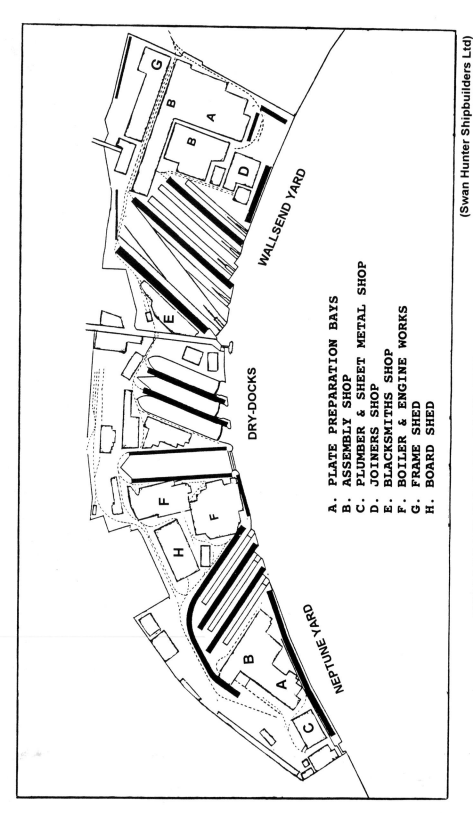

A. PLATE PREPARATION BAYS
B. ASSEMBLY SHOP
C. PLUMBER & SHEET METAL SHOP
D. JOINERS SHOP
E. BLACKSMITHS SHOP
F. BOILER & ENGINE WORKS
G. FRAME SHED
H. BOARD SHED

WALLSEND YARD

DRY-DOCKS

NEPTUNE YARD

SWAN HUNTER SHIPBUILDERS LTD.
NEPTUNE AND WALLSEND YARDS IN 1969

(Swan Hunter Shipbuilders Ltd)

yards, the name being changed once again to Swan Hunter Shipbuilders Ltd early in 1969.

At the Wallsend shipyard in 1967/68 the old berths 1 and 2 with gantry cranes were demolished and replaced with a single realigned berth angled across both of the old ones and capable of building VLCC tankers of 250,000 dwt and 1100 feet in length. The steel production facilities were also comprehensively modernised, including the installation of numerically-controlled plate cutting machines and a panel production line. New craneage was installed in the fabrication shed, and two 180-ton capacity Clarke Chapman cranes were provided alongside the main building berth. A large modern joinery shop was also established to serve all the yards in the Group. (See shipyard plan). The Dry Docks Department had been updated by a new 715 feet no. 4 dry-dock in 1957 and opened by the Duchess of Northumberland. These dry-docks and those of Smiths Docks Co. Ltd, North Shields were operated separately from 1966 as Swan Hunter Shiprepairers Ltd.

The first supertanker keel to be laid down on the new berth was that of *Esso Northumbria* in April,1968, and she was launched by Princess Anne on 2nd May,1969 and left the river for trials watched by huge crowds on 8th February,1970. Seven more tankers of her size were to follow at intervals of one year:- *Esso Hibernia* (1971), *Texaco Great Britain* (1972), *London Lion* (1973), *World Unicorn* (1974), *Windsor Lion* (1975), *Tyne Pride* (1976) and *Everett F. Wells* (1977). Some of these giants had been part of a deal with Maritime Fruit Carriers of Haifa, Israel for an indefinite number of supertankers and fruit reefers. Unfortunately Swan's partner in the 'Swan Maritime' deal got into financial difficulties, leaving the shipbuilder to dispose of those already built, mostly to Russian and Venezuelan owners. In the event thirteen tankers of three sizes were built:- crude carriers of 250,000 dwt and 112,000 dwt; and products tankers of 32,000 dwt.

At the Neptune Yard after the merger new shops were completed to supply the Group with pipes and engineering components, a centralised sheet metal shop was established and an electrical console shop set up. One of the first ships completed after the merger was the car and train ferry *Vortigern* 4371/69 for British Rail. In summer she operated as a car ferry on the Dover to Boulogne route with space for 240 cars, while in winter she operated as a train ferry on the Dover to Dunkirk route. An order for four high-class cargo-liners for the Persian Gulf services of British India was then started. *Manora* 11208/70, *Merkara* 11142/71, *Morvada* 11142/71 and *Mulbera* 11143/71 had some of their cargo space refrigerated, and their service speeds of 19 knots were provided by oil engines, two of which came from Barclay, Curle on the Clyde and two from Hawthorn, Leslie at Newcastle.

Launch of Type 22 destroyers CHATHAM (above) on 20th January,1988 and SHEFFIELD (below) on 26th March,1986.   (Author).

The keel of the last passenger ship to be built on the Tyne was then laid at the Neptune Yard in 1971, and she was launched as *Vistafjord* for the Norwegian America Line on 15th May,1972. Extensive use of aluminium for her superstructure was a feature, as was her designed twin role as a Transatlantic liner and cruise ship. She left the Tyne in May,1973 for Oslo, from where she departed on her maiden voyage to New York on 22nd May,1973. She had accomodation for 550 passengers, and her twin propellers were powered by oil engines made at Wallsend by G. Clark & N.E.M. Ltd, and was later sold to Cunard for cruising.

The Neptune Yard then fitted out the hull of the Barrow-built liner *Copenhagen*, whose Danish owner had gone bankrupt and she was completed as *Odessa* 13253/74 for the Russian Black Sea cruising fleet. The yard then concentrated on naval work starting with the smaller replenishment tankers *Gold Rover* and *Black Rover* in 1974/75 before buiding five Type 42 destroyers and three Type 22 frigates, whose launch and completion dates were:-

	Launch	Completion
COVENTRY	21.6.1974	10.1978
NEWCASTLE	24.4.1975	2.1978
GLASGOW	14.4.1976	3.1979
EXETER	25.4.1978	8.1980
YORK	21.6.1982	7.1984
SHEFFIELD	26.3.1986	12.1988
COVENTRY	8.4.1986	3.1989
CHATHAM	20.1.1988	11.1989

Merchant orders in these gaps included the hull of the heavy lift ship *Starman Anglia* 2777/77 for Blue Star Line Ltd, which was then completed at the Haverton Hill yard on the Tees, the Stephenson Clarke collier *Aldrington* 4334/78, and the tanker *Osco Ingram Osprey* 18959/82 and 30,000 dwt for the Ingram Corporation of the U.S.A., parent group of the Rowbotham coastal tanker fleet. Houlder Brothers diving support ship *Orelia* was launched on 11th December,1982 and completed in June,1984 for Houlder Offshore Ltd. She has a sophisticated computer-controlled dynamic positioning system to hold her steady above a well head using her six 6-cylinder Mirlees oil engines double-reduction geared to three shafts. The cable layer and repair ship *Pacific Guardian* was launched on 13th June,1984 for the Pacific station at Suva,Fiji of Cable & Wireless Ltd. The destroyer *Coventry* was launched by management in the dead of the night on 8th April,1986 to beat a dispute at the yard. After the launch of the Type 22 frigate *Chatham* on 20th January,1988 all production was switched to the Wallsend Yard.

Cable layer PACIFIC GUARDIAN seen leaving the Thames in 1984 for her maiden voyage to
Fiji, and at her launch from the Neptune Yard on 13th June,1984.   (Cable & Wireless Ltd)

Antarctic research ship JAMES CLARK ROSS on her launch day of 1st December,1990 shortly before being sent into the Tyne by H. M. The Queen, fleet replenishement oiler FORT GEORGE is on the right.   (Author).

Cable layer SIR ERIC SHARP slides down the ways at Wallsend on   25th October,1988. (Author)

Swan Hunter Shipbuilders Ltd had become part of the nationalised British Shipbuilders Ltd on 1st July,1977, with the Group payroll standing at 11,000 employees and while the main berth at the Wallsend Yard was building the hull of the aircraft carrier *Illustrious*. She was duly launched on 1st December,1978 by Princess Margaret and her outfitting, first at Wallsend and then at Walker Naval Yard, was speeded up in early 1982 so that she could participate in the Falklands War. The yard had won the order for her sister *Ark Royal* in 1978, and her keel was laid on the same berth and she was launched on 2nd June,1981 by H.M. The Queen Mother and completed at Walker Naval Yard in 1984. Three large merchant ships were then constructed at the Wallsend Yard - the forestry products carrier *Thorseggen* 14578/83 for Thor Dahl A/S,Norway for charter to Norsk-Pacific Inc of Los Angeles for regular cargoes of pulp from Alaska to California; the bulk/container ship *Hoegh Duke* 30061/84 for Leif Hoegh A/S,Oslo; and the ro-ro/container ship *Atlantic Conveyor* 58438/85 for Cunard for Transatlantic service in Atlantic Container Transport and a replacement for a ship of the same name lost in the Falklands War.

Swan Hunter Shipbuilders Ltd was privatised on 20th January,1986 when sold for £5M in a 'management buy-out' to Dr. Roger Vaughan, Peter A. Vaughan, Ken Chapman and Alex Marsh. The workforce stood at 4500 employees and the Wallsend Yard was building the hull of another replacement for a ship lost in the Falklands War - the tank landing ship *Sir Galahad,* launched on 13th December,1986 and completed during 1987. Following privatisation the Yard won orders for four Type 23 frigates *Marlborough,Westminster,Northumberland* and *Richmond* and an oiler/replenishment ship for the Royal Navy, *Fort George*, an Antarctic oceanographic ship *James Clark Ross,* a cable layer/repair ship *Sir Eric Sharp* for Cable & Wireless Ltd, as well as alterations and repair work of patrol boats for overseas customers. H. M. The Queen launched *James Clark Ross* on 1st December,1990 in a colourful ceremony for the National Environmental Research Council as a replacement for the *John Biscoe* of 1956. *Fort George* was the last big launch on the Tyne on 1st March,1991, and the Type 23 frigates *Westminster* and *Northumberland* were launched during 1992 with the final launch being that of their sister frigate *Richmond* on 6th April,1993. Unfortunately Joint Chief Executives Dr. Roger Vaughn and Alex Marsh had to place the company into receivership on 13th May,1993 following the failure of the yard to secure an order for a Landing Platform Helicopter ship. It was alleged that the cash flow of the company was weak due to non-payment of staged payments on R.F.A. *Fort George*, and this the most famous Tyneside shipyard was offered for sale by the receivers. A huge total of 2,700 merchant and naval ships had been built by yards with the Swan Hunter name.

The last launch, sponsor Lady Hill-Norton (above) moves to the launching dias, turns to wave to the crowd (below), then launches the Type 23 frigate RICHMOND on 6th April,1993 thus ending 130 years of shipbuilding tradition at Wallsend. (Author).

CHARLES MITCHELL & COMPANY 1853 - 1882
ARMSTRONG,MITCHELL & CO. LTD. 1882 - 1897 87
ARMSTRONG,WHITWORTH & CO. LTD. 1897-1928 6
VICKERS-ARMSTRONG LTD. 1928 - 1968 223

This section covers three shipyards, the Armstrong warship yard at Elswick, the High Walker Naval Yard, and the Low Walker yard of Charles Mitchell. Charles Mitchell was born in Aberdeen on 20th May,1820 and served his apprenticeship with Simpson & Company, ironfounders of Aberdeen, before moving to Newcastle in September,1842 to work for John H.S. Coutts, also originally from Aberdeen. Charles worked for Coutts until 1844 before moving to London to work for Maudslay,Son & Field and also travelling extensively in France,Germany and Italy. He returned to Newcastle in 1852 to set-up his own Low Walker yard next to the Coutts yard. His first vessel, *Havilah*, was a coaster for the Australian trade and was launched in February,1853. His seventh ship was ordered by German owners as *Hesperus*, but on completion in December,1854 was bought by the Admiralty and sent with a cargo of iron rails from Walker to Balaclava for the Crimean War railway. Initially paddle steamers were built for use on Indian rivers, the Nile in Egypt and on Russian rivers in connection with the Russian Black Sea grain trade. Now successful, Charles married Ann Swan, third child of William and Ann Swan of West Farm,Walker on 9th May,1854 and gained two practical brothers-in-law in Charles S. Swan and Henry F. Swan.

Some 450 ships were completed under the Mitchell name up to 1882, with three being launched in a unique triple launch at the yard in 1856. Yard nos. 15,17 and 18 were launched simultaneously - an event that was never repeated on the Tyne (see illustration) - with Yard 17 and 18, *Eupatoria* of 537 grt and *Sophia* of 413 grt, shown on the left, while Yard 15, *George Robert* of 76 grt, is shown entering the river at centre. The vessel on the right in the middle of the river is a spectator craft. In 1858 two 'kits' for screw steamers were supplied for erection on the Volga under the supervision of Charles S. Swan, while in 1864 Henry F. Swan, who had joined the yard as an apprentice in 1858, was despatched to St. Petersburg to build five small warships. Russian owners were important to the yard with orders from 1868 continuing to flow to the Low Walker yard for small warships, river craft and larger passenger-carrying vessels such as the clipper-bowed *Czar* 2241/83. A total of

twenty four passenger-carrying ships was built by the yard for both Russian and other owners, the first being *Canton* and *Hong Kong*, both of 1881 grt and constructed in 1871.

The first undersea telegraph cables were being laid at this time, and the Hooper Telegraph Company ordered a ship to lay 5000 miles of cable off the South American coast. Mitchell was asked to build her in the short time of three months, and *Hooper* 4935/73 was in fact ready in one hundred days. Siemens of Germany ordered another cable layer 18 months later, the twin-screw *Faraday* 4908/74, and a French cable layer followed as *Puyer Quertier* 1385/79. In 1877 a 1000-ton floating dock was built for the Dutch Government and towed out to Java. The backbone of the yard, however, was tramps for British owners such as Watts,Milburn of Newcastle, who ordered eight tramps with Newcastle and London district names e.g. *Kensington* 908/78; and Hamilton,Fraser of Liverpool who ordered six tramps with names beginning *'INCH'* e.g. *Inchclutha* 1984/79; and with two tramps each for local owners Hunting & Son: *Joseph Ferens* 1803/77 and *Yoxford* 1999/78; and Stag Line: *Robinia* 1816/76 and *Azalea* 1828/77.

The first British gunboat built at the yard was *Staunch* of 1867, and was fitted with a 9" Armstrong muzzle-loading gun, and then some 27 similar gunboats fitted with a 10" Armstrong gun were built as the 'Ant' class by the yard up to 1881. The Japanese cruiser *Tsukuski Kam* was built in 1880, and two cruisers and several gunboats were completed for China in 1881, and the Chilean cruiser *Esmeralda* left the river in 1884, having been designed by George Rendel, Managing Director of Armstrong's Elswick ordnance works. She was the first fruits of a merger between William Armstrong and Charles Mitchell in the new company Armstrong,Mitchell & Co. Ltd launched with a capital of £1.575M in 1882. William Armstrong had established a company at Elswick in 1847, making his reputation initially with hydraulic cranes. The Crimean War gave impetus to the Armstrong Field Gun, and his breech-loading guns, rifling of gun barrels for accuracy of aim, and armour piercing shells and high explosives made him one of the two great armament manufacturers in the world - Armstrong of England at his Elswick works and Krupps of Germany. Plans for a new shipyard for warships only next to the Elswick works were laid in 1883 and the cruiser *Panther* was the first ship launched there in 1885.

The Low Walker yard concentrated on merchant shipbuilding, especially of tankers from 1885. *Gluckauf* for the Deutsch-America Petroleum Company was launched on 16th June,1886 one day ahead of *Bakuin* for Alfred Suart of London at the Gray yard in West Hartlepool. She was completed in July of that year as the world's first ocean-going tanker, having been designed by Henry F. Swan to carry 3500 tons of oil from America or the Black Sea to Europe. The Deutsch-America

**GLUCKAUF of 1886, the world's first bulk oil tanker.
(Tyne & Wear Archives)**

**TRIGONIA (left) of 1898 and COWRIE (below) of 1896, both owned by Shell.
(Tyne & Wear Archives)**

S. S. Cowrie dans le Chantier à Port-Tewfik.

Petroleum Company placed orders for many sister tankers at Low Walker and the yard went on complete over 100 tankers up to the outbreak of war in 1914. Some twenty tankers were for the German register, the Deutsch-America Petroleum Company following *Gluckauf* with *Vorwarts* 2466/86, *Minister Maybach* 2881/87, *Wilkommen* 2817/87, *Energie* 2817/87 and *Paula* 2675/88 and many others. Sixty tankers came under the British flag for owners such as Anglo-Saxon/Shell, Bowring, Burmah Oil, Prince Line, Moss Tankers, Galbraith Pembroke, Lane & Macandrews, Eagle Oil and others. One tanker *Le Coq* 3399/95 was completed for the ownership of Henry F. Swan, Managing Director of the Low Walker yard with management by Lane & Macandrews. Tankers were also completed by the yard for the Belgian, Italian, Dutch, French, Russian, American and Japanese registers.

Two Russian ice-breakers were completed in 1898, *Ermack* 5128/98 and *Sampo* 1339/98, the former fitted with hydraulic elevators for raising and lowering carriages and trucks for the different levels of the river Volga. Perhaps the most spectacular ship built for the Russians was the train ferry *Baikal* 4200/99, which was sent overland in 7200 pieces and re-assembled on the banks of Lake Baikal as part of the Trans-Siberian railway. German and British owners continued to order dry-cargo liners such as:-

EUROPA	1533/80	Hamburg-Amerika Line
INDIA	1551/81	"
AUSTRALIA	2149/81	"
POLYNESIA	2196/81	"
POLARIA	2196/82	"
CALIFORNIA	2196/83	"
ASCANIA	2069/87	"
COLONIA	2069/88	"
ITALIA	3498/89	"
TIJUCA	2452/87	Hamburg-Sud America Line
OLINDA	2452/87	"
ITAPARICA	2544/89	"
ORANJE PRINCE	1868/89	Prince Line
ELBERFELD	2630/89	Deutsche-Australia Line
BARMAN	2646/89	Hansa Line
NEKO	3576/91	Kosmos D/S Ges.
ROLAND	3729/92	Norddeutscher Lloyd
MARK	3835/93	"
DOROTHEA RICKMERS	3738/95	Rickmers Rhederei
VERIA	3229/99	Cunard Line
ATLANTIAN	9399/99	F. Leyland
MOUNT TEMPLE	9792/01	Elder Dempster
SWAZI	4941/01	Bucknall Line
BANTU	4189/01	"
BARALONG	4192/01	"

The first warships from Elswick and Walker Naval Yard, the cruiser PANTHER of 1885 for
Austro-Hungary (above), and the Royal Navy battleship MALAYA of 1916 (Vickers &
Abrahams of Devonport).

The keel of the battleship MALAYA was laid at the Naval Yard by Winston Churchill
on 20th October,1913 and she was launched on 13th May,1915 and completed
in February,1916. Her main propelling machinery was supplied by the Wallsend
Slipway & Engineering Co. Ltd. She served with distinction throughout World War I,
and subsequently in the Mediterranean with the main battle fleet stationed
at Alexandria for operations against Italy in World War II.

GRIQUA	3344/02	Bucknall Line
AMATONGA	3331/03	"
SAINT CUTHBERT	4954/04	Saint Line
MYRMIDON	4965/06	Blue Funnel Line
POLYPHEMUS	4968/07	"
CLAN MACGILLIVRAY	5023/11	Clan Line
CLAN MACARTHUR	5815/12	"
CLAN MACTAVISH	5816/13	"

The Australian coastal passenger steamer *Yongala* 3664/03 could carry 240 passengers, while *Louisiana* 3015/96 was the first North American trader for Danish ferry company DFDS. The Silverdale Company of Canada ordered the Great Lakes steamer *Neebing* 1750/03, and three Norwegian shipowners ordered the large cargo ships *Storstad* 6028/10, *Sandefjord* 6026/11 and *Kim* 5857/12, the latter being converted later into a whale factory ship. The suction dredger *Archer* was completed in 1900, the Isle of Man Steam Packet ferry *Viking* 1951/05 was turbine-propelled while the ferry *Scotia* 1461/01 was completed for Canadian owners. Three floating cranes were built: the 100-ton lifting capacity *Atlas* (1884) and *Titan* (1896) for Mersey Docks & Harbour Board, with *Goliath* (1906) for Rangoon Docks. British tramp owners such as Watts,Watts took *Willesden* 4881/05, *Chatham* 3653/06; and E.C. Thin of Liverpool took *Tropea* 4675/05, *Tremont* 4186/10 and *Tripoli* 4186/10. The cable ship *Restorer* 3180/03 for Cable & Wireless Ltd further demonstrated the yard's willingness to tackle anything that came their way. However the allocation of merchant shipbuilding to Low Walker yard and warship building to the Elswick yard was not clear-cut, for over the 14 years to 1899 Low Walker built 11 small warships.

In 1897, during a period of British naval and armaments expansion Armstrong,Mitchell & Co. Ltd purchased and amalgamated with the Manchester-based armaments firm of Sir Joseph Whitworth & Company to become Sir W.G. Armstrong,Whitworth & Co. Ltd. Charles Mitchell had died in August,1895 while still active and going daily to work at the yard but there were now no Mitchells on the Board. Warship-building at Elswick had expanded from the first cruiser *Panther* of 1885 and her sister *Leopard* of 1886, and these light, fast but heavily-gunned 'Elswick Cruisers' soon gained international customers from Japan, China,Argentina,Norway etc. The Italian cruiser *Piemonte* of 1889 was the fastest in the world at 22 knots at that time, while the Japanese battleship *Yashima* of 1894 could make 20 knots. The first British battleship built at Elswick was the ill-fated *Victoria* of April,1890 and she was followed by *Swiftsure* (1904) and the dreadnought battleships *Superb* (1909) and *Monarch* (1912) and the battlecruiser *Invincible* (1908). Cruisers and smaller warships for the Royal Navy included *Rattler, Wasp, Pandora, Mildura, Sirius, Spartan, Swordfish, Spitfire, Achilles, Lancaster,*

The dreadnought battleship SUPERB seen on completion moored in the Tyne in 1909.

Adventure, Hampshire, Amethyst, Attentive, Newcastle and *Weymouth*. The success of Armstrong-built warships in the Russo-Japanese battle of Tsushima in 1905 brought further orders from foreign navies e.g. the battleship *Minas Geraes* of 1907 for the Brazilian Navy. As warships got larger, the width of Newcastle Swing Bridge opening and the height of the High Level Bridge provided increasing constraints, so a plan was put forward for a new shipyard on a 70 acre site on a bend in the river at High Walker, three miles downstream of the bridges.

Nine building berths were laid out at the Walker Naval Yard with the largest being 1000 feet by 120 feet, with 10-ton cranes on the intervening concrete piers to lift the massive plates. A fitting-out quay was provided downstream of these of 2133 feet length and 32 feet depth of water, ending close to the Low Walker Yard. The layout of blacksmith's, plumber's, joiner's and fitting-out shops is shown in the yard layout drawing. Some 8 million tons of soil had to be removed by barge and dumped at sea in 1913, but work had progressed far enough to allow Winston Churchill, then First Lord of the Admiralty, to lay the keel of the first battleship on 20th October,1913. *Malaya* was launched on 13th May,1915 and completed in February,1916, and on the outbreak of war in August,1914 the Turkish battleship *Sultan Osman*, launched at Elswick in 1913, was lying at Walker Naval Yard and was requisitioned by the Royal Navy and completed as *Agincourt* shortly afterwards. Production built up rapidly as naval orders poured in, including the super-cruisers *Courageous* and *Furious* and soon 3500 men were employed at the Walker Naval Yard in 1915.

The Low Walker yard continued to build tankers and other merchant ships during the war, particularly for the new British Tanker Co. Ltd with five in 1916/17:- *British Emperor, British Princess , British Sovereign, British Ensign* and *British Isles*. The Norwegian tanker *Mantilla* 5660/17 for W. Wilhelmsen was completed for the British-flag fleet of Moss Tankers of Liverpool and then returned to its rightful owner in 1920. Other ships completed were *Abelia* 3650/15 for the Flower Line of Marcus Samuel, *Raranga* 10040/16 for Shaw,Savill & Albion Ltd, and the dry-cargo *Merida* 5951/18 for Bowring. Eleven 'WAR' standard ships were ordered by the Shipping Controller: two 'B' types of 8100 dwt, three 'C' types of 5060 dwt, and three 'Z' tankers and three larger fabricated 'N' types, of which two were sold to Union-Castle Line as *Bratton Castle* and *Bampton Castle* while the third sailed for Glen Line as *Glensanda*.

By the end of the war, the Naval Yard had completed many smaller warships in addition to the battleship *Malaya* and the battlecruisers *Courageous* and *Furious*, the latter also being converted to an aircraft-carrier by the yard between November,1917 and March,1918. Six cruisers, 8 sloops, 9 submarines and smaller craft such as ferries and barges were quickly put into the service of the Royal Navy, as was the ice-breaker *Alexander* 3375/18 - originally ordered by the Russian Government and returned to Russia in 1919. The Elswick Yard only handled uncompleted previous orders and a few submarines, and the last warship ever launched there was the aircraft-carrier *Eagle* on 8th June,1918 and she was then fitted out at Walker Naval Yard before moving to Portsmouth Dockyard for completion in February,1924. She had been laid down as the Chilean battleship *Almirante Cochrane* in 1914, while her sister *Almirante Latorre* was completed at Elswick as the Royal Navy battleship *Canada* in 1915. The first purpose-designed aircraft carrier for the Royal Navy, *Hermes*, was laid down at the Naval Yard in January,1918, launched on 11th September,1919 and fitted out by June,1920 before being towed to Devonport for completion in July,1923.

The deep-water berth at Walker Naval Yard proved its value when the battlecruiser *Lion* arrived at the yard for repair after Jutland. The berth was also used for the post-war modernisation refits and conversion to oil-burning of the Cunarders *Aquitania* in 1920 and *Berengaria* in 1922. In 1920 the yard was switched over to merchant shipbuilding in tandem with the Low Walker yard, the Elswick Yard having been closed down. The first merchant ship completed at the Naval Yard was the Shaw,Savill & Albion cargo-liner *Tairoa* of 7983 grt in July,1920. Four fine passenger liners were then completed in the next few years: *Ausonia* 13912/22 and *Ascania* 14013/25 for Cunard; *Mongolia* 16385/23 for P & O; and *Gripsholm* 17716/25 for Swedish Amerika Line. The turbine-propelled Cunarders carried mostly cabin-class passengers to Canada, while the *Gripsholm* was the first motor-driven passenger liner in Transatlantic service when completed in November,1925 with accomodation for 1593 passengers. *Mongolia* served on the P & O route to Australia via India and was turbine-propelled and had novel features of a fixed swimming pool, an electric lift and electric heaters in passenger cabins.

The world's largest floating dock was built in 1922 for the Southampton Docks of the Southern Railway Company. The displacement tonnage lift weight was 60,000 tons and the huge structure was 960 feet in length, 175 feet overall length and 134 feet clear width at the entrance. The floor area was 3.25 acres, and five sections came from the Naval Yard with the two end sections from the Low Walker Yard. Also from the Naval Yard came four heavy-lift ships for Chr. Smith of Norway:- *Belpareil* 7203/26, *Beljeanne* 7203/26, *Belmoira* 3214/28 and *Belpamela* 3214/28 all powered by Sulzer oil engines; and four general cargo ships: *Frogner* 5301/21 for Fearley & Eger; the Norwegian *Vindeggen* 3124/21 and Danish *Songa* 3116/21 and *Contramaestre Casado* 3282/21 for the Spanish Government. The Channel ferry *Malines* 2969/22, two small Great Lakes traders, three lightships and a survey and

The Tribal class destroyers ESKIMO being launched on 3rd September,1937 with MASHONA to follow in a double launch. (Vickers PLC)

The battleship NELSON completed in 1927 enters the Tyne during the 1930s. (Tyne & Wear Archives).

buoy tender for the Nigerian Government were also built. However tankers predominated, twenty being completed:-

EL OSO	7267/21	Lobitos Oilfields
EL GRILLO	7259/22	"
MIRLO	7455/22	A/S Tankfart(W. Wilhelmsen),Oslo
AMSTERDAM	7352/22	American Petroleum
SCOTTISH STRATH	7417/22	Tankers Ltd 262
SCOTTISH CASTLE	7417/22	"
SAN QUIRINO	5843/23	Eagle Oil
LUBRAFOL	7099/24	SA d'Armament,d'Industrie,Belgium.
ATLANTIC	7342/25	A/S D/S Seljan(Jebsen),Norway
TRICENTROL	5814/23	Trinidad Central Oilfields
ARTHUR W. SEWALL	6030/26	A/S Ivarans Rederi,Norway
TEAKWOOD	6014/27	John I. Jacobs 252
ATHENE	4816/28	Skibs A/S Varild,Norway
BRITISH ENDEAVOUR	4580/27	British Tanker Co. Ltd
BRITISH PROGRESS	4581/27	"
SCOTTISH CHIEF	7006/28	Tankers Ltd 262
SCOTTISH HEATHER	7005/28	"
BINTA	5873/28	A/S Binta,Norway
ALICIA	2694/28	Curacaosche Shell
ADELA	2696/28	"

The only order received by the Naval yard for a warship in the 1920s was the battleship *Nelson* of 35000 tons displacement, and she was laid down immediately after the order was received in 1922, launched in 1925 and completed in September,1927. The Low Walker Yard completed some interesting ships in the 1920s including three more heavy-lift ships for Chr. Smith of Norway: *Beldis* 2902/26, *Belray* 2904/26 and *Belnor* 2871/26 all equipped with Sulzer oil engines, and the Norwegian general cargo ship *Seirstad* 6632/21 for A.F. Klaveness of Oslo. A dozen tankers were completed with seven for Eagle Oil including three of 18000 dwt:- *San Fernando* 13056/19, *San Felix* 13037/21 and *San Fabian* 13031/22, the largest ships ever built by the yard. Three tankers were completed for the Baltic Trading Co. Ltd of London:- *Shirvan* 6017/25, *Shirak* 6023/26 and *Varand* 6023/27; with one each for Lobitos Oilfields *El Aleto* 7203/27 and Steaua Romana of Roumania *Oltenia* 6394/28. The newsprint carriers *Humber Arm* 5758/25 and *Corner Brook* 5759/25 were completed for the newsprint trade from Newfoundland to New York for the American market, and were part of a much larger project that was to lead to the downfall of Armstrong,Whitworth & Co. Ltd itself. In July,1922 the company had formed a separate subsidiary, Newfoundland Power & Paper Utilities Corporation Ltd, to finance a scheme to build a 400 tons/day newsprint mill in Newfoundland. Shares in the new company were to be equally divided between

Armstrong,Whitworth and Reid Paper of New York. Armstrong's would co-operate with two British power companies - Babcock & Wilcox and British Thomson Houston to take-over the engineering company Balfour Beatty to act as their Newfoundland agent. This would provide much-needed work throughout the Armstrong Group - turbines and other heavy products from Elswick and Openshaw in Manchester, electrical equipment from Cromptons, paper-making machinery from Walmsley, and the Armstrong Civil Engineering Division would build a port to ship the newsprint to New York together with dam construction, and Low Walker yard would build two newsprint carriers.

Armstrong,Whitworth & Co. Ltd invested £5M in the mill at Corner Brook on the Humber river in West Newfoundland, but costs escalated and a $1M overdraft was requested in January,1924 from the Bank of Montreal with an option for another sum of equal size. The mill made its first newsprint in July,1925 but by the Autumn losses were mounting and by February,1926 the mill was only producing 265 tons of newsprint/day instead of the projected 400 tons/day. Corner Brook mill was eventually sold after seven months of negotiation in July,1927 to the International Paper Company of New York. Armstrong,Whitworth had lost £2.8M of their investment, but the effect on the cash-flow of the Group as a whole brought down all of the Group as well.

Armstrong,Whitworth & Co. Ltd losses amounted to £625,767 for the first 11 months of 1926, and negotiations for a merger with Vickers of Barrow started in early 1927. On 28th November,1927 proposals for a new Vickers-Armstrong company were approved with Armstrongs receiving £4.5M for their assets and Vickers some £8.5M. Vickers-Armstrong Ltd began trading on 1st January,1928 with Low Walker yard also included, but leased back to a residual Armstrong,Whitworth company, who also acquired the Dobson yard for £95,000 and the Tyne Iron yard for £31,000. Although Walker Naval Yard was closed down in Autumn,1928 after work in hand had been completed due to the scarcity of naval orders, merchant shipbuilding revived in 1928 with 1929 newbuildings tonnage greater than at any time since 1920 for North-East coast yards. The tramps *Sinnington Court* 6910/28 and *Tilsington Court* 6910/28 were completed for Court Line by Low Walker yard just after the yard mergers, and then a further 20 ships were completed by the combined Low Walker,Dobson and Tyne Iron yards under the Armstrong,Whitworth name before all three closed down in 1931. These included the tankers *Laurelwood* 7347/29 for John I. Jacobs and *Anglo-Swede* 8033/30 for Rederi A/B Tanker (Olson & Wright),Stockholm and *Elise* 7910/31 for Bech of Norway; three funnel-less twin-screw refrigerated Westfal-Larsen motor ships: *Brimanger, Hindanger, Villanger* all 4883/29, and the sister tramps *Kitty Taylor* 4640/29 and *Jo Taylor* 4640/33, the

The New York to Bermuda cruise liner MONARCH OF BERMUDA of 1931 (above), and her replacement OCEAN MONARCH of 1951 (below) (B. Fielden).

FURNESS BERMUDA LINE. T.S.S. "OCEAN MONARCH"

latter having lain incomplete for some years during the Depression after the closure of the yards.

The Walker Naval Yard was closed for six years during the wasted years of the Depression from Autumn,1928 to Autumn,1934, only opening during 1930-31 to employ some men to build the classic Furness Bermuda liner *Monarch of Bermuda* 22424/31. The Arroll-built hammer-head crane, which still stands, was erected at the yard in time to fit out the *'Monarch'* at a cost of £93,000. She had three funnels and inordinately high masts and was launched on 17th March,1931 and completed on 7th November,1931 after achieving nearly 21 knots on trials off Newbiggin. She was powered by large Fraser & Chalmers steam turbines linked to General Electric motors passing their power to four screws. She had accomodation for 830 first-class passengers, and it is ironic that she should have been built in the chronic Depression years on Tyneside for the holiday trade from New York to Bermuda for well-to-do Americans. The yard re-opened in Autumn,1934 to lay the keel of the cruiser *Newcastle*, which was completed in March,1937 and her sister *Sheffield* was completed at the yard in August,1937. Six destroyers were also completed: *Hero* (1936), *Hereward* (1936), *Afridi* (1938), *Cossack* (1938), *Eskimo* (1938) and *Mashona* (1939). The last pair provided a boost to publicity by their double launch on 3rd September,1937.

Warship production during World War II was massive with one battleship, four aircraft-carriers, three cruisers, 24 destroyers, one monitor, 16 submarines, and many motor and tank landing craft. The keel of the battleship *King George V* had been laid in January,1937 after the abandonment of Treaty limitations on size, and she was launched in February,1939 by King George VI and completed in December,1940 to serve with distinction in many battles. The carrier *Victorious* was also ordered in 1937 and launched on 14th September,1939 and completed in May,1941 just in time for her Fleet Air Arm aircraft to take part in the hunt for the German super battleship *Bismarck* in the North Atlantic, which was finally sunk by the battleships *King George V* and *Rodney*, sister of *Nelson* built at the yard. The other three carriers were *Colossus* launched in September,1943 and completed in December,1944; *Perseus* launched in March,1944 and completed in September, 1945; and *Hercules* launched in September,1945 when work was suspended after her launch, and she lay incomplete at Portsmouth until sold to India as *Vikrant* in 1961. Orders for sixteen more warships were cancelled at the end of the war.

The Low Waker yard was re-opened in 1942 to build standard 'B' type *Empire* tramps of 10,000 dwt, the first of an initial five being launched as *Empire Standard* on 29th June,1942. The yard became the Tyne branch of the Shipbuilding Corporation at the end of 1943 and completed ten more *Empire* tramps, with the last two being sold on the stocks at the beginning of 1947 to United Africa Co. Ltd (later Palm Line) and completed as *Ashantian* and *Zarian*. In May,1946 a half-ship was launched at the yard, this being a new fore-end for the J. & C. Harrison tramp *Harpagus* 7271/42, which had been mined and broken into two off the Normandy beaches in August,1944. The two halves were then joined together in a Tyne dry-dock. A further few coasters and military oil barges were completed before the yard closed down for the last time in 1948.

The Walker Naval Yard was switched over to merchant shipbuilding during 1946, after orders for many replacement cargo-liners were won from liner companies, who also queued to refurbish surviving liners after long war service as troopers. P & O sent their *Strathaird* and *Strathmore* in 1947/48, and Furness,Withy their *Queen of Bermuda* and *Monarch of Bermuda*. Whereas the former re-entered the New York - Bermuda holiday trade in February,1949, the *'Monarch'* - built at the yard in 1931 - suffered a disastrous fire to her passenger accomodation on 24th March,1947 while in dry-dock at Palmers(Hebburn), owned by Vickers-Armstrong Ltd. She was then purchased by the Ministry of Transport and towed to Southampton to be rebuilt by Thorneycroft as an Australian emigrant carrier as *New Australia*. Two Blue Funnel/Glen Line cargo-liners and three cross-channel ferries were also converted back and overhauled for peace-time use. The first merchant ship to be built after the war was the heavy-lift ship *Empire Athelstan* of 7795 grt in June,1946, and her sister was completed as the Norwegian *Beljeanne* for Chr. Smith at the end of the year. Many cargo-liners followed during the next twenty years, with main customers being Blue Funnel Line and Ellerman:-

AUTOLYCUS	8236/49	CITY OF NEW YORK	8420/47
AUTOMEDON	8236/49	CITY OF HULL	8458/47
PATROCLUS	10109/50	CITY OF CHICAGO	7622/50
PERSEUS	10109/50	CITY OF OTTAWA	7622/50
LAERTES	8270/49	CITY OF PORT ELIZABETH	13363/52
ATREUS	7800/51	CITY OF EXETER	13345/53
ALCINOUS	7799/52	CITY OF YORK	13345/53
LAOMEDON	7864/53	CITY OF DURBAN	13345/54
ADRASTUS	7859/53	CITY OF RIPON	7713/56
LYCAON	7895/54	CITY OF AUCKLAND	8181/58
DEMODOCUS	7968/55	CITY OF EASTBOURNE	10006/62
ANTENOR	7974/57	CITY OF GLASGOW	10081/63
ACHILLES	7974/57		
AJAX	7974/58		
MEMNON	8504/59		
MELAMPUS	8511/60		
PRIAM	12094/66		
PEISANDER	12094/67		

CITY OF PORT ELIZABETH was the first of four passenger/cargo-liners for the South African service of Ellerman Lines in 1952, and the last of the quartet was completed as CITY OF DURBAN in May,1954.   (Vickers PLC & Ellerman Lines)

LS   PROMETHEUS   12094/67
PROTESILAUS   12094/67
RADNORSHIRE   12089/67

19   8   6

and Furness,Withy and subsidiaries; P & O and subsidiaries New Zealand Shipping Co. Ltd and Federal S.N. Co. Ltd:-

62

NOVA SCOTIA 19	7438/47	SURAT	8925/48
NEWFOUNDLAND 19	7437/48	SHILLONG	8934/49
CINGALESE PRINCE	8827/50	HURUNUI	11276/48 6
EASTERN PRINCE	8827/50	HERTFORD	11276/48
PACIFIC RELIANCE 2	9442/51		
PACIFIC NORTHWEST	9442/54		
PACIFIC ENVOY	9439/58		
PACIFIC STRONGHOLD	9439/58		
CANOPIC	11166/54		
ILLYRIC	11256/60		
LAURENTIC	7964/65		

Furness,Withy also placed an order for a smaller replacement for the *Monarch of Bermuda,* which was destroyed by fire in dry-dock at Palmers,Hebburn in 1947 while undergoing overhaul. This was *Ocean Monarch,* launched on 27th July,1950 and able to accomodate 414 first-class passengers. Parsons geared turbines drove twin screws on trials on 23rd March,1951 at a speed in excess of her service speed of 18 knots, and she sailed from New York on 3rd May,1951 on her maiden voyage with holidaymakers for Bermuda. The New Zealand Shipping Co. 6 Ltd had taken delivery of their motor liner *Rangitoto* of 21809 grt two years earlier with accomodation for 100 first-class passengers for their London to Wellington and later Round the World service. Three more liners came from the yard in two beautiful white 'Empresses' for Canadian Pacific, and *Northern Star,* launched by H.M. The Queen Mother on 27th June,1961 and completed in June,1962 for the Round the World service of Shaw,Savill & Albion Ltd. The turbine-propelled *Empress of England* of 25585 grt was completed in March,1957 and could carry 160 first-class and 900 second-class passengers at 21 knots on her regular service to Canada. The *Empress of Canada* of 27284 grt was launched on 10th May,1960 by Mrs. John Diefenbaker, wife of the then Canadian Prime Minister, and completed in March,1961. She was opened by the yard for viewing by the people of Tyneside before she left on her maiden voyage to Canada. However after ten years Transatlantic flights had made her redundant, and she was sold to Carnival Cruises, for whom she sailed out of Miami as *Mardi Gras* until 1992. The engines-aft *Northern Star* also had a very short career of only 12 years after being completed in

Canadian Pacific liner EMPRESS OF CANADA on her launch day of 10th May,1960; and her
earlier but smaller running mate EMPRESS OF ENGLAND of 1957.   (Vickers PLC, W.S.P.L.)

The first Transatlantic motor-driven liner, the Swedish GRIPSHOLM of 1925 (above); and
NORTHERN STAR launched by H. M. The Queen Mother on 27th June,1961.
(Sjofartsmusseet, Gothenburg & Furness, Withy Group)

NORTHERN STAR sailed from Southampton on her maiden voyage on 10th July,1962
on her maiden Round the World voyage to New Zealand via Cape Town, but suffered
turbine trouble from her Parsons turbines with the lubricating oil having to be
subsequently changed. She had a short career of only 13 years and she arrived
at Kaohsiung for scrapping on 11th December,1975.

June,1962 with an unusual light green coloured hull and able to accomodate 1412 passengers, however technical and commercial problems made her uneconomical in a changed world and she went for scrap at Kaohsiung in 1974.

Tanker building had resumed in 1950 at the yard, whose slipways were big enough to accomodate these giants as they quadrupled in carrying capacity over the next 15 years:-

CREDO	16355/51	A/S Jensens Rederi,Norway	GRT
MAJORIAN	16370/51	A/S Julian Rederi,Norway	
SAXONGLADE	13322/52	Niarchos Group	
SAXONDALE	13321/52	"	
SAXONGLEN	13321/53	"	
SAXONMEAD	13321/53	"	
WORLD ENTERPRISE	20536/53	"	
WORLD HARMONY	20992/54	"	
ESSO YORK	17542/55	Esso Petroleum Co. Ltd	
ESSO EXETER	17527/55	"	
ALVENUS	21863/57	Alvian S.S. Co. Ltd	
CURRO	16656/55	A/S Jensens Rederi,Norway	
HINNITES	12186/56	Shell Tankers	
CANTO	16710/58	A/S Jensens Rederi,Norway	
ESSO DURHAM	23862/58	Esso Petroleum Co. Ltd	
ESSO PORTSMOUTH	24125/59	"	
GARONNE	24513/59	Orient S.N. Co. Ltd	
SERENIA	42082/61	Shell Tankers	
ESSO EDINBURGH	31685/63	Esso Petroleum Co. Ltd	
ESSO NEWCASTLE	31685/63	"	
REGENT PEMBROKE	36779/65	Regent Petroleum Co. Ltd	

Serenia was the largest at 71250 dwt and 817 feet in length when launched on 18th October,1960 by Mrs. Richard Wood, wife of the then Minister of Power and was the largest tanker built in Britain at that time. She began her sea trials on 16th June,1961, moving down the Tyne stern-first with tug assistance until she could be turned off Jarrow Slake, and then steamed out to sea, clearing the Tyne Piers in the early evening. She then steamed up the east coast 'north-about' for the Mersey, where she was dry-docked beween 19th June and 28th June. She attained 17.27 knots on a full power trial off the Isle of Arran on 2nd July from her twin Barrow-built steam turbines. Her new eau-de-nil hull colours and twin exhausts aft made her distinctive under the command of Shell Commodore Capt. J.C. Nettleship.

Esso Portsmouth was badly damaged by fire at Milford Haven in 1960 and a new 240 feet hull section was built at the yard and then joined in the brand-new 860 feet dry-dock at Palmers,Hebburn. The gate for the new dock had also been built at the yard and floated down-river in April,1961 with *Esso Portsmouth* the first ship to enter the giant dock, the smaller 715 feet dry-dock at Palmers,Hebburn having been filled in. New 400 feet hull sections were built at the yard in 1962 to convert the two tankers *Saxonglade* and *Saxondale* into the bulk carriers *World Glade* and *World Dale* in Palmers,Hebburn new dock. An order for a tanker of 37000 dwt for P & O in 1963 was transferred to the Barrow yard of Vickers Ltd and completed as *Malwa*.

The largest warship completed in post-WWII years at the yard was the guided missile destroyer *Glamorgan* completed in October,1966 and powered by steam and gas turbines. Four frigates for the Royal Navy were also launched by the yard:- *Eastbourne* (1955), *Scarborough* (1957), *Penelope* (1963), and *Bacchante* (1969), as well as the frigates *Beas* and *Betwa* for the Indian Navy in 1960, the frigate *Rostam* for the Iranian Navy and the corvette *Keta* for the Ghanaian Navy.

The diesel-electric New Zealand train ferry *Aranui* left the yard in April,1966 for the Antipodes, and after completing the five 'P' class cargo-liners for Blue Funnel Line the last pair of ships were then launched by the yard as a separate entity. These were the phosphorus carriers *Albright Pioneer* and *Albright Explorer* both 6870/68 for Albright & Wilson Ltd to supply their works at Portishead. The Geddes Report recommended yard mergers, and Walker Naval Yard became the Walker Yard of Swan Hunter Shipbuilders Ltd with effect from 1st January,1968.

The yard with its very long 1100 feet slipways was ideal for the building of large container ships then being ordered and won orders for six. The first pair were completed in 1969/70 for Cunard for operation in Atlantic Container Line with international partners. *Atlantic Causeway* and *Atlantic Conveyor* both 14946 grt had capacity for 850 containers plus other ro-ro lorries and vehicles. *Dart America* and *Dart Atlantic* both 31036 grt were completed in 1970/71 for the Transatlantic trade of Dart Line, whose partners were Bristol City Line, Compagnie Maritime Belge and Clarke Traffic Services Ltd,Montreal and could carry 1535 containers. *Remuera* was completed in December,1973 for the P & O service to Australia and New Zealand and could carry 1700 refrigerated containers. Two smaller container ships were completed for the Mediterranean trade of Prince Line Ltd in 1979:- *Crown Prince* and *Royal Prince* both of 1599 grt and able to carry 288 containers at a service speed of 15 knots powered by some of the last three-cylinder Doxford oil engines ever built . The refrigerated container ship *Dunedin* of 18140 grt was the last ship launched by the Walker Yard on 15th February,1980 for the joint Shaw Savill - Bank Line service from New Zealand to the West Indies. She was completed in July,1980 with capacity for 768 containers including 358 refrigerated, and a sister *Willowbank* was completed at the same time on the Tees by Smiths Dock Co. Ltd.

The Walker yard had also completed the bulk carriers *Alnwick Castle* 57255/74 for Bamburgh Shipping Co. Ltd,Newcastle and *Begonia* 16329/78 for Stag

Line,North Shields as well as the passenger liner *Rangatira* 9387/72 for the Union Steamship Co. Ltd of New Zealand. A large oiler and replenishment ship for the Iranian Navy, *Kharg*, was launched in November,1977 and completed in April,1980 but her delivery was embargoed by the British Government because of the Iraq-Iran War and she lay alongside the fitting-out berth until released in October,1984. The aircraft carrier *Illustrious* moved up to the Walker Yard from the Wallsend Yard in November,1980 to complete her fitting-out and she was ready to sail to the South Atlantic in June,1982. Her sister *Ark Royal* similarly moved up-river in May,1983 to complete her fitting-out by June,1985. The yard was then put on a 'care and maintenance basis' while negotiations for the sale of the site for industrial redevelopment went ahead. By 1988 the classic shipyard offices had been demolished, and industrial hose and North Sea oil companies had replaced this famous shipyard.

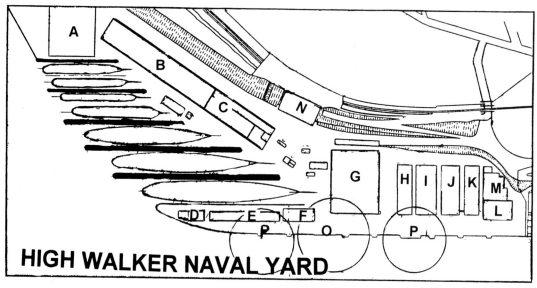

HIGH WALKER NAVAL YARD

(Tyne & Wear Archives)

A. PLATERS SHOP
B. WELDERS SHOP
C. MOULD LOFT
D. FITTERS SHOP
E. PLUMBERS & COPPERSMITHS SHOP
F. POWER STATION
G. FRAME BENDING & ANGLESMITHS SHOP
H. BLACKSMITHS SHOP
I. RIGGERS SHOP
J. ELECTRICIANS SHOP
K. JOINERS SHOP
L. SAWMILLS
M. TIMBER SHEDS
N. OFFICES
O. 250-TON HAMMER HEAD CRANE
P. 30-TON FITTING-OUT CRANES

R. & W. HAWTHORN, LESLIE & CO. LTD.
27

Andrew Leslie was the son of a Shetland crofter who had served an apprenticeship in Aberdeen at the iron works of John Vernon & Company, and then moved to Tyneside to lay out an iron shipyard at Hebburn in 1853. His first ship was the three-masted brigantine *Clarendon* 1000/54, fitted with an auxiliary screw powered by a steam engine of 20 horsepower, her principal shareholder being W.S. Lindsay, M.P. for Tynemouth. His second large ship was *General Williams* 1200/55 which unfortunately foundered off Malta on her second voyage for the Greek & Oriental Steam Navigation Company, which also took all five ships built by the yard in 1860.

Andrew Leslie took various partners such as J.H. Coutts, H.L. Wainwright and Arthur Coote to raise capital, and went on to build some 255 ships under his own name up to his retirement in 1886. The principal customers of his yard were Lamport & Holt of Liverpool, which had 46 cargo-liners built starting with *Copernicus* 1372/61 and ending with *Flamsteed* 3381/92; and the Ocean Steamship Company of Alfred Holt (Blue Funnel Line), which had 30 cargo-liners completed starting with *Diomed* 1848/68 and ending with *Deucalion* 7740/30. Local owners such as William Milburn and his Anglo-Australasian Steam Navigation Co. Ltd ordered 25 ships for the meat trade homewards from Australia, with ten ships between 1880 and 1885 including *Port Jackson* 2644/83 the first of twenty 'PORT's built by the yard up to Milburn's merger into the Commonwealth & Dominion Line in 1916. Other important customers included Adamson & Short of North Shields, who took 11 ships between 1870 and 1878; E.J. Hough of London with eight ships between 1868 and 1873, and Rathbone Brothers of Liverpool who took five ships between 1868 and 1882. The first four ships owned by Danish ferry company DFDS were built at the yard.

The final Leslie paddle steamers were a set of four in 1884 for use on the Amazon: *Para E Amazonas, Oyapock, Acara* and *Araguay* of 400 grt, with the first-named being chosen to convey Prince Albert down the Tyne from Newcastle, where he had opened the Hancock Museum, to North Shields to name the new Albert Edward Dock after himself. The French twin-hulled cross channel steamer *Calais-Douvres* 1925/77 had her paddle wheels located between the hulls and worked the route well into the 1920s!

Russian customers were important to the yard starting with *Azoz* 1414/67 and sometimes accounting for half of the yard production up to 1881. The Russian paddle steamers *Kem* and *Boko* of 1876/77 were followed by the early tanker *Looch* 1446/86, and by several impressive passenger ships for the Russian Volunteer Fleet Association with a speed of 19 knots from two sets of triple expansion engines driving twin propellers and designed to be carriers of 1380 troops in times of war:- *Kostroma* 3513/88, *Orel* 4528/89 , *Saratov* 5309/91, *Petersburg* 5336/94, *Kherson* 6385/95 and *Ekaterinoslav* 5492/96. The final and largest passenger ship for this same owner had even more powerful engines with double triple expansion engines feeding each propeller so that *Smolensk* 7270/01 exceeded well over 20 knots on trials, and she was completed with 16 specially strengthened seatings for guns in times of war when she would carry 1600 troops. Similar powerful engines were also built for the Russian warship *Petropavlovsk*. The Russian Steam Navigating & Trading Company took delivery of five steamers of 2000 grt between 1890 and 1895: *Grand Duke Alexis, Grand Duke Constantine, 2nd Grand Duke Constantine, Grand Duchess Xenia* and *Cezarevitch George*.

A watercolour painting of the yard in 1883.

After Andrew Leslie's retirement in 1886 the yard was merged with the engineering business of Robert & William Hawthorn of Forth Banks, Newcastle to form R. & W. Hawthorn,Leslie & Co. Ltd. Robert Hawthorn had started building engines in 1817, mostly railway locomotives as well as stationary and marine engines. Andrew Leslie ordered 33 out of 78 engines for his ships from the Hawthorn brothers between 1860 and 1870. Benjamin Chapman Browne became a partner with the Hawthorns, and they set-up a second engine building factory at St. Peters in East Newcastle in 1871, and this marine engine side of the business prospered under Francis Carr Marshall.

The first ship built at Hebburn after the merger was *Port Pirie* 3109/86, but unfortunately the yard made losses for the next few years especially on contracts to convert dry-cargo ships into bulk-oil tankers. *Chigwell* and *Petriana* were converted in 1887 for Alfred Suart of London, and another such conversion was made to *Marquis Scicluna*. Profitability was not restored at the yard until after the completion of the twin-screw cruiser *Bellona* for the Admiralty, launched in August, 1890 at a loss of £16,119. A substantial association with the New Zealand frozen meat trade was made with the launching of *Nairnshire* in 1889 for the Scottish Shire Line of Turnbull, Martin & Company and others also followed with the new Linde refrigerating plant for Federal Steam Navigation and the New Zealand Shipping Co. Ltd:-

NAIRNSHIRE	3720/89	Scottish Shire Line
MORAYSHIRE	5576/98	"
PERTHSHIRE	5550/93	"
BUTESHIRE	5574/93	"
BANFFSHIRE	5526/94	Scottish Shire Line
RAKAIA	5628/95	N.Z. Shipping Co. Ltd
WAIMATE	5610/96	"
CORNWALL	5490/96	Federal S.N.
DEVON	5489/96	"
WAKANUI	5576/98	N.Z. Shipping Co. Ltd
MORAYSHIRE	5576/98	Scottish Shire Line
KENT	5464/99	Federal S.N.
SURREY	5455/99	"
KARAMEA	5563/99	N.Z. Shipping Co. Ltd
WHAKATANE	5715/99	"
SUSSEX	5474/00	Federal S.N.
TONGARIRO	7660/01	N.Z. Shipping Co. Ltd
TURAKINA	8027/02	"
AYRSHIRE	7252/03	Scottish Shire Line
DURHAM	5537/03	Federal S.N.

In 1891 Herbert B. Rowell was appointed as Yard Manager to improve its financial performance, and only 21 out of 104 merchant ships built between 1898 and 1918 made losses. Profit from the shipyard however was only 2.4% of turnover between 1899 and 1906, and 5.1% of turnover between 1907 and 1914. At the turn of the century he won orders for cargo-liners for the Transatlantic trade of Frederick Leyland Ltd, headed by shipping millionaire John R. Ellerman; and for the South American trade of the Booth Steamship Co. Ltd, both of Liverpool:-

CANADIAN	9301/00	ANTONY	6439/06
KINGSTONIAN	6564/01	CUTHBERT	3563/06
COLONIAN	6443/01	STEPHEN	4177/10
HANOVERIAN	11960/02	DENIS	4435/11
NESTORIAN	6395/11	PANCRAS	4436/11
NINIAN	6385/11		
NUBIAN	6384/11		
NITONIAN	6381/12		

Antony was a twin-screw passenger ship, and one contract for the Booth company was won by the yard at a price of £54,880 - some £4120 less than the next tender. The accomodation on the Leyland ships for passengers was limited except for *Hanoverian*, which was comparable in numbers and standard of accomodation to Cunard's *Ivernia* built at this time by Swan,Hunter, and which became *Cretic* of White Star in 1903. British India Line and Glen Line each ordered one cargo-liner, *Waipara* 5505/03 and *Glenstrae* 4718/05, while *Cooeyanna* 3922/02 was completed for the Australian passenger/cargo services of McIlwraith,McEarn of Melbourne. Swedish owners were also important at this time e.g. Swedish-Syd-Africa Line and Transatlantic Rederi A/B of W.H. Lundgren; and pioneering ore-carriers for the Rederi A/B Lulea-Ofoten which later became the famous Grangesberg - Oxelosund company:-

ATLANTIC	3340/04	VOLLRATH THAM	5807/09
AUSTRALIC	4010/07	SIR ERNEST CASSEL	7723/10
BALTIC	3294/05	NORBOTTEN	7936/12
HELLENIC	4254/09	MALMBERGET	7936/13
INDIANIC	4271/08		
TASMANIC	3985/07		
BIA	3344/05		

Vollrath Tham and her sisters featured large holds and a special arrangement of gravity discharge ore hoppers to give faster discharge at suitable equipped ports. Ten electric cranes were fitted, each capable of lifting 2.5 tons and giving a full discharge in under two days with their own gear - forerunners of the geared bulk carriers of today. Tramps also featured with the Doxford-designed 'Turret' *Heathdene* 3542/98 for John T. Lunn of Newcastle; and *Holywell* 4867/07 for Tyzack & Branfoot of Sunderland; and *Framlington Court* 4153/11 for the fast-expanding fleet of Court Line Ltd of London.

Profitable warship building began in 1895 of three-funnelled small torpedo boat destroyers with *Sunfish*, and some 45 further examples for the Admiralty followed up to 1918, enabling the advantages of serial production to be gained.

The world's first turbine-driven warship was of this class from the yard - *Viper* of 1899 - equipped with turbines by Tyneside inventor Sir Charles Parsons. Her speed on trials was 35 knots but she was unfortunately wrecked two years later in 1901. The first ever turbine-driven ship was of course the 100 feet long *Turbinia*, built at Wallsend by Sir Charles Parsons in 1894 and demonstrated to their Lordships of the Admiralty at the Jubilee Review of the Fleet in the Solent in 1897 when she averaged 34.5 knots.

Three ships under construction in 1910 with the spire of St. Andrew on left. (R. & W. Hawthorn, Leslie & Co. Ltd)

A total of £100,000 was spent on new equipment for the yard between 1902 and 1912, and two new berths were added of 700 feet in length on ground previously used for storing timber (See Shipyard plan). Seven revolving steel derrick cranes, each 100 feet high, flanked the new slipways, and the dry-dock was extended to a length of 461 feet and a width of 68 feet. A return to tanker building was made in 1913 on these berths with three of 9000 dwt for Andrew Weir:- *Barneson* 6051/13, *Desabla* 6047/13 and *Gymeric* 6138/17.

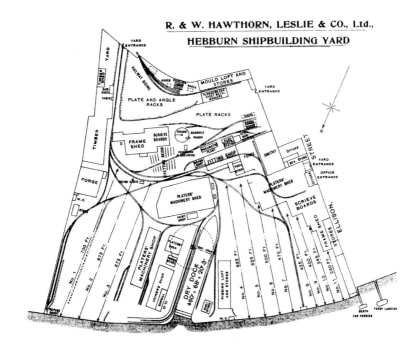

R. & W. HAWTHORN, LESLIE & CO., Ltd.,
HEBBURN SHIPBUILDING YARD

World War I production was impressive with a further twelve merchant ships, two cruisers *Champion* (1915) and *Calypso* (1917), three destroyers and 21 torpedo boat destroyers. The merchant ships were five cargo-liners for Glen Line and Blue Funnel Line, four for Port Line, and two standard WAR 'A' types and two 'B' types completed for British India in 1920 as *Sirsa* and *Surada*.

Sixty ships totalling 272,900 tons were launched during the 1920s of which the most famous were the P & O Indian service express liners *Ranpura* 16585/25 and *Ranchi* 16650/25; and *Andania* 13950/22 for the Canadian service of Cunard. When *Andania* was launched on 1st November, 1921 she was the largest vessel built at Hebburn up to that time and could carry 484 cabin class passengers and 1184 third-class passengers at a speed of 15 knots from two Parsons turbines driving twin screws. *Ranpura* was launched as the first of the pair for P & O on 13th September, 1924 and was completed in April, 1925 with *Ranchi* following in service in July, 1925. They had two funnels of which the aft was a dummy, and were powered by two sets of quadruple expansion steam reciprocating engines driving twin screws to give a service speed of 17 knots. Their deck areas for passengers featured a tennis court and two quoit pitches but no swimming pools, and the traditional attitudes of the day restricted the smoking room to male passengers only. The total passenger capacity was 600 of which 310 were first-class.

Three smaller intermediate liners were completed for the Calcutta/Japan service of British India S.N. Co. Ltd:- *Talma* 10007/23 and *Tilawa* 10006/24 with two closely spaced funnels, and *Talamba* /8018/24 with three funnels. Propulsion was again by quadruple expansion engines to give 12 knots, and they had accomodation for around 60 first-class and 80 second-class passengers and no fewer than 3262 Indian deck passengers could be crammed in ! British India also had two cargo-liners from the yard:- *Shirala* 7841/25 and *Rohna* 8602/26 with the latter having the dubious distinction of being the first ship to be sunk by air-guided torpedo during WWII. Three cargo-liners were also completed for Blue Funnel Line during this period:- *Glaucus* 7644/20, *Autolycus* 7718/22 and *Deucalion* 7740/30; and two for Booth Line:- *Basil* 4862/28 and *Boniface* 4877/28 which were able to make fuel consumption comparisons as *Boniface* was fitted with the first British-built Bauer-Wach exhaust turbine to boost the same steam reciprocating engines as fitted in her sister.

Fourteen tankers and tramps were also completed by the yard in the 1920s and 1930s:-

BADARPUR	8079/21	GLENTWORTH	5677/20
BULYSSES	7519/26	LLANBERIS	5055/27
BULLMOUTH	7519/27	LLANGOLLEN	5056/27
HARPA	3007/30	TRELAWNY	4689/27
AGNITA	3561/30	BENWELL TOWER	4414/27
HELIX	3007/31	FOWBERRY TOWER	4484/29
CAPRELLA	8377/31	KAYESON	4606/29
CAPSA	8229/31	HARPALION	5486/32
DAPHNELLA	8078/38	HARLESDEN	5483/32
DORYSSA	8078/38	HARPALYCUS	5629/35
DARONIA	8139/38	WINDSORWOOD	5395/36
DOLABELLA	8142/39	YORKWOOD	5401/36
CERINTHUS	3878/30	DUMFRIES	5143/35
SAN AMBROSIO	7410/35	BALMORALWOOD	5832/36

The first tanker in the left of the above list was owned by Burmah Oil, and the next eleven by the Anglo-Saxon/Shell Group, a major customer to whom the last two tankers in the list were also on charter. Two engines-aft self-trimming colliers of 7000 dwt were built for the Australian coastal services of Australian Steamships(Pty) Ltd:- *Age* 4734/35 and *Cycle* 3952/38. They had 16 derricks and distinctive goalpost masts at the bow and in front of the aft crew spaces. Other colliers were also built for the North-East coast coal trade:- *William Cash* 1186/29 and *Henry Woodall* 625/35 for Stephenson Clarke; *Kirkwood* 2780/29 and *Pinewood* 2466/30 for France,Fenwick and the gas collier *Suntrap* 939/29. Four vessels were also completed for the Argentine Navy and a number of coasters for

The P & O liner RANCHI of 1925 (above). (E.C.B. Thornton).

The British India liner TALMA of 1923 (above) on service between Calcutta and Japan;
the Burmah Oil tanker BADARPUR of 1921 (below). (P & O ; Hawthorn,Leslie & Co. Ltd)

the Tyne-Tees Steamship Co. Ltd, of which the most famous was the Newcastle to London coastal liner *Bernicia* 1944/23.

The Admiralty ordered a cruiser in March,1926 which was launched in 1928 and completed as *Sussex* early in 1929, providing the equivalent of a years work for 1500 men. In addition two sloops *Bridgewater* and *Sandwich* were completed in 1928 and were followed by ten detroyers:- *Active* (1929), *Antelope* (1929), *Boadicea* (1930), *Blanche*(1930), *Electra*(1934), *Encounter*(1934), *Imogen* and *Imperial*(1936), *Jervis*(1938) and the famous *Kelly*(1938). The latter earned much respect for the yard under the command of Lord Louis Mountbatten when she survived a serious torpedoing off the Norwegian coast and arrived back at the yard for repairs almost awash. She was later sunk by dive-bombers during the German invasion of Greece and Crete. The cruiser *Manchester* was ordered in 1935 at a cost of £1M and completed her trials in March,1938. All of these naval contracts yielded a profit of between 2% and 6% to the yard, but the entire profit for all contracts during the 1930s amounted to only £208,000. Four sloops for Portugal had also been constructed during the disastrous years 1932/34, when the 250-ton coaster *Rock* was the only ship to leave a Hebburn slipway during 1933. The yard workforce shrank to only 650 men, with only 1400 in the combined engineering/shipyard workforce compared to a toal of over 5000 during World War I.

The pick-up in orders after the Depression in 1936 brought an important new customer to the yard in Houlder Brothers. The refrigerated meat carrier *Beacon Grange* was launched in November,1936 for the Plate trade. She was powered by Hawthorn-Werkspoor oil engines and was to be the first of thirteen ships built for this customer. The Union Steamship Co. Ltd of New Zealand contracted to build the smart white-painted twin screw motor vessel *Matua* 4166/36 with accomodation for 48 passengers, and also for the cargo-only *Waipori* 4282/38.

The destroyer *Legion* was the first ship down a Hebburn slipway during World War II on Boxing Day,1939 in a war programme that was to see speeded up production of 41 naval vessels and 17 merchant ships. The largest warship was the light fleet aircraft carrier *Triumph*, and a total of three cruisers *Cleopatra*, *Diadem* and *Naiad*, and 16 destroyers, two fast minelayers, 14 landing craft and three transport ferries. The merchant contribution to the war effort was 15 tankers and two refrigerated meat carriers for Houlder Brothers:- *Rippingham Grange* 10365/43 and *Condesa* 10367/43, both replacements for meat carriers lost earlier in the war. In addition to new ships, there were many conversions such as the Aberdeen & Commonwealth liner *Jervis Bay* into an Armed Merchant Cruiser fitted with 6 inch guns. She was later sunk in an very brave action on 5th November,1940 when Capt. E.S. Fogarty Fegen sacrificed himself and 198 of his crew in defence of HX84 when attacked in the North Atlantic by the German pocket battleship *Admiral Scheer*. Urgent repairs to badly damaged ships such as the destroyer *Kelly* in the dry-dock diverted men from new construction work, and this 'Casualty Clearing Station' docked 120 warships and 112 merchant vessels.

The aircraft carrier *Triumph* steamed out of the Tyne in the Spring of 1946 to be commissioned at Portsmouth on 9th May,1946. She had been launched by Lady Louis Mountbatten on 22nd October,1944 and her overall length of 695 feet made her the longest vessel built to date. Two Battle class destroyers *Agincourt* and *Alamein* were launched just before the end of the war, and spent much time at the fitting-out berth before beginning trials in 1947/48. Three tankers for the Anglo-Saxon Petroleum Co. Ltd were the first vessels launched after the end of the war, and two of these were notable for technical reasons. *Auricula* was the first diesel-engined vessel in the world to burn heavy fuel oil in August,1946, and *Auris* was the first merchant vessel in the world to undertake deep-sea voyages powered by marine gas turbines in October,1951. Altogether 13 of the 50 tankers built at the yard between 1946 and 1968 were for the Anglo-Saxon Petroleum Co. Ltd, with others also chartered to Shell from independent owner tankers. The following deadweight table of tankers built by the yard gives a good impression of the escalating sizes of tankers:-

	DWT	
AURICULA	12290/46	Anglo-Saxon/Shell
LATIA	9220/46	"
AURIS	12290/48	"
LAMPANIA	9220/47	"
LABIOSA	9110/48	"
BRITISH ENDEAVOUR	12250/48	British Tanker Co. Ltd
BRITISH RESOURCE	16200/49	"
ATHELKING	15632/49	Athel Line
LATIRUS	9245/49	Anglo-Saxon/Shell
ATHELMONARCH	15632/50	Athel Line
ATHELBEACH	10350/50	"
ATHELDUCHESS	13125/50	"
BRITISH SEAFARER	16800/51	British Tanker Co. Ltd
BRITISH TALENT	28625/51	"
CLUTHA RIVER	18510/51	British Empire S.N. Co. Ltd
CALTEX LIVERPOOL	17460/52	Overseas Tankship, Texas Oil
CALTEX BAHRAIN	17500/52	"
TYNEFIELD	18700/52	Hunting & Son
CALTEX MANCHESTER	17510/53	Overseas Tankship, Texas Oil
BRITISH FLAG	16750/53	British Tanker Co. Ltd
HAUSTRUM	18050/53	Anglo-Saxon/Shell

	DWT		
BORDER FUSILIER	16190/54	Lowland Tanker Co. Ltd	189
HAUSTELLUM	18150/54	Anglo-Saxon/Shell	
FORTHFIELD	18150/54	Hunting & Son	56
ATHELMERE	10390/54	Athel Line	190
ATHELSTANE	10350/55	"	
VOLA	32170/56	Anglo-Saxon/Shell	
HOROMYA	18250/56	"	
VOLVATELLA	32170/56	"	
BRITISH COURAGE	35572/57	British Tanker Co. Ltd	
HALIA	18250/58	Anglo-Saxon/Shell	
CALTEX NEWCASTLE	18130/57	Overseas Tankship,Texas Oil	
THAMESFIELD 2	33880/58	Hunting & Son	56
DENBY GRANGE	18500/58	Houlder Line	53
ANADARA	19313/59	Anglo-Saxon/Shell	
BRANDON PRIORY	37434/59	Warwick Tanker Co. Ltd	359
KAYESON	47940/60	Kaye,Son & Co. Ltd	234
CLYMENE	19903/61	Hadley Shipping Co. Ltd	362
TIDESPRING	20000/62	Naval Oiler	192
TIDEPOOL	20000/62	"	
BRITISH VENTURE 3	38100/63	British Tanker Co. Ltd	
BRITISH DRAGOON 2	53078/63	"	
BRITISH HAWTHORN	20550/64	"	
OLWEN	30000/64	Naval Oiler	192
OLNA	30000/65	"	
CLERK MAXWELL	9070/66	Ocean Gas Transport Ltd	363
MARIANO ESCOBEDO	9400/67	Petroleos Mexicanos	
WILTSHIRE	12330/68	Bibby Line	195

The design of *British Venture* was altered during her construction to an all-aft superstructure, and she was also the first British motor supertanker, these changes delaying her entry into service by 18 months to April,1963. The longest ships ever launched at Hebburn were *Kayeson* at 711 feet in 1960, and *British Dragoon* at 725 feet on 25th April,1963, both these tankers being 'tight-squeezes' as the Tyne is narrow at this point. *Kayeson* had originally been ordered by Shell as a sister to three tankers of similar dwt then building at Harland & Wolff at Belfast. However the Hebburn yard was unable to accomodate the proposed design length of 753 feet and she was shortened by 42 feet. She was then sold to the "K" Steamship Co. Ltd,London and long-term chartered back to Shell.

The yard pioneered the introduction of tankers carrying liquefied gases, and the dry-cargo *Broughty*, built in 1955 in Holland for the Dundee,Perth & London Shipping Co. Ltd, was taken in hand in 1963 and converted into the first such tanker in the world. She emerged with special tanks capable of carrying 668 tons of liquefied gases and was renamed *Abbas* at the end of the conversion. The yard then went on to build the first large deep-sea gas tanker, *Clerk-Maxwell*

8298/66 for Ocean Gas Transport Co. Ltd with Houlder Brothers as managers. She could carry 9070 tons of liquefied gases, her cargo tanks having a metric capacity of 11751 cu. m., with the cargo coolant temperature being controlled via a large white-painted housing on deck in front of the bridge. A similar gas tanker was completed for Petroleos Mexicanos as *Mariano Escobedo* in 1967, and a larger version of 12320 dwt was ordered by George Gibson & Co. Ltd,Leith for delivery in 1968. However her charter was not conformed and she was sold while under construction to Bibby Line of Liverpool with a two-year charter back to Gibson. She was completed as *Wiltshire* in September,1968 and left the Tyne after trials for Pascagoula to load her first cargo of liquefied ammonia for Antwerp.

The only passenger liner built by the yard in post-WWII years was *Angola* 12932/48 for Companhia Nacional de Navegacao,Lisbon. An exact sister, *Mocambique*, was completed in the following year by Swan,Hunter (q.v.). Dry-cargo customers included Moor Line, managed by Walter Runciman of Newcastle, and Houlder Brothers:-

GLENMOOR	5577/52	HORNBY GRANGE	10785/46
HAZELMOOR	5572/53	DUQUESA	11007/49
INNESMOOR	5574/54	OSWESTRY GRANGE	9406/52
JEDMOOR	5970/58	ROYSTON GRANGE	10261/59
KIRRIEMOOR	5922/60	HARDWICKE GRANGE	10337/60
LINKMOOR	8155/61	OCEAN TRANSPORT	8608/61
ELYSIA	8531/65		

Moor Line purchased the Glasgow-based Anchor Line in July,1965 while *Elysia* was under construction and she kept her Anchor name. *Linkmoor* also took the Anchor Line name of *Eucadia* in 1968. Houlder Brothers *Oswestry Grange* of 1952 and *Ocean Transport* of 1961 were not refrigerated, but served on the Plate service with general cargo. *Royston Grange* was to meet with a tragic end after a collision in the Indio Channel near Montevideo on 11th May,1972 with a fully-loaded tanker of 18000 dwt. The ensuing fireball engulfed all her 63 crew including the wife and daughter of the Chief Steward, and also ten passengers and the Argentinean pilot on board with another eight dead amongst the crew of the tanker.

Port Line ordered three refrigerated meat-carriers for their Australian trade from the yard:- *Port Lyttelton* 7413/46, *Port Auckland* 11945/48 and *Port Adelaide* 8105/50; with one cargo-liner each for Donaldson Line *Cortona* 8289/47, and Elder,Dempster *Salaga* 4810/47. Two bulk carriers of 9500 dwt were completed for Sugar Line Ltd, formed in 1950 by sugar giants Tate & Lyle Ltd and United

Molasses:- *Crystal Gem* 8674/55 and *Crystal Diamond* 8675/56; and two bauxite carriers featured the first all-welded decks from the yard:- *Pathfinder* 6658/49 and *Prospector* 6658/50. Three ferries were completed for British Rail:- *Cambridge Ferry* (1963), *Holyhead Ferry 1* (1965) and *Antrim Princess* (1967).

The Admiralty ordered two frigates, *Llandaff* (1955) and *Argonaut* (1966); four fleet oilers *Tidespring* and *Tidepool* (both 1962), *Olwen* (1964) and *Olna* (1965); and three tank landing ships *Sir Bedivere*, *Sir Tristram* and *Sir Percivale*, completed in 1966/67. The yard was reorganised in 1958 with £1.1M spent on providing assembly areas for welded sections and on new craneage to lift these assemblies into position on a ship on the berth. Sir Robin Rowell, son of a former Yard Manager Herbert Rowell, who had been appointed Yard Manager in 1936 was to remain in that position until the Tyne yard mergers were steered through from 1st January, 1968 following the Geddes report.

Three 'Rover' class replenishment ships for the Royal Navy were then completed by the renamed Hebburn Shipyard of Swan Hunter Shipbuilders Ltd between August, 1969 and July, 1970, *Green Rover, Grey Rover* and *Blue Rover*. Liquid gas tankers *Faraday* of 24750 dwt with tanks of 31215 cu. m. was completed in 1971 for Ocean Gas Transport Co. Ltd (Houlder Brothers); and *Emiliano Zapata* of 2910 dwt for Petroleos Mexicanos in 1970; and *Lincolnshire* of 24556 dwt for Bibby Line in 1972. Chemical tankers *Stolt Lion* of 25650 dwt, and *Chemical Venturer* and *Chemical Explorer* of 28650 dwt of 1972 were followed by two products tankers for Common Brothers of Newcastle in 1973:- *Joseph R. Smallwood* and *Frank D. Moores* both of 31000 tons deadweight.

Two cargo-liners for the Pacific service of Bank Line Ltd were completed in 1973/74:- *Forthbank* and *Clydebank* both of 11405 grt. A start was then made on five products tankers of 32000 dwt for the 'Swan Maritime' deal, of which three were subsequently completed for Russian owners and two for Venezuelan owners between 1975 and 1979. Two forward sections of 112,000 dwt crude carriers were also launched at Hebburn shipyard for joining to the aft sections launched by Walker Naval Yard, the resultant ships being *Yorkshire* of Bibby Line and the Russian *Geroi Sevastopolya*. The liquefied gas tanker *Gandara* of 17650 dwt was completed for P & O in 1976, by which time the first ship from the Hebburn Shipbuilding Dock had been floated out. This was another 112,000 dwt crude carrier, the Russian *Interoceanic I*, the dry-dock in which she had been built being the former 850' x 145' Palmers Hebburn dock, opened in the summer of 1961 for repair work and closed in September, 1970. Cranes of 100 ton capacity were then provided around the dock, and completely new steelworking and outfitting facilities were established, and shipbuilding activities began in 1974 with full production achieved in 1976.

After nationalisation on 1st July,1977 further changes occurred to the old Hawthorn,Leslie shipyard, with the shipyard being split in two and the eastern end of the yard with the largest building berth then amalgamated with the Hebburn Shipbuilding Dock described above. The western end of the old shipyard became the Training and Safety section of British Shipbuilders (North East). After the collapse of the Swan Maritime deal for which much of the steel had already been ordered, three of these contracts were turned into 29000 dwt bulk carriers, two for Bowring *Trinculo* and *Desdemona* both 17940/78, and one for Stag Line, completed as *Begonia* at Walker Naval Yard. The Hebburn Shipbuilding Dock was to have two more ships 'floated-out', the Polish bulk carrier *Kopalnia Gottwald* 10979/79, and the segregated ballast tanker for British Petroleum(Pty) of Australia, *BP Achiever* 66031/83.

The last ships to come from the old Hawthorn,Leslie yard were four carriers of nuclear irridiated fuel for a Japanese charter and managed by James Fisher & Sons Ltd, Barrow. These were the sisters *Pacific Swan, Pacific Crane* and *Pacific Teal*, all of 4550 grt, and the smaller *Mediterranean Shearwater* of 2486 grt, the last of the quartet completing in November,1982 when the yard was placed on a 'care and maintenance basis'.

The segregated ballast tanker BP ACHIEVER of 1983 built in Hebburn Building Dock. (Author).

The irridiated nuclear core carriers PACIFIC SWAN and MEDITERRANEAN SHEARWATER.
(British Shipbuilders Ltd, Author)

PALMERS SHIPBUILDING & IRON CO. LTD.

Charles Mark Palmer was born at South Shields on November 3rd,1822, the son of a prosperous businessman and shipowner trading to India and who had earlier sailed on whalers to the Greenland fisheries. Charles Palmer first worked for his father and then in 1845 joined John Bowes in his colliery and rose to a position in charge when the Marley Hill colliery was taken over in 1847, followed by the collieries of Lord Ravensworth. He then established a shipyard at Jarrow in 1851 with his elder brother George on land leased from a Mr. Carr-Ellison of Hebburn in order to build steam colliers to ship coal to London. Palmer Brothers & Company launched their first ship, the paddle tug *Northumberland* in 1852. The yard achieved some memorable 'first's:-

1.   **First sea-going screw collier**, *John Bowes*, the yard's second ship launched on 30th June,1852 for John Bowes of Barnard Castle, Durham with Charles also having a financial interest in the ship. She could deliver 650 tons of coal/week to the Thames, or the equivalent of eight sailing colliers and greatly helped to reduce the transport costs of North East Coast coal against the rail costs from the Midlands coalfields. *John Bowes* had a very long life under the Spanish flag before foundering as *Villa Selgas* in 1933.

2.   **First rolled armour plates** were produced in 1854 for warships. The outbreak of the Crimean War in 1853 had created a demand for armour-plated warships, and the floating battery *Terror* of 1856 was built to destroy the Russian forts at Cronstadt.

3.   **First double bottoms for water ballast** used in *Vaderland, Nederland* and *Switzerland*, completed between 1872 and 1874, reputedly for carrying oil.

Local dignatories and coal merchants had watched the launch of *John Bowes* from spectator craft in mid-stream, while the Palmer band played on, and soon orders poured in for more colliers. In the next two years the yard built 25 colliers of 12,210 grt, with output increasing to some 22,000 tons by 1860. Charles Palmer purchased 14 collieries to safeguard his supply of coal for his workshops, and also leased land in North Yorkshire which contained ironstone and set-up the Grindle Park Mining Company to work it. He built a special harbour at Port Mulgrave near Staithes to ship the ore back to Jarrow, and also had interests in the Tyne Plate Glass Company to supply ship's glass fittings and the Bede Metal Company to supply copper needed in shipbuilding. He also started an engineering side to the business in 1853, with his first engine going into the collier *Jarrow*. In 1860 a yard was acquired at Howdon which had last been used by Charles Mitchell to build four barges for India in 1857/58, and the Howdon yard was to be used for a considerable percentage of the total output e.g. in 1883, the peak year for Palmers, no fewer than 15 out of 33 ships were built at Howdon. This yard was not finally closed until 1912. Palmers Shipbuilding & Iron Co. Ltd was incorporated in 1865 as a limited liability company with Manchester interests holding most of the shares with Palmer as Chairman and Managing Director.

Charles Mark Palmer staged a spectacular launch of four ships in August,1863, going one better than the triple launch of Charles Mitchell in 1856 at Low Walker, and two better than the many double launches staged by Andrew Leslie at Hebburn. He was elected M.P. for North Durham in 1874 and subsequently served for a long time as M.P. for Jarrow, where he was made Mayor in 1875. His brother George subsequently retired from the business and Charles carried on and greatly enlarged the works by the addition of engine works, iron rolling mills and blast furnaces. However heavy losses of £33,000 in 1890/91 caused his resignation in 1893 at the age of 71 years. He had erected a hospital at Jarrow in 1870 for the exclusive use of his shipyard employees known as Palmers Memorial Hospital in memory of his first wife. A bronze statue of the founder was sited in the hospital grounds in 1903 after his death, and was later moved to the riverfront at Jarrow, where it can still be seen.

Five beautiful sailing ships were built: *Scotsman, Otterspool, Four Winds, Dovenby Hall* of 1884 and *Lydgate* of 1893, and the main types of ship initially built were colliers for customers such as Lord Joicey; Marquis of Londonderry; W. Cory & Son; J. Fenwick; Harris & Dixon, London. Tramps were built for Newcastle owners Hall Brothers; Nelson,Donkin & Company; Hugh Roberts and his North Shipping Co. Ltd; Joseph Temperley & Company; Hunting & Son; and Stephens & Mawson. Cardiff tramp owners included Morel & Company, John Cory, Anning Brothers, Evan Thomas Radcliffe; and others such as Lindsay,Gracie & Company,Leith; Wilson & Company,Hull; King Line and Court Line. Coastal steamers were completed for the Tyne Steamship Company, later the Tyne-Tees Shipping Co. Ltd, of which Palmer became Chairman, and for whom the coastal liner *Sir William Stephenson* 1540/06 was built. Hall Brothers paid a tribute to Sir Charles Mark Palmer by naming their last tramp built by him as *Lady Palmer* of 2752

The launch of the armour-plated H.M.S TRIUMPH of 1870 from Palmers yard.

grt and completed in October,1889. Two years later another customer of the yard paid a tribute to another great Tyneside genius, Sir William Armstrong of Armstrong,Mitchell & Co. Ltd, by naming their ship *Lady Armstrong* of 3219 grt and completed in July,1891 for Adam,Hamilton & Company of Greenock.

Liner companies had also ordered ships with six small steamers for Norddeutscher Lloyd in 1857/58: *Adler, Moewe, Schwan, Schwalbe, Weser* and *Hudson* all of 523 grt. The Galway liners *Connaught* and *Leinster*, later *Hibernia*, were built in 1860 but Palmer made a bad financial loss on these contracts. In 1861 he secured a contract from the Italian Government to construct mail steamers for a service between Italy and Alexandria. He played an important part in establishing the National Line, another director being Thomas Ismay, founder of the White Star Line, and four Transatlantic liners were built by the yard, with others for the competing Guion Line of Liverpool :-

CANADA	4276/63	National Line
ERIN	4577/65	"
ENGLAND	4898/65	"
IRELAND	3985/67	"
CITY OF LINCOLN	3008/67	Guion Line
NEVADA	3121/68	"
WYOMING	3700/70	"
WISCONSIN	3700/70	"
MONTANA	4321/72	"
DAKOTA	4332/73	"

unfortunately the compound engines and water-tube boilers of *Montana* and *Dakota* proved to be a technical failure, and the ships had to be reboiled with the engines downrated and an order for a similar pair from the yard was cancelled. A large troopship, *Jumna*, was built for the Indian service of the British Government in 1866; with the New Zealand Shipping Company building *Orari* and *Otaki* in 1875.

The yard was a major builder of warships for the Royal Navy starting with *Terror* (1856), the iron-clad frigates *Defence* (1862), *Cerberus* (1868), *Gorgon* (1871), the armour-plated wooden sheathed frigates *Swiftsure* and *Triumph* of 1870, the belted cruisers *Orlando* and *Undaunted* of 1886, cruisers *Retribution* (1890), *Pique* (1890), *Rainbow* (1890), *Pegasus* (1898), *Pyramus* (1898), *Sapphire* (1905), battleships *Resolution* (1893), *Revenge* (1894), *Russell* (1903), *Lord Nelson* (1908), *Hercules* (1911), and battlecruiser *Queen Mary* of 1913. Many small torpedo boat destroyers were also built, and the output during World War I was one battleship, *Resolution* of 1916, one cruiser *Dauntless*, three monitors, 18 destroyers and two submarines.

Tankers figured prominently in the yard output after the rush to build true bulk-oil tankers had started after the completion of *Gluckauf* in July,1886 at the Armstrong,Mitchell yard. The yard had the second highest output of 18 tankers in the North-East up to 1906, and some of the first tankers from Palmers were:-

DWT

RION	2186/89	Stephens & Mawson,Newcastle 236
LA CAMPINE	2542/89	AmericanPetroleumCompany,Holland
ASTRAKHAN	3438/92	H.E. Moss,Liverpool 59
ARAS	3210/93	Stephens & Mawson,Newcastle 236
AMERICAN	3897/93	AmericanPetroleumCompany,Holland
ROTTERDAM	4272/95	"
NEW YORK	7050/02	American Petroleum Company,Holland
PROMETHEUS	7002/03	Deutsche American Petroleum Gmbh
ASHTABULA	7015/03	Anglo-American Oil Company 365
HESPERUS	6389/08	"
F.A. TAMPLIN	3999/11	T.W. Tamplin,Liverpool 364
OSAGE	5051/12	Deutsche American Petroleum Gmbh
PAUNCE	4972/12	"
ARCA	4839/12	Anglo-Saxon/Shell
HERMES	3768/14	La Corona Pet. Maats (Dutch Shell)
DONAX I	3717/13	Anglo-Saxon/Shell
AUNGBAN	5125/13	Burmah Oil 193
MARICOPA	6967/13	W. Wilhelmsen,Norway
SAN VALERIO	6433/13	Eagle Oil
SAN ZEFERINO	6430/14	"
SAN MELITO	10160/14	"
SAN HILARIO	10160/14	"
LUMINA	5856/17	H.E. Moss,Liverpool 59
MADRONO	5854/17	W. Wilhelmsen,Norway.
CADILLAC	11105/17	Anglo-American Oil Company 365
SARANAC	11150/17	"

Hermes was completed in October,1914 for the Dutch Shell company of La Corona Petroleum Maats as a twin-screw tanker fitted with one of the first Werkspoor oil engines made in Amsterdam. The four largest tankers *San Melito, San Hilario, Cadillac* and *Saranac* were among the largest tankers built in the world at this time. Many cargo-liners were completed for the West African trade of Elder,Dempster; and the world-wide trades of Ellerman Lines:-

MONTCALM	5477/97	CITY OF MADRAS	4684/03
MONTEREY	5443/97	CITY OF BOMBAY	5186/10
MONTEAGLE	5467/98	CITY OF DURHAM	5356/11
MONTFORT	5481/99	CITY OF LINCOLN	5867/11
SAPELE	3152/04	CITY OF BIRMINGHAM	7498/12
ADDAH	3148/04	CITY OF MARSEILLES	8250/12
CHAMA	3151/05	CITY OF MYSORE	5294/14
EBANI	4862/12	CITY OF FLORENCE	5399/13
EBOE	4866/12	ROUMELIAN	2687/14

Hamburg-Amerika Line had nine cargo-liners of 5600 grt completed by the yard as their 'A' class between 1896 and 1901: *Asturia, Adria, Armenia, Andalusia, Arabia, Abyssinia, Acilia, Alexandria* and *Arlemisia*. *Bosnia* 7440/98 , *Belgia* 7507/00 and *Brasilia* 6682/06 formed their 'B' class with the first pair having been laid down as 'speculation ships' by Sir Christopher Furness of West Hartlepool but were sold to Hamburg-Amerika Line while under construction - the same fate happening to more hulls ordered by Furness from Alexander Stephen & Sons Ltd on the Clyde, completing as *Bengalia* 7690/98 and *Bethania* 7519/99. Sir Christopher Furness had a small 6% holding in the yard between 1903 and 1911, and had *Guardiana* 6852/06 completed at the yard, but his *Adriana* 5420/07 was again sold under construction, this time to Messageries Maritime of Marseilles as *Meinam*. The British Shipowners Company of Liverpool had three cargo-liners completed at the yard in time to be used as troopships in the Boer War:- *British Prince* 7324/99, *British Princess* 7326/99 and *British Empire* 7437/01 with the latter becoming the Cunarder *Flavia* in 1916. P & O had the passenger carrying cargo-liners *Borneo* 4690/95 and *Socotra* 6044/96 built at the yard - the latter being a twin-screw ship. Allan Line ordered a passenger cargo-liner for their Glasgow to Montreal route, and completed as *Hurenian* 6859/01, while R.P. Houston built two cargo-liners for his South African services: *Hypatia* 5662/01 and *Hyacinthus* 5756/02. J. Marke Wood & Sons of Liverpool had six ships of between 4000 and 5000 grt built at the yard in the ten years between 1894 and 1904: *Abana, Amana, Adana, Anapa, Asama* and *Acara*.

Electric overhead trolley cranes on elliptical-shaped gantries were introduced on the berths in 1906, and the production of tramps and cargo-liners in succeeding years was speeded up:-

The Dreadnought battleship HERCULES being launched after being named by Lady Furness on 10th May, 1910;
(William Parry and the Bede Gallery)

HERCULES on trials showing her ten 12" guns. (Tyne & Wear Archives)

BARRINGTON COURT	4367/06	Court Line,London 26
HYMETTUS	4782/06	Currie,Melbourne
MEINAM	5456/07	Messageries Maritime,Marseilles
FRANCES DUNCAN	2384/07	J.T. Duncan,Cardiff 366
PARKHAVEN	2655/08	Van Uden,Rotterdam
JANUS	4824/10	Currie,Melbourne
TORILLA	6679/11	British India 42
ERDELY	4247/11	Hungarian Levant Line
CLAN MACEWEN	5140/12	Clan Line 18
KAFUE	6044/12	Bucknall Line 357
KARROO	6127/12	"
CROXTETH HALL 2	5872/13	Hall Line 186

in addition to those ships mentioned earlier. The seven-berth shipyard of Robert Stephenson at Hebburn (q.v.) had lain idle for two or three years and was leased in 1911, together with their 715 feet dry-dock, the largest on the North-East Coast, to complement the smaller Palmer dry-dock at Jarrow. The Stephenson yard was then purchased in 1912 for merchant ship production.

The phenomenal warship production during World War I included one battleship *Resolution* (1916), one cruiser *Dauntless*, three monitors, 18 destroyers and two submarines. Merchant ship output included two cargo-liners for the New Zealand trade of the Federal Steam Navigation Co. Ltd: *Kent* 9857/17 and *Surrey* 9783/17; the cargo-liner *City of Winchester* 7981/17 for Ellerman Lines; and a large cargo ship for Italian owners Sicula Americana, *San Gennaro* 10917/17, which was converted into the liner *Colombo* in 1921. Five standard *WAR* 'Z' tankers were completed for the Shipping Controller, for whom the tanker *British Light* 6470/17 was also completed and managed by the British Tanker Co. Ltd. Five 'B' type dry-cargo ships were completed at Hebburn and two at Jarrow for liner companies such as Bank Line, P & O, British India and The Cairn Line of Steamships Ltd. The small yard of the Amble Shipbuilding Co. Ltd at Amble,Northumberland was purchased during the war, and a 560 feet dry-dock was operated at Swansea from 1922. A start was made after the war on cargo-liners for Blue Funnel and Ellerman Line , with many of these handsome ships being turbine propelled with turbines built at the yard:-

AUTOMEDON 2	7628/22	CITY OF PEKIN 2	6960/20
MEDON	5915/23	CITY OF PITTSBURG	7377/22
MELAMPUS	6336/24	CITY OF LANCASTER	3040/24
MERIONES	7671/22	CITY OF DUNDEE 2	5273/21
ANTENOR 3	11174/25		

Tramp LANGLEEBROOK of 1930 (above), and tanker BRITISH ARDOUR of 1928 (below). (Solomon).

Shell tanker PECTEN of 1927 (above), and tanker LUCERNA of 1930 (below).

with *Antenor* being twin-screw and powered by four steam turbines, *City of Pittsburg* had three steam turbines DR geared to a single screw shaft, while *City of Dundee* was powered by two steam turbines DR geared to a single screw shaft and had been completed as *Sandon Hall* for Hall Line. Blue Star Line took three cargo-liners *Africstar* 11900/26, *Stuartstar* 10646/26 and *Tuscan Star* with the first-pair being turbine propelled to twin screws while the third was a motorship with two 8-cylinder 2SCSA Sulzer oil engines linked to twin propellers. The yard also completed the twin-screw cargo-liner *Maimoa* 11291/20 for Shaw,Savill & Albion Ltd; and two examples of turbine-powered tramps - a rarity among the tramp fleets - in *Pear Branch* 4786/21 and *Plum Branch* 4798/21 for the Nautilus Steam Shipping Co. Ltd (F.W. Ritson), Sunderland. Three cargo ships were built for overseas owners Societe d'Affreteurs of France: *Bacchus* 5047/20, *Silene* 5019/20 and *Phoebus* 5006/21, and two for W. Wilhelmsen, Norway: *Tana* 5538/21 and *Tugela* 5559/21; while local owner Frederick Carrick and his Medomsley Shipping Co. Ltd had six tramps built at the yard between the summer of 1924 and 1930:- *Medomsley, Langleeford, Hedgehope, Langleetarn, Langleecrag* and *Langleebrook*.

    The large British cable-layer *Faraday* of 5533 grt was completed in April,1923 for Siemens Brothers,London. She was launched on 16th February,1923 with a cruiser stern and three decks including a shelter deck above the holds for the cable drums, and was powered by two triple expansion steam engines driving two screws. However, tankers predominated in post-WWI years:-

SAN GASPAR	12910/21	Eagle Oil
SAN GERARDO	12915/22	"
SAN MACEDONIO	5938/22	"
SAN MANUEL	5923/22	"
BRITISH CORPORAL	6972/22	British Tanker Co. Ltd
BRITISH SERGEANT	5868/22	"
BRITISH MARINER	6996/22	"
BRITISH PREMIER	5872/22	"
BRITISH GENERAL	6989/22	"
BRITISH CAPTAIN	6968/23	"
BRITISH OFFICER	6990/22	"
BRITISH AVIATOR	6998/24	"
BRITISH YEOMAN	6990/23	"
BRITISH CHEMIST	6997/25	"
BRITISH INVENTOR	7101/26	"
BRITISH INDUSTRY	4297/27	"

BRITISH FREEDOM	6985/28	British Tanker Co. Ltd
BRITISH LOYALTY	6993/28	"
BRITISH HONOUR	6991/28	"
BRITISH JUSTICE	6982/28	"
BRITISH ARDOUR	7124/28	"
BRITISH CHIVALRY	7118/29	"
BRITISH SCIENCE	7138/31	"
BRITISH SPLENDOUR	7138/31	"
BRITISH STRENGTH	7139/31	"
BEACONSTREET	7432/27	Beacon Oil Co.Ltd,Montreal
PECTEN	7725/27	Anglo-Saxon/Shell
PATELLA	7468/27	"
CABIMAS	1976/24	Venezuela Gulf Oil
PARAGUANA	1977/24	"
ZAPARA	2036/26	"
TOAS	2036/26	"
SUCRE	2646/26	"
BOLIVAR	2651/27	"
URDANETA	2647/27	"
PAEZ	2649/27	"
MONAGAS	2650/27	"
ARAGUA	2650/27	"
PERIJA	2647/27	"
ACOSTA	2634/27	"
CATATUMBO	3163/28	"
APURE	3164/28	"
CARONI	3164/28	"
LUMINETTA	6159/27	Moss Tankers
LUSTROUS	6156/27	"
LUCULUS	6546/29	"
LUXOR	6554/30	"
LUCERNA	6556/30	"
CHEYENNE	8825/30	Anglo-American Oil
APPALACHEE	8826/30	"
PETER HURLL	12043/30	Baltic-Amerika Pet. Import Gmbh

The giant Eagle Oil tankers *San Gaspar* and *San Gerardo* were turbine-propelled, as was half of the fleet built for the British Tanker Co. Ltd. *Beaconstreet* was completed in July,1927 as the first bracketless tanker designed by Sir Joseph Isherwood, and had a triple expansion steam engine built by the yard. The small Venezuela Gulf Oil tankers were shallow draft and twin screw, and designed to take oil from the upper reaches of Lake Venezuela out to refineries on nearby Dutch islands. They had twin triple expansion steam engines supplied by Sunderland engineers MacColl & Pollock Ltd. The tanker *Peter Hurll* was the thousandth ship launched by Palmers on 24th July,1930. The spar-decked cargo ship *Selje* of 6698 grt was completed for Norwegian owners in 1930, and the last merchant ship built at the yard was the tanker *British Strength* completed on 28th April,1931 at the height of the Depression. The yard was left with two destoyers on the order book, similar to the 'B' class *Boreas* and *Brazen*, completed by the yard in 1930. *Diana* was completed during 1932 and the last launch took place on 19th July,1932 when the destroyer *Duchess* slid into the water and she was completed in 1933. However the largest warship built after WWI had been the 8" gun cruiser *York*, launched on 17th July,1928 by H.M. The Queen Mother and completed during 1929, and later sunk by German dive-bombers during the invasion of Crete.

As Palmers was the main employer for Jarrow the effect of mass unemployment during the bitter years following the complete closure of the shipyard, engine works, blast furnaces and rolling mills in 1933 was catastrophic for the town. Men roamed the streets aimlessly in their hundreds and thousands while politicians refused to offer any help, and it was left to the compassion of a single man, Sir John Jarvis, High Sheriff of Surrey, to step in with financial support. He bought a vessel due for scrapping with his own money and sent it immediately to the yard in 1934. A year later he personally paid £100,000 for the White Star liner *Olympic*, sister of the ill-fated *Titanic*, and resold her to a Sheffield scrap metal company for the same sum on condition she was broken up at Jarrow, where she arrived in October,1935. His magnificent gesture ensured regular wages for some shipyard workers for the next 18 months. He also met half the cost of dredging the river at Jarrow from his relief fund, the remaining half being paid by the Tyne Improvement Commission. Sir John Jarvis again came to the aid of the town in 1938 when he bought the Cunard liner *Berengaria* and sent her to Jarrow for demolition.

The Palmer shipyard was acquired by National Shipbuilders Security Ltd in 1933 and demolished in 1935, the unique elliptical-shaped cranes going for scrap to a Sheffield company. The 715 feet dry-dock at Hebburn, formerly owned by the Robert Stephenson yard which was taken over by Palmers in 1912, was taken over by Vickers-Armstrong Ltd and continued to trade as Palmers(Hebburn)Ltd. The dry-dock had seen a delicate surgery operation performed to the ageing Anglo-American oil tankers *Cadillac* and *Saranac* at the beginning of the Depression in 1930. The mid-sections cargo tanks were cut out and rebuilt with new sections built at the shipyard, which had also built the giant tankers in 1917.

Launch of the cruiser YORK on 17th July, 1928 by H. M. The Queen Mother. (Palmers)

JOHN READHEAD & SONS LTD. 95

This famous shipbuilding name was first established in 1865 as a partnership between John Readhead and John Softley in a small yard near South Shields harbour in an area known as the Lawe. John Readhead had first worked as a millwright, but at the age of 32 years had started training as a shipwright in the Lawe yard of Thomas Marshall. After 15 years experience, the time was right to start shipbuilding for himself and Readhead & Softley started trading on 1st March,1865 with £2860 of their own capital in another small yard at the Lawe.

The first ship completed was a small collier brig named *Unus* 183/65 for Hodge & Williamson of South Shields. The first iron screw steamer was completed in 1868, and the barque *Lizzie Leslie* 370/68 attained fame as the first ship ever classed by Lloyd's Register as 100A1. The steam tug *Washington* was built in 1870 for service on the Thames, after which she returned to the river of her birth, towing until scrapped in 1952 at the age of 82 years. The partnership with Softley was dissolved in 1872 after building 87 small craft.

The Spanish coaster *Sagunto* of 1875 had an even longer life, her iron hull resisting rust and her original Readhead-built engine was still propelling her around the Spanish coasts at 9 knots over 90 years later! The tug *President* saw service at Limerick and on the Tyne in a career of 83 years. The Lawe yard was restricted as regards length of ship built, and so John Readhead moved upriver in 1881 to the western part of South Shields next to Tyne Dock. The last ship constructed at the Lawe was *Lynton* 1284/81 for Chapman & Miller, Newcastle, and the first ship constructed at the West Yard was *Jane Kelsall* 1278/81 for William D.C. Balls & Son of North Shields.

A long association with Edward Hain of St. Ives,Cornwall had already begun with *Trewidden* 1271/78 and *Tregenna* 1332/80 from the Lawe yard, which then prospered at the West Yard as their main customer with no fewer than 85 further tramps over a period of 84 years - making it one of the greatest shipowner/shipbuilder links of British maritime history. Other important customers at this time were Moor Line (Walter Runciman) with 29 tramps built, the first being *Blakemoor* 1702/89 and the last *Zurichmoor* 4455/25; and C.T. Bowring, London with nine tramps built, the first being *Tafna* 2231/87 and the last *Ronda* 4943/20; and Chapman of Newcastle with seven tramps built, the first being *Lynton* 1284/81 and the last *Demeterton* 14636/67;J. & C. Harrison,London with four tramps built, the first being *Harport* 3986/07 and the last   *Harpalyce* 4708/30; and Prince Line, North Shields with three ships built: *Danish Prince*   1618/84, *Asturian Prince* 3301/93 and *Trojan Prince* 3273/96. One shipowner, Franz Rahtkens, even named

The Readhead yard in 1890 (top), and the visit of H. M. The King in 1917 (middle), and in 1964 showing SAXONIA of Cunard (bottom). (J. Readhead & Sons Ltd.)

The improvement in yard cranage from the old sheerlegs crane at the right of the upper photograph for lifting aboard engines and boilers is illustrated by the modern 60-ton crane to the left of the bridge of SAXONIA in the lower photograph. The other 40-ton and tower 10-ton cranes are spread across the berths and the yard from the pre-fabrication sheds on the left to the engine works on the right.

his ship after the founder of the yard *John Readhead* 1622/82, and other customers included Scrutton & Sons,London; the Cuban Steamship Co. Ltd,London; R. Harrowing of Whitby; R.MacAndrew & Company,London; W. & C.T. Jones, Cardiff; with also exports for foreign owners such as Bergh & Helland,Bergen ; Cie des Bateaux a Vapeur du Nord,Dunkirk and Stathatos Brothers,Greece.

The founder,Alderman John Readhead J.P., died on 9th March,1894 aged 76 years and his four sons James,Robert,John and William carried on the family business with James in charge of the shipyard and Robert in charge of the engine works. John Readhead & Sons Ltd was incorporated in 1909 with a nominal capital of £300,000 in shares mostly held by the four brothers. Their main customer, Hain, had 17 tramps completed from this date up to the outbreak of World War I, when the yard came under Admiralty control. Some 20 tramps were constructed during the Great War with a total deadweight of 156,000 tons and included six *WAR* 'B' types, the 9000 dwt refuelling tanker *Oletta* - the only deep-sea tanker ever built by the yard - and three fast 'P' class submarine chasers capable of 22 knots. A boost to the war morale of the workforce was provided by the visit to the yard of King George V on 17th June,1917 as part of a tour of Tyneside.

Two royal vistors came to the yard after peace had been restored in 1920, Princess Marie Louise and Prince Albert (later King George VI), and they were shown round by James Readhead, who was later knighted in 1922. The main customer, Hain, had been taken over by P & O in 1917, and the new owners began a policy of using other shipyards and ordered less tramps from Readhead - five in total with *Min* 4694/22 completed for the associated Mercantile Steamship Co. Ltd. The yard was sustained in the 1920s by other customers with orders for four tramps from Runciman, three from Constantine Line of Middlesbrough, two from North Shipping Co. Ltd,Newcastle, and single orders from Bowring; Charlton,McAllum; Balls & Stansfield,North Shields whose *Eastville* was their last new tramp, and owners abroad such as Cie des Bateaux a Vapeur du Nord,Dunkirk, and Sota y Aznar,Bilbao:-

ARTESIEN	5420/21	Cie des Bateaux du Nord
ROUBASIEN	5430/21	"
ALTUNA MENDI	6193/22	Sota y Aznar
ANBOTO MENDI	6247/24	"
PEARLMOOR	4581/23	Runciman 3 3
QUEENMOOR	4862/24	"
YORKMOOR	4457/25	"
ZURICHMOOR	4455/25	"
HAZELWOOD	3744/27	J. Constantine 2\5
KIRNWOOD	3741/28	"
GOODWOOD	5008/28	"

NORTH CORNWALL	4304/24	North Shpg. Co. Ltd	174
NORTH DEVON	3658/24	"	
RONDA	4943/20	Bowring	216
HARTSIDE	3786/24	Charlton, McAllum	218
EASTVILLE	3709/25	Balls & Stansfield	219

They were mostly well-deckers, as was the 'spec' ship sold on the stocks to Strick Line for £65,000 but then sold on by Frank Strick to Turnbull, Scott & Co. Ltd for £75,000 and completed in November, 1926 as *Southgate*. This was the first contact in a long association between Stricks and Readheads which saw them becoming their main customer with no fewer than 44 orders. Some 16 Mediterranean tramps with names ending *'A'* and Persian Gulf traders with names ending *'Stan'* were then completed between 1927 and 1931 for Strick Line and associated companies.

Sir James Readhead died on 18th March, 1930 aged 77 years after a long illness, and his son Sir James Halder Readhead succeeded him as Chairman of the company. During the Depression the Readhead family continued to live in some style in Westoe Village, South Shields, but after the completion of *Lorca* 4875/31 and *Camerata* 4875/31 for companies owned by Frank C. Strick, only the apprentices at the shipyard were kept on with the whole workforce laid off. However Sir James H. Readhead put the apprentices to good use, building a 'speculation' ship albeit at an extremely slow pace, which was launched two years later and completed in November, 1934 for Bank Line Ltd as *Tynebank* 4651/34.

The yard thus remained effectively closed, except for apprentices, for five years until 1936 with grass growing on all three slipways. In January, 1936 at last an order was announced from Strick Line for two cargo-liners, which were completed as *Armanistan* 6805/37 and *Baltistan* 6803/37 with low pressure exhaust turbines to boost their triple expansion engines. The long anticipated pick-up in orders then began with five orders for cargo-liners from Bank Line Ltd, four from Strick Line and a tramp for Sir Arthur Sutherland:-

TIELBANK	5083/37	Bank Line	61
TESTBANK	5083/37	"	
TEVIOTBANK	5087/38	"	
THORNLIEBANK	5569/39	"	
THURSOBANK	5575/40	"	
SHAHRISTAN	6935/38	Strick Line	179 27
TURKISTAN	6935/39	"	
AFGHANISTAN	6992/40	"	
BALUCHISTAN	6750/40	"	
SUTHERLAND	5083/38	Sutherland S.S. Co. Ltd	217

Long associations were formed with Hain Line, pictured is TREGENNA of 1949 (above); and with Strick Line, pictured is SERBISTAN of 1966 (below).   (A. Duncan)

A move to gain some room for expansion was made in 1937 by acquiring Smiths Docks Co. Ltd old dry-docks, which separated the building berths from the repair yard. The dry-docks were then filled in with ballast from the nearby Johnston hill. The repair yard had continued to operate during the Depression, and what little work was obtained helped the cash-flow position of the company enough to survive. An interesting repair job was made at the end of 1937 to the Constantine owned tramp *Kingswood* 5055/29 which had suffered a serious blow-out of the donkey boiler after a massive engine room explosion. The boiler travelled in a forward direction through all the forward bulkheads a distance of some 164 feet before becoming embedded in the shell plating of the forepeak and causing a large hole in the starboard side of the forepeak. After temporary repairs in Australia, the tramp was towed home to the Readhead yard, where the boiler was restored to its correct position. The repair yard during the first year of war was, however, soon at full stretch coping with a succession of serious damage to colliers and tramps from torpedoes and mines. Severe buckling of the dock gates to no. 2 dry-dock, which can still be seen today, was caused by German air-raid damage during the night of April 9th/10th,1941.

Sir James H. Readhead died during May,1940 and he was succeeded as Chairman of the company by Christopher Southall, and Harold Towers, son-in-law of Sir James, as Managing Director. Harold Towers had joined the shipyard as an apprentice in 1936, married the daughter of the boss and been elected to the Board in 1936. A more enlightened approach to management was then made during the difficult war years, including permission for office staff to use the bridge over the street outside the shipyard to cross to the offices on the other side - once only the exclusive preserve of the Readhead family!

The contribution to the shipbuilding war effort from 1939 to 1945 was 31 tramps with a total carrying capacity of 307,000 tons, and two special repair ships for the Navy of similar size, and two *'Chant'* coastal tankers. The dry-docks had been continually in use repairing the shattered hulls of colliers, tramps and banana boats. Nine of the tramps were completed to Readhead designs, the remainder being 11 of the 'B' type and three of the 'C' type and two 'D' type of the standard *'Empire'* tramp of 10,000 tons dwt. The repair ship *Moray Firth* was built and engined by the yard, whereas her sister *Beauly Firth* was moved up-river to the Palmers yard for fitting-out. Six ships were completed for private owners, including three for Strick Line, one for Bank Line, one for the North Shipping Co. Ltd of Newcastle, and one paper carrier for Runciman(London) Ltd.

The first launch after peace had returned was the first of three cargo-liners for British India S.N. Co. Ltd, *Palikonda*, on 22nd June,1945 and she was followed

The Strick Line cargo-liner ARMANISTAN ready for launch in 1949. (J. Readhead & Sons Ltd)

by *Obra* and *Okhla* in 1946. After this order was completed, orders for some 66 cargo-liners and tramps were secured during the next twenty years to 1966 for well-known shipowners such as Strick Line (20 ships), H.Hogarth (6 ships),Hain (5 ships), Stag Line (4 ships), Bristol City Steamers (3 ships), Hudson S.S. Co. Ltd (3 ships), France,Fenwick (3 ships), Cunard Line (2 ships) and T.& J. Harrison (2 ships). Export orders were six tramps for Greek owners, two for Norwegian, two for French, two for Irish and one for a Danish owner. The yard developed a new design known as a 'strengthened raised quarter-decker', which featured a five hold engines-aft design ideally suited for the heavy grain and sugar trades. These were constructed for William France,Fenwick as *Rookwood* 6246/52, *Rushwood* 6208/53, *Granwood* 7920/59; Hudson Steamship Co. Ltd as *Hudson Deep* 6198/52 and *Hudson Point* 7863/57; and for Stag Line as *Camellia* 6161/53, *Cydonia* 6231/55, *Gloxinia* 7665/58 and *Photinia* 7676/61. This last ship also provided much conversion work for the Dry Docks Department, as she was twice converted at great expense to lay power cables between the North and South Islands in New Zealand and also between Trinidad and Tobago on charter to British Insulated Callender's Cable Company.

The launch of SAXONIA of Cunard in 1964. (Shields Gazette)

The most prestigious of these post-WWII orders was that for two sister cargo-liners for Cunard Line of 7080 dwt. *Media* was launched first on 20th June,1963 with

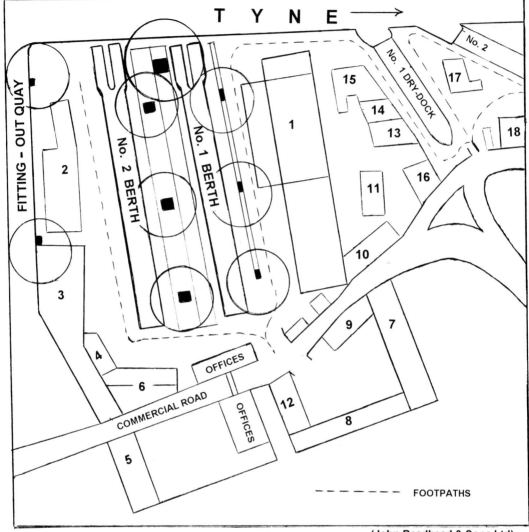

(John Readhead & Sons Ltd)

READHEAD SHIPYARD IN 1965

1. MAIN FABRICATION SHED
2. No. 2 FABRICATION SHED
3. ENGINE WORKS
4. BLACKSMITH
5. PLUMBERS SHOP
6. JOINERS SHOP
7. PLATERS SHOP
8. TIMBER SHED
9. SHEET METAL SHOP
10. SAWMILL
11. BOILER HOUSE
12. ELECTRICIANS SHOP
13. CARPENTERS SHOP
14. PLUMBERS SHOP
15. COLD BENDING SHED
16. DRY-DOCK OFFICE
17. FITTERS SHOP
18. PLATERS SHOP

Saxonia following later in the year, and their diesel engines were constructed at the Newcastle factory of Hawthorn,Leslie (Engineers) Ltd. This reflected a trend in engine building away from the Engine Works of the Readhead yard, where previously to 1957 all newbuildings with the exception of two ships had been engined by the yard.   The manufacture of steam reciprocating machinery was discontinued shortly afterwards, and by 1963 the number of building berths was reduced from three to two.   The old centre berth now accomodated improved cranage to lift prefabricated sections, with double width gantry stands for two 60-ton, one 40-ton and a 10-ton monotower crane.   Modernisation included a new prefabrication shed, a cold frame bending machine, a flame planing machine for plate edges, and extension of the building berths. This was rewarded by two orders for bulk carriers of 21110 dwt and 25012 dwt obtained in 1965. The first bulker was completed as *Demeterton* in May,1967 for Chapman & Willan, Newcastle, and the other as *Himmerland* for Dansk-Fransk A/S D/S of Denmark later in 1967. A larger bulker of 26603 dwt was then constructed for Stag Line of North Shields and completed in October,1968 as *Zinnia* at a cost of £1.625M.

The Readhead yard was taken over by Swan Hunter Shipbuilders Ltd as from 1st January,1968 as a result of the merger recommendations of the Geddes Report. The South Shields yard then consisted of two building berths capable of building ships up to 625 feet in length, a 480 feet long dry-dock and a 330 feet long dry-dock. The bigger dry-dock was able to give pre-delivery dry-docking to two small container ships completed later that year for the Harwich to Zeebrugge service of British Rail Shipping & International Services. *Sea Freightliners I* and *II* could carry 218 twenty foot containers with a deadweight of 3213 tons and gross tonnage of 4034 tons.

Two long-established customers took delivery of their final ships from the yard between 1969 and 1972.   Strick Line took delivery of their cargo-liner *Tabaristan* on 7th May,1969 some seven weeks ahead of schedule at a cost of £2M and fitted with a very large Stulcken heavy-lift derrick amidships and four deck cranes, while her sister *Nigaristan* delivered in 1970 had a total of eight deck cranes and no Stulcken. *Nigaristan* was the last of 44 Strick Line ships from the yard and her powerful 6-cylinder Doxford oil engine gave over 18 knots on trials. British India Line , part of P & O as was Strick Line, took delivery of four cargo-liners *Amra* and *Aska* of 13921 dwt in 1969/70, and the reefers *Zaida* and *Zira* of 6634 dwt in 1972.

The yard benefitted from full order books at the Deptford yard of Sunderland Shipbuilders Ltd, the preferred shipbuilder for a engines-aft tramp of 15000 dwt for W.A. Souter & Co. Ltd, Newcastle. A repeat order for an identical ship built at

Sunderland in 1968 was completed by the yard as *Sheaf Field* 9372/71. Swan Hunter Shipbuilders Ltd then won orders for six cargo-liners of 15216 dwt for Bank Line, of which three were built at South Shields: *Corabank* 11405/73, *Moraybank* 11405/73 and *Ivybank* 11405/74. Common Brothers of Newcastle took delivery of four tankers of 31000 dwt from Swan Hunter Shipbuilders Ltd at this time, two from Hebburn, and two from the Readhead yard with the first launched as *Strait of Canso* on 25th April,1975 and the second launched as *Hindustan* on 12th May,1976.

The order book was now empty, but a reprieve for the yard came in the shape of an order for a coaster for Fred Everard, which was launched as *Singularity* on 17th March,1977 and completed in June of that year just before the Tyne yards were nationalised on 1st July,1977. The South Shields yard then concentrated purely on repair work as part of Tyne Shiprepair Ltd, but it was closed by British Shipbuilders during 1982. It was then leased back to a company created by the Readhead workforce, but when they got into financial difficulties eighteen months later the repair yard was taken over by Tyne Dock Engineering Co. Ltd. The shipbuilding yard has since been stripped but is still in business as McNulty Marine for North Sea oil rig modification work.

Bank Line cargo-liner IVYBANK of 1974 en-route to the Pacific. (A. Weir & Co.)

TYNE IRON SHIPBUILDING CO. LTD. 126

In 1871 two brothers, H.A.B. Cole and R.F. Cole, from the south of England took over the Willington Quay shipyard of William B. Hornsby from Sunderland, who in turn had taken it over from the Marshall Brothers of South Shields, and which had originally been established by Thomas Adamson in 1852. The Cole brothers built six iron screw steamers of Newcastle registry up to 1876 under manager William J. Bone - the first was *Cleveland* 1067/72 for Nelson & Company and the last was *Lord Eslington* 1722/76. The Tyne Iron SB Co. Ltd was then set-up later in 1876 by William J. Bone, and completed six ships during 1877, four of these to a standard design of 1700 grt and capable of carrying 2500 tons of cargo e.g. *Lord Derby* 1731/77 for Newcastle owners.

The main types of ships built were tramps, colliers and some tankers. The main customers were:- Stag Line of North Shields with 23 ships, the first being *Laurestina* 1919/77 and the last *Gloxinia* 3380/20; Hunting & Son of Newcastle with 14 ships, the first being *Yoxford* 1878/80 and the last *Wellfield* 6054/23; Stephens, Sutton Ltd with 12 tramps, the first being *Rowland* 1367/78 and the last *Roddam* 3218/12; Rowland & Marwood, Whitby with four tramps, the first being *Wileysike* 2501/88 and the last *Ingleside* 3736/10; International Line, Whitby managed by Christopher Marwood with four tramps:- *Leucadia* 3748/10, *Etolia* 3733/11, *Florentia* 3688/12 and *Thessalia* 3691/12.

Other customers were J.D. Milburn of Newcastle with his Australian traders *Port Augusta* 2875/86, *Port Denison* 3435/96, *Port Albert* 3514/97 and *Port Phillip* 3103/97; Fisher, Renwick of Newcastle with *Ella Sayer* 2549/98 and *Sentry* 1014/24; Newton Brothers & Company of London with *Energia* 3177/83; The Clan Line Steamers Ltd of Glasgow with *Clan Murray* 2108/81 launched as *Muriel*; West Hartlepool Steam Navigation Co. Ltd with *Guildhall* 2609/98 and *Haddonhall* 2608/98; and many Scandinavian and German owners such as L. Krogius of Sweden with *Ceres* 1068/89, and Wilhelm Wilhelmsen of Norway with several ships; and Hamburg-America Line with *Helvetica* 2825/89; and A/S Kjobenhavn (Peter L. Fisker), Copenhagen with *Euxinia* 3754/99.

The yard grew from an initial four acres to include all of the land to the east of the Clelands yard, and was well equipped and had good labour relations and was ranked among the leading Tyneside yards. The first tanker built by the yard was *Duffield* 3767/93 for Hunting & Son of Newcastle, who ordered her in 1889 but her design took much time to complete. She was followed over the years by eight more tankers for these owners.

West Hartlepool tramp GUILDHALL of 1898 (above), and Prince Line tanker RUSSIAN PRINCE of 1912 (below).

William Bone remained in charge until 1901 when J. Bourn formerly of Armstrong,Mitchell & Co. Ltd took over as Manager with G.F. Mulherion as General Manager and they remained in charge until the yard's closure. The immediate pre-WWI years brought a flood of orders for tramps and included two cargo-liners for the Booth Steamship Co. Ltd of Liverpool *Christopher* 4416/10 and *Aidan* 4545/11, and two for Elder Dempster completed as *Gaboon* 3297/15 and *Gambia* 3296/15, as well as Fred Olsen's *Bra-Kar* 4777/11 for use in carrying granite blocks from Norway to South America returning with grain and coffee. Tramps and their owners included:-

LLANDUDNO	4187/10	Evan Thomas Radcliffe,Cardiff
DUNRAVEN	3117/10	"
ESSEX BARON	4307/14	Meldrum & Swinson,London
PROPHET	3226/12	Houlder,Middleton of London
HANNAH	3697/13	Rahtkens Shpg. Co.,M'brough
RUEL	4029/13	Turnbull Brothers,Cardiff
ORLA	4033/14	A. Bergvall,Norway

and four tankers were built during this period :-

RUSSIAN PRINCE	4158/12	Prince Line
ROUMANIAN PRINCE	4143/13	"
SILVIA	5268/13	C.T. Bowring
ELBRUZ	4881/14	Soc Anon d'Armament, d'Industrie et de Commerce

the latter being an unusual design of twin-screw tanker for Belgian owners and fitted with an early oil engine and was the first motor driven tanker built on Tyneside.

Output during World War I was 10 tramps of which seven were *WAR* 'C' types; three naval patrol boats and two naval tankers *Philol* 1178/16 and *Scotol* 1177/16. The last *WAR* 'C' type was completed in January,1920 and was followed later that year by another to that design for Stag Line, *Gloxinia* 3380/20. However she did not start trading immediately and moved down-river to the dry-dock of Smiths Dock Co. Ltd,North Shields for conversion into a tanker. Orders were taken for four ships for the French owner Cie Francais des Chemins de Fer Paris-Orleans,Nantes and completed as:- *Vendome* 4730/20, *Chateauroux* 4730/21, *Lorient* 4185/21 and *Poitiers* 4184/21.

Two tankers were completed for Hunting & Son of Newcastle, *Oilfield* 5387/23 and *Wellfield* 5633/23, the latter being the biggest ship ever built at the yard, and two colliers for the South Metropolitan Gas Board, *Camberwell* 1568/24 and *Redriff* 1560/25, and a coaster for Fisher,Renwick *Sentry* 1014/24. However the slump of the early 1920s continued without relent with no ships completed in 1926 and the yard was forced to close after the completion of its last ship *Kenton* of 3930 grt in January,1927 for International South American Steamship Co. Ltd (A. Stott & Co),Newcastle. The yard had completed just over 200 ships and was sold in 1928 to Armstrong,Whitworth & Co. Ltd to complete a few more tramps under Armstrong yard numbers up to final closure in 1933. The yard was then sold to National Shipbuilders Security Ltd and dismantled in 1935.

One of the largest tankers built by Tyne Iron was OILFIELD of 1923 owned by Hunting of Newcastle. (J. Clarkson).

NORTHUMBERLAND SHIPBUILDING CO. LTD.

Harry S. Edwards & Sons, with repair yards at both North Shields and South Shields, laid out a shipbuilding yard at Howdon-on-Tyne in 1883, and completed some 75 ships between then and 1898, the first being *Merchant Prince* of 1722 grt for James Knott of North Shields and his Prince Line. One of the largest ships built by Edwards was *Markomannia* 3470/90 for Hamburg-America Line, having been laid-down for F. Stumore of London as *Benwell Tower*. Edwards died in 1898 and his yard at Howdon, which had latterly been at reduced output, was acquired by Rowland Hodge, previously yard manager for C.S. Swan & Hunter at Wallsend. He transferred the ownership of the yard to a new company with the Northumberland name for £6,000 in shares with Sir Christopher Furness, the West Hartlepool shipowner taking a controlling interest. Ships built by the yard for Furness group companies, or known to have been laid down as speculative ventures accounted for 34% of buildings, 51 out of 148 ships built before WWI. Those actually completed for Furness,Withy & Co. Ltd and subsidiaries Manchester Liners Ltd, British Maritime Trust Ltd, Chesapeake & Ohio Steamship Co. Ltd, Neptune Steam Navigation Co. Ltd numbered twenty four ships, and those for Houlder Line and subsidiary Empire Transport Co. Ltd numbered twelve ships.

Ships were built by the yard to individual designs, but two standard designs emerged, the first for spar-deckers and two-deckers of 4300 grt on dimensions of 360' length and 48' beam with a deadweight of 7300 tons. *Rosalie* was the first of the type when launched in December,1899 for John Cory of Cardiff, and she was followed by *Rhodesia* 4313/00, *Ruperra* 4232/01 and *Roath* 4306/01 for the same owner. The design was stretched in 1907 by 20 feet in length increasing the deadweight to 7500 tons, starting with *Graciana* 4265/07 for Furness. Over 90 examples were built, some being strengthened as two-deckers and mostly laid down as speculative ventures for Furness, although a large majority of the 36 actually completed for the Furness group were of this type. Ships were completed to this type for other customers e.g.:- Watts,Watts & Co. Ltd; T. Dunlop,Glasgow; B.J. Sutherland,Newcastle; Court Line; J. Mathias & Sons,Cardiff; Agincourt Steamship Co. Ltd,London; New York & Pacific Steamship Co. Ltd and many others.

The second standard design was for shelter-deckers of 4800 grt on dimensions of 410' length and 52' beam with a deadweight of 9700 tons. *Rotterdam* of 1907 was the first of the type for Furness, for whom the yard also built *Brantford* 4844/09 and *Savannah* 4849/09. Eleven of this type were built in the years before World War I, examples for other customers were *Queen Louise* 4879/12 for

QUEEN ALEXANDRA of 1901 of the Glasgow fleet of Thomas Dunlop.   (W.S.P.L.)

ROATH of 1901 owned by John Cory of Cardiff.   (W.I.M.M.)

T. Dunlop,Glasgow and *Harmatris* 4863/12 for J. & C. Harrison,London, the remaining examples being mostly for overseas owners:- *Galileo* 4768/07, *Gerania* 4800/09, *Francisco* 4760/10, *Marengo* 4832/10, *Buenaventura* 4881/13 and *Frimley* 4880/13.

The yard also built some steamers for the Great Lakes e.g. *A.E. Ames* 1637/03, and the twin-funnelled Greek emigrant steamer *Patris* 4390/09, whose triple expansion engines produced a creditable 16 knots in service. The yard was unique during the war in that it was allowed by the Shipping Controller to build to its own standard design of shelter-decker tramp, which was given the official category of 'F1'. Some 14 examples of the 'F1' were built, with most completing for commercial owners such as Union-Castle Line, Union Steamship Co. Ltd of New Zealand, Saint Line and others until 1920. Three *WAR* 'A' and 'B' types were also completed, and those for private owners included *Maenwen* launched on 15th December,1917 for W. & C.T. Jones Steamship Co. Ltd,Cardiff but sold during fitting-out to The Clan Line Steamers Ltd,Glasgow and completed in March,1918 as *Clan Macvicar*. Clan Line also took delivery of *Clan Macvey* 5830/18, *Clan Mackay* 6580/17 and *Clan Mackenzie* 6500/17 from the yard. *Grelfryda* 4976/17 and *Greltoria* 5143/17 were also completed for James C. Gould of Cardiff.

In November,1918 the Furness Group sold the yard to new owners led by R.A. Workman of Workman,Clark & Co.,Belfast for £835,000 and associated with London merchant bankers Sperling & Company, who used the Northumberland company to create a shipbuilding combine, the largest in Britain under Sir Alexander Kennedy. The Northumberland Shipbuilding Co. Ltd as a public company acquired majority holdings in William Doxford & Sons Ltd,Sunderland followed by Fairfield of Govan; Workman,Clark of Belfast; Blythswood Shipbuilding Company; Monmouth Shipbuilding Company and the Lancashire Iron & Steel Company. When purchased in 1918 the Northumberland share capital was £500,000, but within a year this had been increased to £7M with £5.5M of this in preference shares. The yard continued to build tramps for British and overseas owners:-

GIOVANNA FLORIO	5141/20	J.V. Florio,Palermo
CADORE	5876/20	Lloyd Adriatico
SAN MICHELE	5157/20	Soc. Veneziana,Venice
ADAMELLO	5872/20	Lloyd Adriatico
MONTE NEVOSO	5843/20	"
DALEMOOR	5870/22	Runciman,Newcastle
EASTMOOR	5796/22	"
FERNMOOR	5812/22	"
ORANGEMOOR	5775/23	"
SKIPSEA	5108/22	Brown,Atkinson of Hull
OVERSTONE	3940/24	C. Radcliffe,Cardiff

SAINT ANDREW of 1919 was a standard 'F1' type unique to the Northumberland yard (above), and PONTYPRIDD of 1924 (below) was a typical Cardiff tramp of the 1920s. (A.Duncan & W.S.P.L.)

SNOWDON	3979/24	C. Radcliffe,Cardiff
TACITO	8331/24	Cia Combustibles,B/Aires
DRAMMENSFJORD	4346/24	Norwegian-Amerika Line
PONTYPRIDD	4458/24	Morel,Cardiff 209
GARDEPEE	4517/25	"
AMICUS	3660/25	W. Seager,Cardiff 225
CAMPUS	3667/25	"

The tanker *Modum* 4479/23 was completed for Norwegian owners and became *Peruviana* shortly afterwards in the Furness,Withy fleet before being sold a year later to the Argentine. The Sperling combine collapsed during 1925 as orders had been hard to find in the disastrous freight market of the early and mid 1920s. The optimism of the directors in 1918 had been misplaced as they were unable to serve their debenture and preference shareholders. The problem was exarcebated by the Northumberland Company having ordered too much steel plate from Dorman,Long & Company - some 300,000 tons of which only half was needed and the steelmaker was compensated to the tune of £300,000. *Chelsea* was the last tramp completed in November,1925 and the yard was idle during 1926 and a receiver was appointed. A new company was formed during the following year - Northumberland Shipbuilding Co.(1927) Ltd - and the yard was re-opened. It now had seven berths and could build ships up to 600 feet in length, and then completed the following tramps:-

GEDDINGTON COURT	6903/28	Court Line 26
QUARRINGTON COURT	6900/28	"
FISCUS	4815/28	W. Seager,Cardiff 225
SALVUS	4815/28	"
NOLISEMENT	5084/28	Morel,Cardiff 209
ALLENDE	5081/29	"
CRESSINGTON COURT	4971/29	Court Line 26
DALLINGTON COURT	6889/29	"
BURNHOPE	3859/29	Burnett,Newcastle 226
TYNEMOUTH	4409/29	"
THEMONI	3875/29	Kassos S.N. Co.,Syra
HADIOTIS	4386/29	"
PETERSFIELD	5073/30	Woods,Taylor & Brown 227
REDSEA	5224/30	Brown Atkinson,Hull 216
KINGSWOOD	5055/29	J. Constantine 215
WEARWOOD	4578/30	"
MAPLEWOOD	4562/30	"
BRIARWOOD	4013/30	"

AMICUS (above) was built in 1925 for Sir William Seager of Cardff, and TYNEMOUTH (below) was one of the last ships built by the yard (W.I.M.M. and W.S.P.L.)

and some coasters for Coast Line. *Briarwood* was the last ship launched on 27th May,1930 and after her completion in July,1930 the yard was sold to National Shipbuilders Security Ltd and later dismantled. Some 343 ships had been built by the yard under the Northumberland name, plus a further 75 under the Harry S. Edwards name.

WILLIAM DOBSON & CO. LTD. 279

William Dobson attained a senior position in the Low Walker yard of Charles Mitchell, and then established his own yard just upstream of the Mitchell yard at Wincomblee village in 1883. The yard's first ship was the tramp *Bosphorus* of 2490 grt for local owners Hall Brothers of Newcastle. Other early buildings included steam hopper barges for the River Ouse; a tug and two barges for Portugal; two sailing ships - one fitted for carrying gas tar - and a steamer for the gas tar trade; small tankers for the Caspian Sea; 'kit-built' shallow draught steamers for Russia and China; passenger and cargo ships for the White Sea and Black Sea trades of Russian owners. These unusual specialist ships and Russian contracts indicate that Dobson retained, or exploited, contacts and experience gained during his years working for Mitchell. The yard never challenged the bigger Tyne yards in terms of output, but a steady stream of cargo-liners was produced for well-known customers such as DFDS of Denmark with *Florida* 4401/98 and *Pennsylvania* 3759/07 for their North American services; Prince Line with *Soldier Prince* 3118/01 and *Sailor Prince* 3119/01; Elder,Dempster with *Nyanga* 3066/00; Swedish East Asiatic Company with *Delagoa* 3542/14; Danish East Asiatic Company with *Rhodesia* 4112/14 and Cayo Line,London with *Cayo Romano* 3675/11.

Tramps however were the yard's bread and butter, and included German owners such as Syndikat Rhederei,Hamburg with *Alster* 3618/06 and Norwegian owners such as P.A. Gron of Sandefjord with *Ocean* 4314/08, as well as the following British tramp owners:-

SUTHERLAND	2279/92	Sutherland S.S. Co. Ltd,Newcastle 217
LORD ORMONDE	3914/99	Irish Shipowners Co. Ltd,Belfast 385
RODNEY	3472/01	Trafalgar S.S. Co. Ltd,London 228
LORD ROBERTS	4166/01	Irish Shipowners Co. Ltd,Belfast 385
MICKLEY	2441/02	J.C. Adam,Newcastle 229
MATFEN	2498/03	"
CAPE ANTIBES	2549/03	Lyle Shipping Co. Ltd,Glasgow 52
LARGO LAW	3974/07	Thomas Law & Co.,Glasgow 230
CANADIAN 2	3214/07	J.W. Norcross,Newcastle 231

Paddle steamers being built in 1897 at the Dobson yard. (Mrs. V. Dobson) (Tyne & Wear Archives)

SAILOR PRINCE of 1901 owned by Prince Line.

CADUCEUS of 1927 owned by Hall Brothers of Newcastle. (Solomon)

CYDONIA	3085/10	Stag Line,North Shields 25
LINARIA	3081/11	"
YARROWDALE	4652/12	Mackill S.S. Co. Ltd,Glasgow 232
WILLASTON	5658/14	Wirral Transport Co. Ltd 233

The tanker *Luz Blanca* of 4868 grt, completed in August,1913 for the London & Pacific Petroleum Co. Ltd,London was one of the very few deep-sea tankers built at the yard. One speciality built in large numbers was colliers for customers such as William Cory & Son, William France,Fenwick & Co.; Stephenson,Clarke; Ridley,Son & Tully; Sharp Steamship Co. Ltd; Metropolitan Gas Company; Commercial Gas Company; Wandsworth & Putney Gas Company and other gas and light companies. Several coasters were built for the Lancashire and Yorkshire Railway Co. Ltd, and Thomas Wilson & Sons,Hull, and short-sea traders were also built for Bergen Line of Norway, Worms et Cie,France; Fearnley & Eger, Norway; Ybarra & Co.,Spain; DFDS of Denmark; and other Austro-Hungarian,Belgian,Dutch, Russian and Norwegian owners.

World War I saw a mixture of private and Government orders, the latter replacing the former as they were completed. *East Wales* 4321/15 was completed for Gibbs & Co. Ltd,Cardiff; *Mottisfont* 5692/16 for Harris & Dixon Ltd; and the three sister tramps *Clintonia* 3106/17, *Euphorbia* 3109/17 and *Begonia* 2929/18 for Stag Line of North Shields. Those completed for the Shipping Controller were three *WAR* 'B' types of which the last was completed as *Ballena* in February,1920, and three *WAR* 'C' types. The total war production was 16 tramps and a number of 'X' lighters for the use of the armed forces.

An order was then received for five general cargo ships from Gebr. Van Uden of Holland which were completed as *Parkhaven* 4803/20, *Delfshaven* 4805/21, *Yselhaven* 4802/21, *Schiehaven* 4807/22 and *Lekhaven* 4802/21. Another tramp completed as *Rio Grande* 3667/20 became *Heina* in the Mowinckel fleet of Norway soon after completion. The coaster *Sapper* 1036/23 was completed for the Manchester to London service of Fisher,Renwick; and another for R.H. Penney of Shoreham, *Algol* 1566/24. Orders for tramps became scarce as the slump continued into the mid-1920s, and the last tramps completed at the yard as an independent builder were:-

JAMESON	3585/24	Kaye,Son & Co. Ltd,London 234
CHATTON	3569/25	"
EAST WALES	4358/25	Gibbs & Co. Ltd,Cardiff 235
WEST WALES 2	4353/25	"
ROYAL CROWN 1	4364/27	Hall Brothers,Newcastle 152
CADUCEUS	4364/27	"
WHITE CREST	4365/28	"

381

with the last tramp completing as *Penrose* 4393/28 for the Chellew Steam Navigation Co. Ltd in August,1928, with the yard then posessing four slipways of between 200 and 450 feet in length. The yard was then taken over by Armstrong,Whitworth & Co. Ltd (q.v.) together with the Tyne Iron Shipbuilding yard, and several more ships were then completed under the Armstrong name in each yard until closure in 1931. The yard had built over two hundred ships and was then purchased by National Shipbuilders Security in 1935 and demolished.

CLELAND'S (SUCCESSORS) LTD. 456

This yard was noted for spectacular sideways launches from its cramped site next to Willington Gut. William Cleland had Clydeside origins and was initially a manager for T. & W. Smith of North Shields. In the 1860s he moved to the yard of Palmer Brothers at Howdon, but after Palmers became a limited company in 1865 he left to begin business for himself in 1867 and registered William Cleland's Graving Dock in 1872. The yard carried on a ship-repairing and slipway business, only building one ship, *The Princess* 563/73, a raised quarterdecker steamer. In 1932 at the height of the Depression, William Cleland's Graving Dock was offered for sale, and was bought for £3,000 by the Craggs family of the Goole Shipbuilding & Repairing Co. Ltd later in the year.

As Cleland's (Successors) Ltd shipbuilding was commenced in 1934, building coasters such as *Mytongate* 410/38 for the Hull Gates Shipping Co. Ltd. The World War II output consisted of five coasters, thirteen tugs and a ferry and barge. Three coasters were then constructed for the Hull Gates company during 1947/48, but the main output between 1946 and 1950 was 60 barges of 80 feet length each for services with the oil companies Burmah Oil, BP and Shell. In 1954 a new pre-fabrication hall was added to the yard facilities, and in 1957 the main slipway for stern-first launches was extended, and a new yard was built on an adjoining site to the west for two broadside launching berths, each 120 feet long by 40 feet wide. The improvements had cost £1M and *Queensgate* was the first coaster launched broadside in 1959. Yard output consisted of coasters, coastal tankers, tugs, barges, drilling platforms, towing launches, tenders and yachts. By 1960 some 200 small craft had been built with the yard possessing three berths of which the largest was 350 feet in length, and employing some 700 men. The London & Rochester Trading Co. Ltd (Crescent Shipping) had six coasters built , with several more for Fred. T.

One of the last ships from the Cleland yard, the oil-rig supply vessel SUFFOLK PRINCE of 1982 shown alongside the yard. (Author).

The Meditteranean trader COTSWOLD PRINCE of 1970 from Clelands. (J. Clarkson)

Everard & Sons, three for Comben,Longstaff, with one more building for Monroe Brothers,Liverpool and completed in 1961 as *Kylebank*.

Cleland's by 1960 were marketing their standard design coaster known as *'EXCELSHIP* 2600' of 2600 dwt, and achieved considerable success with traditional coaster owners for whom the following were built:-

CORNISHBROOK	1595/61	Comben,Longstaff
CHESTERBROOK	1594/63	"
CAERNARVONBROOK	1594/64	"
CLAREBROOK	1594/64	"
CORKBROOK	1594/64	"
PENELOPE EVERARD	1583/62	Fred. T. Everard
GILLIAN EVERARD	1590/62	"
ROSEMARY EVERARD	1599/63	"
ETHEL EVERARD	1599/66	"
MARCHON ENTERPRISE	1599/61	Albright & Wilson
MARCHON VENTURER	1599/62	"
GLANTON	1594/64	Sharp S.S. Co. Ltd,Newcastle

In 1967 the Craggs family sold the Cleland's yard and their Goole yard to Swan,Hunter & Wigham Richardson Ltd, both yards then becoming the Small Ship Division of Swan Hunter and later joined by the Grangemouth Dockyard. A small standard coaster type of 412 dwt was marketed from 1968 with four being sold to Tower Shipping Co. Ltd,London and two to Fred. T. Everard & Sons. The yard then commenced building trawlers and during 1970 to 1975 two were built for Boyd Line of Hull - *Arctic Crusader* and *Arctic Reiver* - and eight for J. Marr & Son Ltd,Lowestoft: *Gavina, Luneda, Jacinta, Cordelia, Northella, Farnella, Fyldea* and *Junella* with the last named being the last trawler ever launched on the Tyne in 1975.

Three twin-hold motor vessels of 2600 dwt were completed for the Mediterranean services of Prince Line and Furness,Withy Ltd in 1970. *Cotswold Prince, Mendip Prince* and *Chiltern Prince* were built at Cleland's with a fourth sister, *Malvern Prince*, coming from the Grangemouth Dockyard. They were smart vessels with light grey hulls and sharply raked funnels showing to advantage the Prince of Wales feathers. Four derricks were fitted with one hinged to a goalpost mast located on the top of the bridge. The yard then started to build oil-rig supply ships and anchor handling tugs for the North Sea oilfields, four of the last examples being *Cambridge Service, Norwich Service, Suffolk Prince* and *Suffolk Princess* of 1981/82. Shell (U.K.) Ltd took two coastal tankers in 1981, *Shell Marketer* and *Shell Technician* of 300 dwt.

The twin-hold design of *Suavity* 1594/73 and 3272 dwt for Fred T. Everard was improved further for a series of coasters built for Stephenson Clarke Ltd with two of 3860 dwt - *Birling* and *Emerald* both 1584/77 - and two of 4300 dwt - *Harting* 1584/81 and *Steyning* 1589/83. The larger collier *Ashington* of 6570 dwt delivered in April,1979 to the same owners was the largest ship built by the yard. *Steyning* was the last ship launched on 9th August,1983 and completed on 20th October,1983 when the yard was closed. The site has since being used by a variety of oil rig building companies.

WOOD,SKINNER & CO. LTD.,Bill Quay.

James Skinner had experience of shipbuilding at the former Coutts yard at Low Walker and later as a manager for Andrew Leslie at Hebburn, and William Wood had been cashier at the yard of Schlesinger,Davis next to C.S. Swan & Hunter at Wallsend. They opened a yard with six slipways in 1883 at Bill Quay, which was expanded in the early 1920s to eight slipways with the largest for tramps up to 500 feet in length. At first the yard built coasters and short-sea traders, either in iron or steel, with many of them of the quarter-deck and well-deck designs then popular e.g. *Transit* 1334/89 for W. Wilhelmsen,Tonsberg and the Norwegian shipowner's first purpose-built ship. Scandinavian contracts formed a major part of the yard order book for two decades. The most important local customer was the Burnett Steamship Co. Ltd of Newcastle founded by John Walter Burnett and his brother Norman Burnett. They ordered a small steamer in 1889 from the yard which was delivered in November of that year as *Angelus* of 724 grt. She was the first of 30 colliers and short-sea traders for Burnett from the yard, and the long association of 32 years with all their ships coming from Wood,Skinner was only broken by the liquidation of the shipbuilder in 1925.

1901 was an exceptional year for the yard with 11 vessels launched ranging from small tramps of over 2000 grt to trawlers of 150 grt for Irvin or Purdy of North Shields. Some classic small coasters were built e.g. *Helmsman* 458/03 for Rowbotham, and *Coaster* 269/03 for 'T' Steam Coaster Fleet,Newcastle and *Lewis* 346/03 and *Eddie* 219/04 for Stephenson,Clarke. Two very large self-trimming colliers were built in 1912: *Fulgens* 2512/12 for Gas,Light & Coke Company, and *Combe* 2030/12 for Stephenson,Clarke. Output during WWI included 12 self-trimming colliers of 1700 - 2000 grt, including *Flamma* 1874/17 for the Gas,Light & Coke Company; two 'Insect' class gunboats; and a total of six *WAR* 'C' and 'D'

Vessels under construction at the Wood,Skinner yard. (National Maritime Museum).

A long association was formed between Wood,Skinner and the Burnett Steamship Co. Ltd of
Newcastle, pictured is WALLSEND of 1893 on trials.

vessels. Post-war work relied heavily on the Gas,Light & Coke Company, Burnett,Sharp and Stephenson,Clarke:-

ETHYLENE	936/21	Gas,Light & Coke
GASLIGHT	1696/20	"
WHITEMANTLE	1692/20	"
BIRTLEY	2872/23	Burnett S.S. Co. Ltd
TOWNELEY	2865/23	"
MARSDEN	2897/24	"
HEBBURN	2881/24	"
ASHLEY	1323/24	Stephenson,Clarke
SANDYSIKE	1694/22	Sharp S.S. Co. Ltd
ROTHA	1699/23	"
USWORTH	1985/25	R.S. Dalgleish Ltd,Newcastle

The yard failed financially during 1925 after building 330 small vessels and gaining a good reputation for colliers. The gaunt frames of the last collier remained on one of the slipways to rust away until finally broken up in the late 1930s.

T.& W. SMITH, North Shields

The yard was established in 1782 as wooden shiprepairers and builders, and became a major Tyne yard building East Indiamen and warships in addition to ropemaking. In 1891 a limited liability company of the same name was formed and turned primarily to shiprepairing. In 1899 the yard amalgamated with the Bull Ring repair yards of Harry S. Edwards & Sons, and Edwards Brothers (his sons) to form Smiths Dock Co. Ltd, the largest shiprepairing business in the world. Edwards Brothers yard lay sandwiched between H.S. Edwards and T. & W. Smith. The Smith yard had become iron shipbuilders in the 1850s e.g. *Zingari* 424/54 for Jackson of Hartlepool; an iron corvette for the Government of Haiti; paddle steamer *Lady Tyler* for Harwich/Rotterdam service. Coasters of the quarterdeck design were built in the 1870s, and steam trawlers for North Shields owners were built in large numbers until after the turn of the century, and engined by Shields Engineering Co. Ltd, North Shields. The trawlers *King Edward* of 1902 and *Lawrenny Castle* of 1908 are still listed in Lloyds Register of Shipping as fishing around Spanish and Portuguese coasts. The coaster *Lochside* was completed in 1905 to carry beer from the Lochside brewery at Montrose to Newcastle, and the last ship, the coaster

Mountcharles, was launched in the Autumn of 1909. A new yard commenced shipbuilding in 1910 as Smiths Docks Co. Ltd at South Bank on the Tees (q.v.).

J.T. ELTRINGHAM, South Shields

James Toward Eltringham established a yard at High Holborn in South Shields after serving an apprenticeship at Palmers and built seven small craft totalling 217 tons in his first year of 1864. In 1878 he reputedly built the first steam trawler in the world, *Normandie* of 550 grt. He built many tenders for passenger liner companies after 1900, and including *Flying Breeze* of 1913 for the Alexandra Towing Co. Ltd, Liverpool. Many tugs were built e.g. *Great Emperor* (1909) for service on the Tyne, with around six to ten tugs and trawlers built annually. In 1907 the 26th trawler was delivered to the Prince Fishing Co. Ltd,North Shields. In all, 299 ships were built at the cramped South Shields yard, and the firm then moved to the former Palmer yard at Howdon in 1914. Wartime work for the Admiralty included fast patrol boats and the minesweeper *Harrow* of 1918, and small tramps of 3500 dwt e.g. *Beaumaris* 2372/17 which had been ordered by Fearnley & Eger,Oslo but which was completed for the Shipping Controller with Furness,Withy & Co. Ltd as managers. The company was reconstructed financially in 1919 but the yard closed during the severe recession of 1922 when five berths of between 140 and 340 feet were owned. One of the last ships built was the 4600 dwt collier *Dalewood* for William France,Fenwick & Co. Ltd.

HEPPLE & Co.,South Shields

The firm had a small yard at North Shields from around 1884 but moved to South Shields in 1899, next to Brigham & Cowan Ltd. Their speciality was paddle tugs, steam trawlers and small craft of shallow draft. The paddle tugs *J.C. Stevenson* and *Coble Dene* were built for the Tyne Improvement Commission. A small centre-bucket dredger was built for China in 1909 and a tug for Turkey in 'kit' form in 1920. After this date the yard with two berths of 100 feet and 150 feet in length was mainly a shiprepairer and was sold in 1924 to neighbours Brigham & Cowan Ltd.

J. & D. MORRIS, Pelaw Main

This yard was largely concerned with shiprepairing in the 19th century, but by 1914 had started shipbuilding and during WWI completed five standard 'C1' coasters. After the war there were three berths for building steel steam coasters of 300 - 400 grt, typical of these was *Whickham* of 1922 for J. Morrison; *Jolly Marie, Norman* and *Laura*, all built in 1920 for Walford Shipping Co. Ltd. In 1923 the yard went into liquidation with its largest vessel to date, *Greyfriars* for Newbiggin Steamship Co. Ltd, Newcastle partly-framed; she was then completed by T. Mitchison. A lengthy boilermaker strike during 1923 contributed to the yard closure that year, and the yard was demolished in 1925.

NEWCASTLE SHIPBUILDING CO. Ltd

Newcastle shipowner Sir John Crass, and Harald Merrylee and N. Hunter-Doeg formed this company on 30th August,1919 to take advantage of an expected boom in shipbuilding after WWI. The small shiprepairing business of Huntley was purchased at Hebburn with one slip and a few workshops to the west of the Hawthorn,Leslie yard. An ambitious plan for initially three berths and then for another seven berths was formed with tanker contracts in the offing. Two new fitting-out berths and a river frontage of 1500 feet were planned, and some 60,000 tons of ballast had to be removed before layout of the new yard could begin. A large joiners shop, platers shed, furnace, beam shed with mould loft above were erected. The first three berths were nearly complete in January,1920 and the first keel was laid on 26th February,1920 of the Spanish tramp *Zabalbide* for Compania Maritima,Bilbao. On the following day the keel of the Norwegian cargo ship *Ravnefjell* was laid, and the keel of a sister in March. The first launch took place on 23rd December,1920 of *Zabalbide*, the yard being also officially opened that day by Rear Admiral Sir Edward F. Inglefield. *Ravnefjell* was launched in January,1921 and the keel of the first of three tankers of 10250 dwt was laid. However the freight market was now in slump, and on 9th April,1921 the yard failed financially, and the two vessels already launched remained alongside until 1922. *Zabalbide* was then towed to Irvine's yard at Hartlepool for completion, and *Ravnefjell* was completed at Hebburn by the Forth Shipbuilding Company. The third hull lay on the slipway for another four years before being broken up, a fate shared by the partly-constructed tanker.

J.P. RENNOLDSON & Sons, South Shields

In 1863 J.P. Rennoldson established a slipway for small wooden craft near the Lawe, South Shields. He commenced iron shipbuilding in the 1870s, and in 1890 the yard was reconstructed to build paddle and screw tugs, which were engined at the yard. Screw tugs were built for Australia, and *Titan* of 1899 for the Suez Canal Company, *Hercules* (1907), *George V* (1915) for service on the Tyne, the ill-fated Tyne pilot-cutter *Protector*, a series of salvage tugs for Dover Harbour Board, and *Galatea* for Mersey Docks & Harbour Board. In 1916 the yard had four berths, the longest being 230 feet in length, but the yard failed financially in 1929.

CHARLES RENNOLDSON & Co, South Shields

Charles Rennoldson served his apprenticeship at the Lawe shipyard of Softley, and was then a partner in J.P. Rennoldson's yard for 38 years, designing high-class tugs, salvage steamers, yachts and coasters. His own new yard was opened in 1913 and was well equipped and gained four orders:- *Elwy* of 330 dwt and a sister coaster for Liverpool owners, a small passenger tender for P & O, and another small cargo ship. The twin-screw tug and salvage steamer *Lady Duncannon* followed, then a minesweeper and two small ice-breakers for Russia. The war effort included the minesweeper *Southwold* of 1918 and two standard coasters, *Canterbury Bell* 703/19 and *Tyne Bell* 1535/20. The colliers *Thisbe* 1710/19 for Newcastle owners and *Afterglow* 936/20 for the Gas, Light & Coke Company were among larger vessels built before Charles Rennoldson died in 1924, his yard remained open until 1929.

ROBERT STEPHENSON & Co. Ltd, Hebburn

Robert Stephenson was the son of George Stephenson, the railway locomotive pioneer, and they owned a thriving locomotive business at Forth Banks, Newcastle. Marine engines were also built, and they acquired in the mid-1880s a riverside site of an existing yard at Hebburn to expand this side of the business. Some examples of vessels built were the clipper-bowed *Cheruskia* 3245/90 for Hamburg-America Line, having been laid down as *Glencaladh Tower* for

F. Stumore & Company, London; *Matatua* 3393/90 for Shaw, Savill & Albion Co. Ltd; *Endeavour* 2519/88 for McIntyre Brothers, Newcastle; and well-decker *Cornhill* 589/91 for Warkworth Steamship Co. Ltd, Newcastle. Tramps up to 6000 dwt were built, including a quartet for King Line in 1905/06: *King Arthur* 2589/05, *King Edward* 4357/06, *King Howel* 4343/06 and *King Malcolm* 4351/06. Four more tramps of this size were completed in 1907, and then the Great Lakes steamer *Beaverton* 1886/08 for Canada S.S. Line was one of the last ships built. At its closure there were seven small berths, which were leased by Palmers in 1911 and then purchased in 1912. Some 120 ships had been built on the Tyne under the Stephenson name.

T. MITCHISON LTD, Gateshead

This yard was founded as a shiprepairer in 1919 at Friars Goose slipway, and the yard also completed the collier *Greyfriars* in 1924 after the closure of the J. & D. Morris yard. The yard was taken over by James Burness & Company of London and shipbuilding commenced in 1955. Two motor tugs and a coaster were the first vessels, and altogether some 50 trawlers, tugs and barges were completed until closure occurred in 1964, with two trawlers in 1963 for the Pelagic Fishing Co. Ltd of North Shields, *Relko* and *Pelamid*. *Relko* was towed away to the Clyde for completion by the Greenock Dockyard Co. Ltd in July, 1963.

RYTON MARINE LTD, Davy Bank

In the early 1970s three covered berths, two of 220 feet in length and one of 280 feet, were fitted out for shipbuilding on the North bank of the Tyne at Wallsend to the west of the North East Marine Engineering Co. Ltd engine plant by Ryton Engineering Co. Ltd. Their first craft was the North Shields ferry *Freda Cunningham*, and then two small stern trawlers, the second being *Bernicia* for Newcastle University. A tug for the Clyde was followed by the last vessel, the Cowes ferry *Netley Abbey* for Red Funnel Steamers Ltd, Southampton in 1974.

BLYTH SHIPBUILDING & DRY DOCKS CO. LTD.

Shipbuilding began on this site around 1811 on the south bank of the river Blyth at what today is known as Wimborne Quay. The yard was acquired by Beaumont & Drummond in the 1840s, and in 1863 by Hodgson & Soulsby who repaired and built small wooden sailing ships. They took over the Robinson yard in 1879 and then built the first two iron ships at Blyth in 1880, two hoppers for the Russian Government. The next ship was the iron collier *Speedwell* 974/80 for a Cardiff owner, and the yard was turned into a limited liability company, Blyth Shipbuilding & Dry Docks Co. Ltd in 1883. The first ship built by the new company was *Pontypridd* of 1681 grt and completed in April,1883 for Morel Brothers & Company,Cardiff. The fifth ship completed in May,1884 was *Rothiemay* of 1690 grt for Stephens & Mawson of Newcastle. Daniel Stephens was the senior partner and he was to place orders for a dozen tramps with the yard, leading eventually to his purchasing the majority of the shares, and becoming a Director and finally Chairman.

Charles Hill & Sons, the Bristol shipbuilders and shipowners, had *Exeter City* 2140/87 built at the yard, and other early customers included T.B. Williams of London with *Godmunding* 1264/88; Philipps,Philipps & Co. Ltd with *King Alfred* 1189/89 - the first of many King Line tramps; T. & W. Pinkney of Sunderland with *Prodano* 2476/90; the Arrow Shipping Co. Ltd (Dent & Co.),Newcastle with *Croft* 2675/91; and the Smith Steamship Co. Ltd,Glasgow with *Kilmorack* 2091/91. Ships were also built for Norwegian, Swedish, Danish, Russian, Cuban, Dutch and Australian owners, with cargo-liners and tramps of over 3000 grt and 4500 dwt being built from 1896 :-

ARDOVA	3038/96	E.F. & W. Roberts,Liverpool
CRAIGNEUK/ INCA	3028/97	Bowring, London 76
WILLIAM BROADLEY	3060/98	Stephens & Mawson,Newcastle 236
MOORABOOL	3000/99	Huddart Parker,Melbourne
EVERINGHAM	3041/99	East Yorkshire Steamship Co. Ltd
BARWON	3000/01	Huddart Parker,Melbourne
EGYPTIAN PRINCE	3117/02	Prince Line,Newcastle 108
HORNSEA	3040/04	Brown Atkinson,Hull
RAVENSTONE	3049/05	Stephens Sutton Ltd,Newcastle 203
MEDOMSLEY	3048/06	F. Carrick, Newcastle 237
DE GREVE	3016/07	Konink. Paket. Maats.,Batavia
WERRIBEE	3871/09	Huddart,Parker, Melbourne
ROTHLEY	3942/11	Stephens,Sutton Ltd,Newcastle 203
WEST WALES	4331/12	Gibbs & Co.,Cardiff 235
INGLEMOOR	4331/12	W. Runciman,Newcastle 33
RIDLEY	3323/13	Stephens,Sutton Ltd,Newcastle 203

Arch-decker SHEAF FIELD of 1906 (above), and 'corrugated' tramp RIO DORADO of 1924   (below).

RYTON   3991/13   Stephens, Sutton Ltd, Newcastle Ꙁ ᴏ ʒ

Colliers were also built at the yard for a number of shipowners e.g. Ridley, Son & Tully of Newcastle ordered eleven with the first being *Greenwood* 1117/03 and the last *Aydon* 1928/23; Furness, Withy & Co. Ltd with *Ludworth* 1301/07, *Ryhope* 1334/07 and *Thornley* 1310/07; Sharp Steamship Co. Ltd, Newcastle with *Elterwater* 1228/07, *Ellerbeck* 1499/10, *Elsdon* 1522/14 and *Elwick* 1717/17; William Cory & Sons with *Crayford* 1209/11 and *Deptford* 1208/12. The yard built a number of 'Arch-decker' colliers to a design by Ayre & Ballard where the upper deck was arched from stem to stern with the longitudinal arch giving extra strength and long, unobstructed holds as stringers and hold pillars were unnecessary. Seven of this type were built for William A. Souter & Co. Ltd, Newcastle starting with *Sheaf Field* 1533/06 and ending with *Sheaf Water* 2730/25, and two for Walter Runciman & Co. Ltd, Newcastle *Tullochmoor* 2729/24 and *Uskmoor* 2730/24.

Petter Olsen, brother of the more famous Fredrik Olsen of Oslo, ordered *Borgland* 2991/13 for their A/S Borga to carry Norwegian granite blocks to Buenos Aires to make streets and harbours in Argentina, loading grain homewards. The completion of the Newcastle tramp *Ryton* in December, 1913 for Daniel Stephens left a further option on the order book which was destined for fame for entirely different reasons. She was purchased on the stocks in May, 1914 by the Admiralty and launched on 5th September, 1914 as the seaplane carrier *Ark Royal*. She was commissioned three months later and served throughout World War I able to carry eight seaplanes with cranes to lift them from the holds to sea and back on board. She was converted into the depot ship *Pegasus* in 1923, and served as a catapult ship and accomodation during World War II.

The Blyth yard completed nine tramps and colliers during the Great War as well as four torpedo boat destroyers including *Verbena* and the surveying vessel *Merry Hampton* and ten lighters for the Admiralty. Largest were the tramps *Hebburn* 4372/15 and *Roseden* 4333/18, the latter being the last to the order of Daniel Stephens, Chairman of the yard. The remaining five of eight standard 'C' tramps were completed throughout 1919 and 1920 with the last being completed as the Spanish *Delfina* in January, 1921. Two 'D' type standard colliers had also been built.

The yard then received orders for seven colliers of 2500 dwt from Soc. Navale Caennaise, Caen and completed between 1920 and 1925 as *Hebe*, *Niobe*, *Francaise*, *Caennaise*, *Ornaise*, *Gallium* and *Thisbe*. Four new 'corrugated' tramps of 6000 dwt were completed for the Thompson Steam Shipping Co. Ltd managed by Sir William Petersen of Newcastle: *Rio Azul* 4088/21, *Rio Blanco* 4086/22, *Rio*

Claro 4086/22 and *Rio Dorado* 4570/24. These tramps had two or three horizontal bulges running the full length of the hull to give a better flow of water to the propeller and thus increased speed. However the poor freight rates of the 1920s led to the closure of the yard in May,1925 when a receiver was appointed after the completion of the Russian owned *Sergei Kiroff* 4211/25. The Chairman and majority shareholder, Daniel Stephens, was now over 80 years of age, and he died shortly afterwards on 19th March,1926.

The Newcastle shipowner Robert Stanley Dalgleish then acquired the yard in November,1926, changing the name to Cowpen Dry Docks & Shipbuilding Co. Ltd and amalgamated it with the Ritson's Shipbuilding & Engineering Co. Ltd, which had optimistically laid down three berths in the early 1920s but had only repaired ships during its brief life. R.S. Dalgleish then ordered one steam tramp from the yard for delivery in October,1928 as *Isleworth* 4919/28, with the ten acres of adjoining land of the defunct Ritson's yard giving him room for expansion. The first two ships built under the new title were completed at the end of 1927 as *Stillwater* and *Surewater,* both 1739/27 and Great Lakes traders, and then four tramps were delivered to Ropner of West Hartlepool as *Ashby* 4871/28, *Gullpool* 4870/28, *Cragpool* 5127/28 and *Rushpool* 5125/28. Two colliers were completed in 1929 for William Cory as *Corglen* and *Corbrook*, and the yard then closed in 1930 after the completion of the German collier *Friesland* 2662/30 and the Newcastle tramp *Holmside* 3433/30 for the Burnett Steamship Co. Ltd.

The yard remained closed for seven long years until reactivated in the summer of 1937 under the old Blyth name to build a large number of boom defence vessels and minesweepers and other craft for the Admiralty. These continued to be built until 1942, when the first of five *'River'* class frigates was completed followed by seven *'Castle'* class frigates with the last completed in July,1945. Three 'B' type standard coasters of 1200 dwt were also completed as well as a large tank landing craft and two tugs. The repair side of the yard handled the conversion of the German cargo-liner *Hannover* captured in the West Indies and converted into the first British escort carrier *Audacity* in 1941.

In 1947 the yard, now owned by Mollers (Hong Kong) Ltd, built two tugs and the lighthouse tender *Ready* 1500/47 for Trinity House. The yard now had four berths, the longest being 500 feet in length, and five dry-docks of which the largest was 468 feet in length and 60 feet wide. The new owners of the yard then placed orders for two turbine-driven cargo-liners of 10770 dwt for their shipping subsidiary, Lancashire Shipping Co. Ltd. The first was completed as their *Penrith Castle* 7731/49 in October,1949 but the other was sold during construction to the Pacific Steam Navigation Co. Ltd and completed as *Cuzco* 8038/50. Some smaller

Colliers PULBOROUGH of 1965 built at Blyth and CLIFF QUAY of 1951 built by Pickersgill (above) and London tramp HARBOROUGH of 1956 built at Blyth (below).

shelterdecker general cargo ships were completed for Scandinavian, Polish and Portuguese owners, and the yard launched the first of a number of tankers in 1949 and completed as :-

NELLY MAERSK	8223/50	Maersk Line,Denmark
ROSA MAERSK	8192/50	"
EDDYROCK	2173/53	Admiralty
EDDYNESS	2173/54	"
WILLIAM G. WALKLEY	12624/54	Ampol Petroleum Ltd,London
VARDEFJELL	11991/54	Olsen & Ugelstad,Oslo
HADA	11974/56	J. Ludwig Mowinckels,Bergen
BLYTH ADVENTURER	12523/58	Mollers Ltd
CORHAVEN	12676/58	William Cory
HAMILTON TRADER	12500/59	Mollers Ltd
PLUMLEAF	12692/60	William Cory (Admiralty charter)

The main berth of the yard was extended to 550 feet in length in 1954 to build the larger tankers as well as four ore-carriers for the St. Denis Shipping Co. Ltd of William Cory & Sons Ltd, *Queensgarth, Monksgarth, Dukesgarth* and *Knightsgarth* completed between 1959/61. Two machinery-aft steam bulk carriers were completed for the Australian Government, *Timbarra* 7530/54 and *Talinga* 7582/55, and two paper carriers for Runciman of London, *Isaac Carter* 5626/52 and *Caxton* 5729/58. Tramps *Harborough* 6800/56 and *Harpalycus* 6680/59 were completed for J. & C. Harrison, London, and *King Aegeus* 8429/56 and *King Theseus* 9153/57 for M.P. Nomikos of Greece.

Four coastal tankers were completed during 1961 for Stephenson Clarke Ltd and William Cory & Sons Ltd, while the main berth was being extended again to 625 feet in length and 75 feet in width. Orders were then received for two bulk carriers of 23500 dwt, and completed as *Chapel River* 16398/62 in September,1962 and *Pacific Princess* 16400/65 in January,1965. Two pilot tenders were completed for India in 1964, *Sagar* and *Samudra*, and then the yard started construction of three colliers of 7700 dwt, *Pulborough* 4995/65 and *Rogate* 4997/67 for Stephenson Clarke Ltd, and *Corchester* 4840/65 for William Cory & Sons Ltd. A grab dredger and two hoppers were completed for the port of Calcutta in 1966, and three trailing suction dredgers for Westminster Dredging Ltd, of which the last was completed in March,1967 when the yard closed down. Repair work and shipbreaking was then carried on by various companies in the dry-docks, and the shipbuilding berths were demolished to make room for a paper and timber storage area for the Port of Blyth.

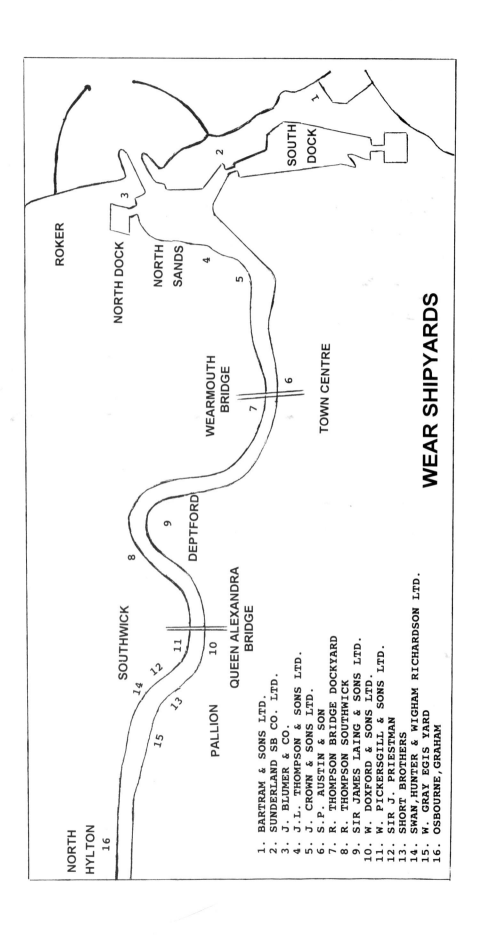

WEAR SHIPYARDS

1. BARTRAM & SONS LTD.
2. SUNDERLAND SB CO. LTD.
3. J. BLUMER & CO.
4. J.L. THOMPSON & SONS LTD.
5. J. CROWN & SONS LTD.
6. S.P. AUSTIN & SON
7. R. THOMPSON BRIDGE DOCKYARD
8. R. THOMPSON SOUTHWICK
9. SIR JAMES LAING & SONS LTD.
10. W. DOXFORD & SONS LTD.
11. W. PICKERSGILL & SONS LTD.
12. SIR J. PRIESTMAN
13. SHORT BROTHERS
14. SWAN, HUNTER & WIGHAM RICHARDSON LTD.
15. W. GRAY EGIS YARD
16. OSBOURNE, GRAHAM

W. DOXFORD & SONS LTD.

The upper reaches of the Wear in 1840 at what is now Washington were industrial instead of the present rural scene, and it was here that William Doxford first tried his hand at wooden shipbuilding. Many established wooden shipbuilders went bankrupt during a long slump in the 1840s, but Doxford came through and moved downriver to larger premises at Pallion to the west of his later shipyard. A larger site was purchased in 1870 and five berths were laid down on what became known as the West Yard. In 1872 Doxford received his first order from the Admiralty for three composite wood/iron steam gunboats, and he then built the larger corvette *Magician* in 1875.

Several notable fast sailing clippers were built, and in the late 1880s broad-beamed steel barques with deep draft suitable for the Australian grain trade were constructed by the yard, of which the last was the *Manchester* launched in 1892. Iron and steel tramps predominated, however, such as *Benton* 759/72 for Newcastle owners, *Rumney* 812/80 for John Cory of Cardiff, *Lesreaulx* 1316/80 and *Collivaud* 1413/82 for Morel of Cardiff, *Glanrheidol* 1005/83 for John Mathias of Cardiff, *Abington* 2053/82 for Raeburn & Verel, Glasgow, *Alphonse Parran* 1943/89 for Frank C. Strick and *Benisaf* 1934/89 for Bowring of London. Liner companies also came to William Doxford e.g. Allan Line of Glasgow for *Grecian* 3613/79, her compound steam engines were also some of the first made at the shipyard, which had added a marine engine and boiler side to the business in 1878.

William Doxford died in 1882 and the business was then run by his four sons, William Theodore Doxford, Alfred, Robert and Charles in partnership. Robert was an engineer who had previously served his apprenticeship under Sir William Allan at the Scotia Works on the south bank of the river near the harbour. The eldest son William Theodore Doxford had been educated at Bramhall College and was in overall charge of the yard, and converted the partnership into a limited liability company, William Doxford & Sons Ltd, from 1st January, 1891 with himself (later knighted) as Managing Director. The first ship completed after the incorporation was *Hawkes Bay* 4583 grt of February, 1891 for Tyser Line Ltd (Tyser & Co.), London; followed by three for The Clan Line Steamers Ltd, Glasgow launched during the first four months:- *Clan Macneil* 2519/91, *Clan Macleod* 2517/91, and *Clan Macintyre* 2514/91 - with the Clan Line soon becoming the most important customer of the yard.

The end of the sailing ship era saw all manner of experiments in hull design of which the 'whaleback' design of Capt. Macdougall of Duluth was one of the strangest. Doxford built one of this design with very low freeboard in 1892,

Sagamore, for William Johnston & Co. Ltd of Liverpool. The Suez Canal measurement of dues based on deck area prompted Arthur Haver, Doxford's Chief Naval Architect, to draw the lines of a 'Turret'. This had a narrow turret of about five feet in height and half the breadth of the ship superimposed on a hull of normal proportions. The main deck was the then called the 'harbour deck' as the ship was secured from here while in harbour, and the top of the turret was called the 'turret deck'. The serious shortcoming of the design was the lack of stability at large angles of roll, with the loss of buoyancy at the smaller hull side giving a lesser ability to withstand rolling forces. As the vulnerable hatch covers were well above the waterline, this normally did not matter, but care had to be taken when loading with a full cargo to ensure that the centre of gravity was kept low. The loss of the *Clan Ranald* in 1909 off Australia, and *Clan Gordon* in 1919 off North Carolina and others were due to this lack of stability, or the failure by the Master to follow loading instructions issued by the shipyard in 1910 after the loss of *Clan Ranald*.

Walter Runciman of Newcastle made the first conditional contract with William Doxford for a 'Turret' ship, but due to early opposition from underwriters and Lloyd's Classification Committee the contract was dropped. After offering favourable credit terms including taking old ships in part-exchange, no buyers were forthcoming and it became clear to Doxford that he would have to partly finance a company to build a prototype, and this he did with Capt. William Petersen, a Danish immigrant then resident in Newcastle. The Turret Steam Shipping Co. Ltd was formed to own the first ship of 3200 dwt, *Turret*, and she was commanded by Capt. William Petersen on her maiden voyage in 1892. He commented favourably on her behaviour at sea, however shipowner mistrust of the design was considerable and three more vessels for his company were constructed, *Turret Age* 2210/93, *Turret Bay* 2211/94 and *Turret Bell* 2211/94 before shipowners at last showed interest. George Horsley & Son of Hartlepool and Angier Line of London were the first to place orders, with the latter soon influencing other shipowners to try the design. Sir Charles Cayzer and his Clan Line Steamers Ltd of Glasgow was much impressed after trying two of the Angier ships for a year in 1896, and over the next ten years from 1897 he placed orders for 30 to the design of varying sizes. The main 'Turret' shipowners over the 19 years that the design was built by the yard to 1911 were:-

Clan Line,Glasgow	30 built and two purchased.
Moor Line,Newcastle	11 built and one purchased.
B.J. Sutherland,Newcastle	9 built and 11 purchased.
Turret S.S. Co. Ltd	8 built and four purchased.
E. Nicholl,Cardiff	7 built.
G. Horsley,Hartlepool	7 built.
Axel Brostrom,Sweden	7 built.

W.H. Muller, Holland	5 built.
F.W. Ritson, Sunderland	4 built.
British India Line, London	3 built.
W. Johnston, Liverpool	3 built.
J. Temperley, Newcastle	3 built.
Hans Heinrich Schmidt, Germany	3 built.
Stephens, Sutton & Stephens, Newcastle	2 built.
G. Jacques, Newcastle	2 built.

One large ship completed at this time was not a 'Turret', *Algoa* 7604/96 and 11500 dwt was completed for Algoa Steamship Co. Ltd (Crow, Rudolph), Liverpool. A fire in 1901 destroyed the Engine Works, which were replaced by a larger and more modern plant within three months with capacity for the production of 30 sets of marine engines/year. Some 65 'Turret's had been completed by the beginning of 1902 when it was decided to lay out a new East Yard of three berths, and to scrap the original five berths of the West Yard and replace them with three berths of greater length and width to enable ships up to 12,000 dwt to be built. The new East Yard was equipped with high gantry cranes, and a new fitting-out quay equipped with a 100-ton radial crane was provided between the two Yards (See Shipyard plan). The East Yard and the revamped West Yard came into full production in 1903/04 enabling the ore-carrying *Grangesberg* of 10,000 dwt to be built and completed in March, 1903 for W.H. Muller, and the seven-hatch coal carriers *Queda*, *Quiloa* and *Querimba* of 11,600 dwt to be completed for British India in 1905. The average size of a 'Turret' remained however in the 6000/7000 dwt range, but a change in the Board of Trade rules in 1910 took the commercial advantage away from the design. The open shelterdecker was then favoured because the 'tween deck was exempted from tonnage measurement by the fitting of special openings called tonnage hatches. The greater deadweight capacity of the closed shelterdecker was also attractive, and the open/closed shelterdecker became the standard cargo ship design until replaced by the bulk carrier in the 1960s.

The last 'Turret' completed was *Orangemoor* of 4134 grt for Walter Runciman of Newcastle in June, 1911 - the last of 176 from the Doxford shipyard with another six built by other shipyards under licence. The financial stability of the Doxford shipyard at this point of time had owed everything to this unusual design of tramp. The combined East and West yards had achieved their greatest production of 106,000 tons of ships during 1906, and the yard had the highest production of any shipyard in the world in 1905 and 1907. A collier built for the Hamburg firm of Sauber Brothers, *Emma Sauber* 2474/09, featured a patented type of discharge system. The ship had large self-trimming hatches and holds of the hopper type with

Doxford Turrets CLAN LINDSAY of 1902 (above) and GARRYVALE of 1907 (below), the latter seen under Finnish colours (W.S.P.L. & J. Clarkson).

PALLION AND SOUTHWICK SHIPYARDS IN 1909

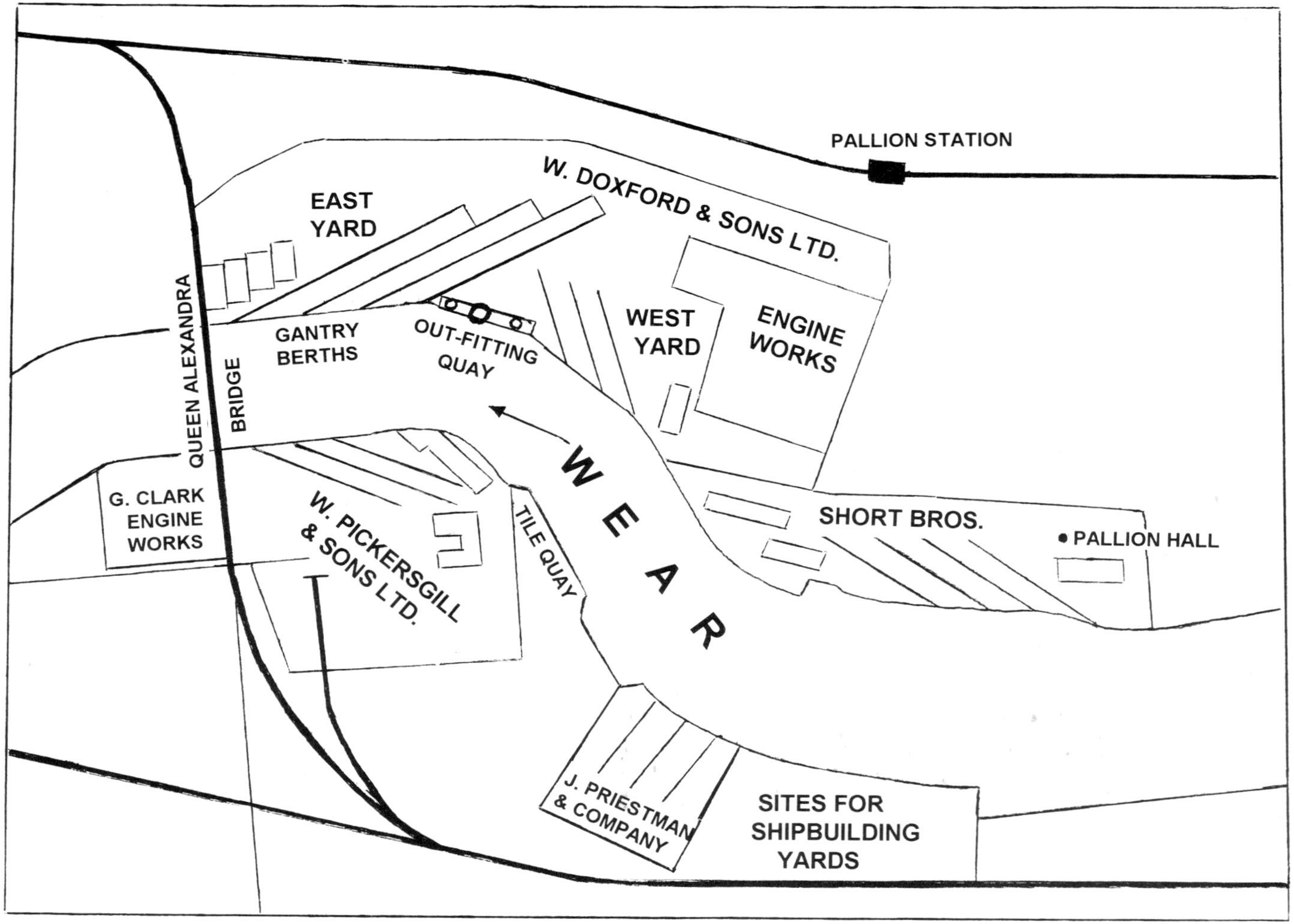

PALLION STATION

W. DOXFORD & SONS LTD.

ENGINE WORKS

WEST YARD

EAST YARD

GANTRY BERTHS

OUT-FITTING QUAY

SHORT BROS.

• PALLION HALL

W E A R

TILE QUAY

J. PRIESTMAN & COMPANY

SITES FOR SHIPBUILDING YARDS

W. PICKERSGILL & SONS LTD.

BRIDGE

QUEEN ALEXANDRA

G. CLARK ENGINE WORKS

(Author)

wing water ballast tanks and a specially designed conveyor system on the bottom of the holds so that she could discharge herself via delivery chutes overboard.

A high level of orders continued after 1911 when freight rates were once again buoyant, and customers included the following well-known liner and tramp shipowners up to the outbreak of WWI:-

Ship	Yard No./Year	Owner	
CAIRNGOWAN	4017/11	Cairn Line of Steamships Ltd	194
CAIRNDHU	4019/11	"	
CLAN MACKENZIE	5018/11	Clan Line Steamers Ltd	18
CLAN MACRAE 2	5058/12	"	
CLAN DAVIDSON	5058/12	"	
GIFFORD	5110/13	Bank Line	61
CAIRNROSS	4016/13	Cairn Line of Steamships Ltd	194
TUSCAN PRINCE	5275/13	Prince Line	108
MOORISH PRINCE	5943/14	"	
ANDREAS	5445/14	L.A. Embiricos	
CLAN OGILVY 2	5890/14	Clan Line Steamers Ltd	18
INDIAN CITY	4637/14	Reardon Smith,Cardiff	177
BLAND HALL	4259/14	E. Nicholl,Cardiff	238
ALBERT HALL	4258/14	"	
WELBECK HALL	4259/14	"	
SOUTHERNDOWN	4438/14	Morel,Cardiff	209

Cairnross was the first turbine-powered cargo ship in the world, when completed in January,1913, powered by two steam turbines by the Parsons Marine Turbine Co. Ltd, Wallsend. The Norwegian tankers *Breifond* 5711/14 and *Aztec* 5624/14 were completed before the outbreak of war fitted with cylindrical tanks for owners Sigval Bergesen and Ragnvald Blakstad.

Some 21 torpedo boat destroyers were completed during the war by the yard, with another *Shikari* launched in July,1919 and completed by Chatham Dockyard. Five merchant ships were completed for Greek owners:- *Lord Byron* 3200/16, *Admiral Cochrane* 6564/17, *Admiral Codrington* 6599/17 and *Admiral Church* 6599/17 for the Byron Steamship Co. Ltd; and *Assimacos* for the Ambatielos brothers. Benjamin J. Sutherland, the Newcastle shipowner had sold 'Turret' ships for Doxfords until his death in 1909, and his company continued to order ships from the Doxford yard during the war, and sold on two ships to the Clan Line Steamers 18 Ltd:- *Clan Macmaster* 4137/17, which had been launched as *Sutherland*, and *Clan Macmillan* 6560/18, which had been launched as *Dumfries* for B.J. Sutherland & Co. Ltd. Some 19 'WAR' standard types were then ordered during the second half of the war by the Shipping Controller - nine 'A' type, three 'B' type and seven larger 'F' type - with eight of the 'A' and 'B' and three of the 'F' completed to private ownership

View of the Doxford yard showing torpedo boat destroyers under construction on the gantry crane berths in 1915.
(Tyne & Wear Archives)

between the end of the war and up to the end of 1920. These shipowners were B.J. Sutherland, Chapman, British India Line, King Line and Greek owners.

Sir William Theodore Doxford had died in 1916, having been in charge of the yard for 34 years. He had also been the local Member of Parliament between 1895 and 1906; President of the North East Coast Institution of Shipbuilders & Engineers; and Vice-President of the Royal Institute of Naval Architects. His son Albert Ernest Doxford succeeded him as Managing Director, however a majority holding in Doxfords was taken in 1919 by the Northumberland Shipbuilding Co. Ltd (q.v.) and the Sperling Group with the Doxford family interest sold and Albert Ernest Doxford retiring from the business. However the Doxford name continued to be used for the shipyard and engine works. The 1920 freight rate collapse led to the cancellation of 19 of 33 orders placed by Norwegian shipowners for standard 9300 dwt shelterdeckers of 420 feet in length. Prices of the remainder fell dramatically from £250,000 to around £85,000 with Rederi A/B Transatlantic (G. Carlsson), Gothenburg purchasing three of these contracts plus an option on a fourth, and amending the engines on three of them from steam to 4-cylinder Doxford opposed piston oil engine. The first of these was launched on 28th September, 1920 as the first large single-screw motorship in the world as *Yngaren* and completed in March, 1921. In service, her fuel consumption was 9 tons of oil/day for an average speed of 10.5 knots. Doxfords had begun testing a series of experimental one-cylinder oil engines in 1909, and experimental submarine oil engines and generators had been built during WWI, the total investment in research to 1920 being £100,000. The second large single-screw motorship in the world was purchased by Furness, Withy & Co. Ltd from B.J. Sutherland & Co., Newcastle while building and was completed in February, 1922 as *Dominion Miller*. The third large motorship of this type was *Eknaren* for Transatlantic of Sweden, launched on 25th July, 1922 and completed in September, 1922. Transatlantic's third contract was completed as the steamer *Anten* and the fourth contract was finally cancelled in 1928. The remaining contracts for 9300 dwt shelterdeckers were completed as steamers at this time:-

KINCARDINE	6503/20	B.J. Sutherland, Newcastle ᐡᒫᐣ
SYDLAND	6561/20	Axel Brostrom, Sweden
KALKEN	6560/20	J. & V. Floric, Palermo
GRANDE GAARD	6584/20	A/S Henrik Osterwold, Norway
ANTEN	6590/20	Transatlantic Rederi, Sweden
HALLGRIM	6630/21	P. Kleppes Rederi, Norway
HALLGYN	6433/21	"
ERVIKEN	6595/21	H.J. Wallem, Norway
ROMDALSTHORN	6408/21	D/S Britannia, Norway

TILTHORN	6408/21	D/S Britannia, Norway
BLYTHMOOR	6582/22	Moor Line, Newcastle
ALNMOOR	6500/22	"
CASTLEMOOR	6574/22	"

33 RUNCIMAN

The next motortramps were completed for Moor Line (Walter Runciman) as *Vinemoor* in January,1924 and *Westmoor* in November,1924 both 4359 grt, and for Furness,Withy & Co. Ltd as *Pacific Shipper* 6304/24 and *Pacific Trader* 6327/24, and three more options for motorships were sold by Furness to Silver Line Ltd and completed as *Silverelm* 4351/24, *Silverfir* 4347/24 and *Silvercedar* 4354/24, with Doxford opposed-piston oil engines powering a further ten Silver Line ships built by other Sunderland yards up to 1930. However the collapse of the Sperling Group owners of the yard, in 1924 and the poor shipping market meant that the Doxford yard closed down after the last launch in September,1924 and did not re-open until April,1927.

When new orders were received the economics of shipowning favoured a choice of the cheaper triple expansion steam engine, built by a variety of Sunderland engine builders, for Doxford-built ships of the late 1920s:-

STONEGATE	5044/28	Turnbull,Scott of London
FORTHBRIDGE	5140/28	Crosby,Son of Hartlepool
CARICA MILICA	6378/28	Jugoslavenska Lloyd
TRIGLAV	6363/28	"
AVALA	6379/28	"
ESSEX MANOR	5001/30	Meldrum & Swinson,London
VINNIE	2552/29	Chr. Knudsen Rederi,Norway
GRACECHURCH	4318/30	James,Muers & Co. Ltd,London

The launch of the Norwegian VINNIE in 1929 (Sunderland Museum).

however some shipowners were still keen to try the new 4-cylinder opposed-piston oil engine e.g. Reardon Smith of Cardiff and Runciman of Newcastle:-

NORTHMOOR	4392/28	W. Runciman,Newcastle
INNESMOOR	4392/28	"
GLENMOOR	4392/28	"
JEDMOOR	4392/28	"
EAST LYNN	4685/28	Reardon Smith,Cardiff
FRESNO CITY	4955/29	"
VANCOUVER CITY	4955/30	"
JUNE	4323/29	Hans Hannevig,Oslo
JULIET	4323/29	"
FRESHMOOR	1074/28	Harris & Dixon,London
PEGASUS	9504/30	Transoil SS(R.Sorman),Gothenburg
MINISTER WEDDEL	6833/30	Norsk Trans(O.E.Sonne),Oslo
IMA	6842/30	Skibs A/S Ima (S. Marcussen),Oslo
BETH	6852/30	A/S Bill (L. Gill-Johannesen),Oslo
KATY	6826/31	A/S Modens (I. Christensen),Oslo
LISE	6826/31	A/S Lise (I. Christensen),Oslo

The last six in the above list were tankers for Scandinavian owners. *Freshmoor* was fitted with a three-cylinder version of the Doxford oil engine, which was later also to power the famous Doxford Economy motortramp, designed during the Depression by Managing Director, J. Ramsay Gebbie, and later Chairman until the 1960s. Doxfords had closed again in 1931 and grass was growing on the six slipways of the combined East and West yards. The backroom boffins of both the shipyard and the engine works however were hard at work producing an economical motortramp with maximum possible efficiency from hull and machinery. The higher building cost for the new tramp of £100,000 would be offset by lower operating costs to produce operating profits for shipowners during difficult trading conditions with capital costs paid for by the Scrap & Build scheme of 1935.

The Doxford Economy tramp design was completed in 1934 and she was a flush-decker with five hatches and four holds, two of which and a deep tank were in front of the composite deckhouse and two aft, served by ten derricks and ten steam winches on two masts and a pair of kingposts. Officers and engineers accomodation was amidships with the crew located aft. Electric welding of plates was used by the shipyard for the first time, although the decks and other strong points were still rivetted. Her dimensions were 412.2 feet length, 54.2 feet breadth and a loaded draft of 26.5 feet, 4932 grt with a cargo carrying capacity of 9200 tons. She was powered by a three-cylinder two-stroke cycle single-acting Doxford opposed piston oil engine of 1800 bhp to give a service speed of 10 knots on 6.5 tons of oil/day. The first of the new design was named *Sutherland* at her launch on 6th

December, 1934 for Sir Arthur Sutherland, and she was to be followed by five more of the design for this Newcastle shipowner, with the total number of the standard design being 30 with ten of these financed by the Government schemes:-

SUTHERLAND	4956/35	Sutherland, Newcastle 217
KINROSS	4956/35	"
CAITHNESS	4970/35	"
STIRLING	4995/35	"
PEEBLES	4982/36	"
ROSS	4978/36	"
–KIRRIEMOOR	4970/35	Runciman, Newcastle 37
–FERNMOOR	4972/36	"
RUGELEY	4985/36	Stephens Sutton, Newcastle 203
RILEY	4993/36	"
RIPLEY	4997/36	"
RIDLEY	4993/37	"
ROTHLEY	4996/36	Stephens, Sutton, Newcastle
TROMA	5029/37	A/S J. Ludwig Mowinckels, Bergen
RODSLEY	5000/39	Stephens Sutton, Newcastle 208
RAWNSLEY	4998/40	Stephens, Sutton, Newcastle
ROOKLEY	4998/40	"
REAVELEY	4998/40	"
QUEEN MAUD	4976/36	T. Dunlop, Glasgow 57
WEARPOOL	4982/37	Ropner, Hartlepool 29
MOORBY	4992/36	"
SKIPSEA	4974/36	W. Brown, Atkinson, Hull 216

The Doxford Economy motortramp KIRRIEMOOR of 1935. (B. Fielden).

JERSEY	4986/36	Morel,Cardiff 209
FOREST	4998/37	"
STATIRA	4852/37	Chellew S.N.,Cardiff 244
LADY GLANELY	5497/38	Tatem,Cardiff 245
CLIFTONHALL	5062/38	West Hartlepool S.N. 246
WILLOWBANK	5041/39	Bank Line,London 61
HANNINGTON COURT	5449/39	Court Line,London 26
DERWENTHALL	4938/40	West Hartlepool S.N. 246

and other Doxford motorships of this time had similar hulls but were fitted with the larger 4-cylinder opposed-piston oil engine e.g. *Eskbank* 5137/37, *Ettrickbank* 5138/37, *Teesbank* 5136/37 for Bank Line; *Kaipara* 5883/38 for Union SS Co. Ltd of New Zealand; *S. Thome* 5179/38 for Comm. Nacional Navegacao,Portugal; the twin-screw *Nonsuco* 5212/38 for North Negros Sugar Company,Manila and *Port Montreal* 5882/37 for Port Line Ltd. The small fruiters *Posarica* 1893/38 and *Palomares* 1896/38 were fitted with five-cylinder Doxford oil engines for Macandrews & Co.,London; and the tanker *British Genius* 8553/39 was fitted with a four-cylinder version for the British Tanker Co. Ltd. Two overseas owners preferred the well-tried triple expansion engine: N.V. Stoomvaarts Maat. (Vinke & Co) with *Ittersum* 5199/38 and Vlasov (Alva SS) with *Starstone* 5702/38.

An improved Doxford Economy tramp design of 9500 dwt was completed in 1938 with 'split-superstructure' profile with number 3 hold between the bridge and engineers accomodation. Their oil engine was uprated to 2500 bhp giving 12 knots on 9.5 tons of oil/day, and some 85 of this standard design were to be built throughout the war and up to 1954, some of the first being:-

KASSOS	5215/39	Kassos S.N.,Greece
MERCHANT PRINCE	5229/39	Lykiardopulo,London
LA ESTANCIA	5185/40	Buries Markes Ltd,London 247
LA CORDILLERA	5185/40	"
EIGNON	5218/39	Morel,Cardiff 209
CATRINE	5218/39	"
SUTHERLAND	5170/40	Sutherland,Newcastle 217
DUKE OF ATHENS	5217/40	S. Livanos,Greece
PUTNEY HILL	5215/40	Counties Ship Mgmt.,London 48
TOWER GRANGE	5226/40	"
FULTALA	5051/40	British India 42
ANTAR	5222/41	T. Bowen Rees 248
DALTONHALL	5175/41	West Hartlepool S.N. 246
ATLANTIC CITY	5133/41	Reardon Smith,Cardiff 177
EASTERN CITY	5185/41	"
DAGHESTAN	7248/41	Common Brothers,Newcastle 67
KAFIRISTAN	7250/41	"

DALTONHALL of 1941 was a 'stretched' Doxford Economy motortramp.

The Pallion yards and their six berths were continuosly improved during the war years with sheds,lofts and stores being added and only a new canteen was to be destroyed by a direct bomb hit. A total of 75 merchant ships of over half a million tons were completed up to May,1945, with steel consumed running at around 40,000 tons/year and the highest figure of production being in 1942. Fitting-out work was more extensive as ships had to be fitted with defensive armament, but an extra fitting-out quay was gained in 1946 when the Palmers Hill engine works of John Dickinson & Sons Ltd was purchased on the north bank of the river next to the Monkwearmouth bridge.

The resumption of building to private contract in 1946 saw many orders won for the standard Doxford Economy tramp as well as for other designs for replacements for war losses. Soc. Generale de Commerciel & Industriel Transports, Lisbon ordered four to a smaller design and completed in 1948 as *Braganca, Braga, Borba* and *Belas* all of 4404 grt. The Pallion yard of Doxford went on to complete a total of 123 ships, 23 of these being tankers, over the next twenty years from 1946. The most important customers were Bank Line Ltd with 28 ships; T. & J. Harrison with 17 ships, Reardon Smith with 10 ships, Hain S.S. Co. Ltd with four ships; J. & C. Harrison with three more ships to add to the five completed during the war for this

London tramp owner. Smaller numbers of tramps were built for Runciman; Buries Markes; West Hartlepool Steam Navigation Co. Ltd; Morel; and the tanker owners included the British Tanker Co. Ltd, Overseas Tankship (Caltex), Lowland Tanker Co. Ltd, Hunting & Son and Prince Line. The Doxford main 3-cylinder oil engine manufactured at the Pallion Engine Works had underpinned the success of the shipyard with over 140 engines of the 3-cylinder version built between 1935 and 1955. Licencees in ten countries including the U.S.A. made the engine one of the most popular diesel engines in the world. Some of the last examples of this type of engine went into the last 'split-profile' Doxford Economy completed in 1954, with Greek owners then leading the way with orders for tramps of 13,000 dwt and cargo-liners of 16,600 dwt:-

AGHIA MARINA	8796/54	Rethymnis - Kulukundis
AGHIOS NICOLAOS	8848/55	"
AGHIOS SPYRIDON	9951/57	"
DONA OURANIA	8850/56	Chandris Group
DONA MARGARITA	8716/56	"
DONA EDIE	9746/57	Chandris Group
DONA KATERINA	9953/57	"
MISS CHANDRIS	9855/59	"
STAMATIOS G. EMBIRICOS	8878/56	Embiricos
PEARL CLIPPER	8963/60	N.G. Livanos
PEARL TRADER	10122/62	"
PEARL MERCHANT	11199/63	"
YANNIS	11195/63	Chandris
KATHERINE	11198/64	N.G. Livanos
PEARL ISLAND	11199/64	"
ALIKI LIVANOS	11195/65	"

Nearly all were supplied with larger Doxford oil engines, although Sulzer diesels were beginning to be specified for Pallion-built ships. Two subsidiaries had been set-up in 1956, William Doxford & Sons(Shipbuilders) Ltd and William Doxford & Sons(Engineers) Ltd, and in 1961 the parent company joined the Laing and Thompson yards as Doxford & Sunderland Shipbuilding & Engineering Co. Ltd. A large 9-cylinder Doxford 'J' oil engine of 30,000 bhp was fitted as the first of its type into the tanker *North Sands* built for the Group by the North Sands yard in 1966, when a full merger of the yards occurred. More cargo-liners were built at Pallion :-

WORCESTERSHIRE 2	9931/65	Bibby Line 195
COVENTRY CITY	7643/66	Bristol City Line 111
TORONTO CITY	7643/66	"
DERBYSHIRE	9931/66	Bibby Line 195
WARWICKSHIRE 2	10682/67	"
MAGICIAN	8454/68	T. & J. Harrison, Liverpool 35

The Bibby Line cargo-liner WARWICKSHIRE of 1967 (above), and the Bristol City Line cargo-liner COVENTRY CITY of 1966 (below), both photographed on trials. (Turners Ltd).

15

WORCESTERSHIRE ready for launch under the gantry cranes in 1965.

HISTORIAN 5	8454/68	T. & J. Harrison, Liverpool 3 5
DUNHUANG	11421/67	Cosco, China
JINSHA	11170/67	"
SHIRRABANK	7591/66	Bank Line 61
TEVIOTBANK 2	7591/67	"
N.G. LIVANOS	11025/67	N.G. Livanos
NICHOLAS J.LIVANOS	11025/68	"
MARIGO R	10840/69	Rethymnis & Kulukundis
IKTINOS	11489/70	Lyras Brothers
IASON	11489/70	"
FINIX	11489/70	Fafalios
FEAX	11489/70	"
FAETHON	11489/71	"
BENEFACTOR 2	11506/71	T. & J. Harrison 3 5
ATALANTI	11001/72	Vernicos - Evgenidis
HEREFORDSHIRE	11453/72	Bibby Line 195
LANCASHIRE 2	11451/72	Bibby Line 195

Company advertisement of the 1960s.

26

The Doxford & Sunderland Group was taken over by Court Line in 1972, by which time plans were well advanced to demolish the old East Yard at Pallion and replace it with a shipbuilding hall capable of simultaneous building of two ships alongside each other up to 30,000 dwt. *Lancashire* was the last ship build under the old gantry cranes in 1972, which were demolished during 1973 and work on the new yard commenced on 1st October,1973. Orders for four cargo-liners for Bank Line: *61* *Fleetbank, Cloverbank, Birchbank* and *Beaverbank*; and one for T. & J. Harrison Ltd, *35* *Craftsman,* were transferred to the Deptford Yard of Laing. The dimensions of the new building hall were 181 metres long, 50 metres wide and 32 metres in height.

The dock gate itself weighed 385 tonnes, and the first unit of the next Bank Line cargo-liner was able to be laid on 29th June,1975. She was floated out as *Cedarbank* at the official opening of the new Hall on 8th April,1976 and completed later in 1976.

The Doxford & Sunderland Group had been renamed Sunderland Shipbuilders Ltd on 5th March,1973 after its take-over by Court Line Ltd. The first Chairman was James Venus, formerly Managing Director of Appledore Shipbuilders in Devon - also part of Court Line shipbuilding interests, and the Managing Director was J. P. Gillfillan. Unfortunately Court Line collapsed with massive debts in 1974, and the Government then took over the three Sunderland yards in 1975 and then merged them into British Shipbuilders Ltd on 1st July,1977. The new Pallion yard completed further cargo-liners for Bank Line with *Fenbank* the fiftieth Bank Line ship completed in 1978, and for the Shipping Corporation of India, before switching to build seven of the standard B30 bulk carriers in 1981:-

NOSIRA LIN	18040/81	Nosira Shipping Co. Ltd
NOSIRA SHARON	18039/81	"
NOSIRA MADELEINE	18040/82	"
BROOMPARK	18190/82	J. & J. Denholm,Glasgow 60
DARYA MA	17720/83	Kissinchand Chellaram,Hong Kong
ALBERTA	17882/84	Pegasus Ocean Services,Greece
RADNIK	17882/84	Jugoslavenska Oceanska Plovidba

The Pallion Engineering Works of Doxford had been producing 3-cylinder oil engines of 5500 bhp at 220 rpm in the 1970s for small container ships owned by Ellerman Lines and Prince Line. A contract was also won for nine 4-cylinder Doxford oil engines from the Argentinean shipowner Empresa Lineas Maritimas (ELMA) for 'SD14's being built under licence at Dundee and Ensenada in Argentina. These developed 8000 bhp at 124 rpm to give a service speed of 15.5 knots. However the popularity of the Doxford oil engine had fallen to such an extent that the last Doxford oil engine was lifted aboard the bulker *Canadian Pioneer* in 1980, and the Pallion Engineering Works became a 'spare-part' operation only.

The Pallion yard then began to look in 1984 at the lucrative North Sea oil services market. An order for two sophisticated oil well maintenance ships was won from Stena Line of Sweden, these being completed in 1986 as *Stena Seawell* and *Stena Wellservicer* of 9200 grt. These had a large helideck over the forward accomodation and a large twin crane at the stern made by Whessoe of Darlington. They spent some time laid-up in the Tyne before taking up their first North Sea oil charter, and the Pallion yard itself had also run out of customers. Fortunately a Danish order was won for an unspecified number of ferries by North East

Shipbuilders Ltd, the name of the merged Sunderland Shipbuilders Ltd and Austin & Pickersgill Ltd from 1986. These Danish ferries featured a novel type of propulsion with no engine room and instead sets of electric generators in small yellow containers on the main deck driving the propellers. It was agreed that the Pallion Yard should build the Series III type of the *Supaflex* ferry, with the former Austin & Pickersgill Yard at Southwick building the Series IV. However political decisions by the British Government forced the closure of the Sunderland yards in 1988 when only 15 of the ferries had been completed.

Heavy and mounting losses by British Shipbuilders Ltd over the ten years since nationalisation on 1st July,1977 had made the British Government unwilling to sink any more public money into the state shipbuilding company. However their privatisation strategy for British Shipbuilders Ltd hinged on the fact that the European Economic Community would only subsidise the privatisation on condition that North East Shipbuilders Ltd was closed down. British and foreign shipping interests were more than willing to buy the Sunderland yards and were astonished that the British Government insisted on closing them down instead of sale to private interests. It has since been alleged that Lord Young, Minister for the Department of Trade and Industry, made a secret deal with the EEC to save the ailing Govan Yard on the Clyde by selling it to Norwegian buyers in return for the obliteration of the Sunderland shipbuilding capacity. The town of Sunderland would receive £45M in EEC grants to retrain the shipyard workforce and attract inward investment to the town. Shipbuilding at both the Pallion Yard and Southwick Yard came to an abrupt end towards the end of 1988, throwing some 6,000 shipyard workers out of work. The Pallion Yard has since been used for engineering work by Pallion Engineering Ltd, but this venture unfortunately failed financially.

STENA WELLSERVICER fitting-out at Manor Quay with the crane ship in the background. (Author)

Night-time scene of work proceeding on two Bank Line cargo-liners in the new Pallion Shipbuilding Hall.
(British Shipbuilders Ltd)

Two views of
FIRBANK
emerging
from the Hall
in 1976 .
(A. Weir & Co)

JOSEPH L. THOMPSON & SONS LTD 3ₒ

This North Sands yard became the largest and most famous of all the shipbuilding yards on this historic site on the north bank of the river in an arc round to the North Dock that launched directly into the inner harbour. It had been established in 1846 by Robert Thompson, an experienced shipbuilder and yard manager on the Tyne as well as the Wear, who set-up in business with his three sons as Robert Thompson & Sons, and their first ship was the small sailing ship *Pearl* of 240 tons. She took eleven weeks to build by Robert Thompson, his three sons and four employees and showed a profit of £200. His son of the same name, Robert, left in 1854 to set-up his own yard at Southwick (See Robert Thompson & Sons Ltd). Robert senior died in 1860 and shortly afterwards the business came under the control of his son Joseph Lowes Thompson. The yard changed its title to Joseph L. Thompson in February,1871 and the first ship built under this title was their first iron ship *Celsus* for J.H. Culliford of Sunderland. The last sailing ships were built by the yard in 1876, *Brier Holme* of 920 tons for Hine Brothers, and *G.B.S.* of 596 tons for George B. Sully.

Joseph L. Thompson retired in 1875, and the business was carried on by his three sons Robert, Joseph Lowes and Charles. The yard achieved the highest output of any Wear shipbuilder in 1882, and in 1883 produced sixteen ships of 30,495 tons. The yard continued to acquire ground including the site of William Pile's yard and Peter Austin's yard, and soon acquired the whole of the North Sands, where previously seven yards had been in operation. The yard enlarged its slipways to build bigger steamers and began to build in steel in 1884 when the Manor Quay was completed to give the yard a substantial river frontage for the fitting-out and repair of vessels. Half of the yard output in 1885 was in steel and by 1888 no more iron ships were built.

Joseph L. Thompson II retired in 1893, having introduced electrical plant into the yard, and extended the business interests to the Sunderland Forge & Engineering Co. Ltd, Skinningrove Iron Co. Ltd and as shipowners in the Alpha Steamship Co. Ltd. His brother Robert remained as Manager and he formed a limited liability company, Joseph L. Thompson & Sons Ltd, registered on 12th July,1894. He invited James Marr, who had joined the yard 17 years earlier, and Peter Phorson on to the Board of Directors. Sir James Marr became Chairman and Managing Director of the yard in 1901, and also joined the Board of Sir James Laing & Sons Ltd in 1909. The first ship completed by the new company was *Amyl* 2474/94 for W. Tulley of Hull; and a yard output of 35,597 in 1894 made the yard the leading Wear shipbuilder again and also the fourth largest in the world for the

The London tramp REMBRANDT of 1886 owned by Frederic Bolton framed in the classic setting of the Clifton Suspension Bridge at Bristol; and her sister RUBENS of 1887 on trials (below).

The Whitby tramp RED CROSS of 1890 was a flush-decker (above), whereas the London-owned ZINGARA of 1898 (below) was a three-island ship. (F.W. Hawks).

third year in succession.   By this time the yard had acquired some important customers who placed repeat orders, including the local owners Tyzack & Branfoot with 10 ships, the first being *Edmonsley* 1526/84 and the last *Shadwell* 4091/03; Turner,Brightman of London with 12 ships, the first being *Zeta* 2334/88 and the last *Zinal* 5729/20. Whitby shipowners were important to the yard with John H. Barry placing orders for ten ships from *Larpool* 1288/80 to *John H. Barry* 3083/99; Rowland & Marwood ordered 11 ships from *Resolution* 1913/88 to *Burnholme* 3474/04; Christopher Marwood and the International Line Steamship Co. Ltd some eight ships from *Northumbria* 1912/88 to *Nuceria* 4702/14; and Robinson & Rowland took delivery of three ships in 1883/84; with the Harrowing family also taking three ships.

London shipowner Frederic Bolton named all of his tramps after painters, naming his first ever ship *Raphael* 1860/85 at the North Sands yard in June,1885. She was fitted with compound steam engines, but the next from the yard *Rembrandt* 1828/86 had the more powerful triple expansion engines. His next *Rubens* 2077/87 was the first built of steel, but she had an unlucky start for having returned from trials she was rammed and sunk at her moorings in the river by a collier, but was soon raised to begin her career. A further six ships were built for this owner by the yard, the last being *Ribera* 3500/04. Miss Gladys Bacon launched the first ship from the yard for Hartlepool shipowner Sivewright,Bacon & Company in October,1898 as *Salfordia* 3666/98, and a further five ships were launched for companies managed by Sivewright,Bacon. Harris & Dixon Ltd, the London shipowner, broker and tanker charterer had their first ship built at the yard in 1909, *Brinkburn* 3827/09, and subsequently took delivery of another ten tramps over the next ten years including *Batsford* 4782/14. Tramps *King Lud* 3650/06 and *King John* 3644/06 were delivered to King Line of London, and *Don Cesar* 3655/06 and *Don Emilio* 3651/06 to the associated Buenos Aires & Pacific Railway Co. Ltd. Tramps were also built for local owners such as James Westoll and Viginty T. Thompson.

Liner shipowners also flocked to the yard for ships e.g. for the passenger/cargo liner *Euterpe* 2291/86 for Lloyd Austro-Hungarian; Prince Line of North Shields with *Tudor Prince* 1521/84, Johnston Line of Liverpool with *Avonmore* 2209/89 and two others; William Milburn of Newcastle and his Anglo-Australian Line of meat carriers with *Port Chalmers* 4154/91 and *Port Stephens* 3554/94. Overseas shipowners such as J. M. de Y Barra of Spain were also important, taking nine ships between 1885 and 1893, the first being *Cabo Palos* 1562/85 and the last *Cabo Tortosa* 1496/93. *Vega* 1164/95 was launched on 9th March,1895 and delivered in June of that year to Bergen Line of Norway for their regular Newcastle to Bergen and Trondheim sailings, extended in high summer to

North Cape cruises. Three ships were delivered to German owners in the following year, Rickmers Line of Hamburg taking *Maria Rickmers* 4888/96 and *Ellen Rickmers* 5350/96, and the Hamburg-Pacfic Line of Hamburg taking *Luciana* 4801/96.

At the turn of the century the yard built almost exclusively for the Transatlantic trades, with Point Line (Simpson,Spence & Young),London building *Pinners Point* 3921/95, *Crown Point* 5219/00, *Eagle Point* 5222/00, *North Point* 5216/00 and *East Point* 4234/00 for their Virginia - U.K. trade. American companies such as the North Atlantic Steamship Co. Ltd (Thomas Hogan & Sons) and the New York & Pacific Steamship Co. Ltd (Grace Line) took fifteen ships:-

MASCONOMO	4183/98	CAPAC	3052/93
MARIPOSA	4696/99	CONDOR	3053/93
MONOMOY	4831/01	CACIQUE	3052/94
MANITOBA	4687/01	COYA	3040/95
MONTAUK	3387/01	CELIA	5004/04
MATTEAWAN	3390/01	CURACA	6386/12
MADAWASKA	4120/02	CHINCHA	6395/12
MIRAMICHI	3604/02		

The yard in terms of tonnage had been head of the river throughout the 1890s with 1898 output standing at 40,815 tons, but lost its position to Laing in 1900 with 40,307 tons and then to Doxford after 1904. Cunard Line ordered one ship in 1902 which was completed as *Brescia* 3235/03, and another ship completed for Transatlantic service in that year was *Pennine Range* 3397/03 for the locally owned Neptune Steam Navigation Co. Ltd, which ran a service between Rotterdam and Baltimore with a call at the Tyne for bunkers. The average output for the four years between 1904 and 1907 was 46,266 tons, and the 1907 output of 12 ships of 48,178 tons was a record for the yard, which stood until the Great War, as the freight slump until 1910 reduced the output.

Robert Thompson, yard manager, died in 1908 and was survived by a daughter and four sons, of which Norman Thompson and Cyril Thompson joined the yard. Tramps continued to be completed e.g. *Northern* 4731/12 for Harris & Dixon of London, with Scandinavian shipowners such as Wilhelm Wilhelmsen of Norway taking *Terrier* 5122/10; and W.H. Lundgren of Sweden taking two ships for his Swedish-Syd-Africa Line and Transatlantic Rederi A/B, *Nordic* 4182/14 and *Sydic* 4177/14. Four pioneering ore-carriers were built for the Rederi A/B Lulea-Ofoten, which later became the famous Grangesberg - Oxelosund company: *Murjek* 4124/12, *Kiruna* 4638/13, *Narvik* 4235/14 and *Boden* 4235/14.

The yard output during the Great War was 17 ships of 91,486 tons, with three for the Mercantile Steamship Co. Ltd,London:- *Foyle* 4739/15, *Boyne* 4445/15

Silver Line had thirteen ships built on the Wear in the 1920s for their Round the World service, pictured is SILVERBELLE of 1927 with deck cargo (above); The Whitby tramp RUNSWICK of 1930 (below) with fore and aft well-decks.

and *Pruth* 4698/15. Harris & Dixon Ltd took delivery of *Holbrook* 6655/17 and *Dunbridge* 6650/17, while *Eastern City* 5992/17 was completed for Reardon Smith of Cardiff. Norwegian shipowners such as Wilhelm Wilhelmsen also had ships on order with the yard when war broke out, and three of 8810 dwt came under British management during the war and were returned to their rightful owners at the end of the war e.g. *Abercorn* 5424/16, while *Tenterden* 4127/17 of 7050 dwt was returned similarly to Jacob R. Olsen. The Admiralty took the tanker *Bornol* of 6767 dwt and the Shipping Controller ordered three standard WAR 'C' tramps and five 'F' ships, the last three of which were completed as *City of Melbourne* 6419/19 for Ellerman Lines, *Radnorshire* 6723/19 for Royal Mail Line and *Lord Guilford* 6635/19 for the Byron Steamship Co. Ltd.

The following ships were ordered in the post-war boom at very high prices and very good profit to the yard e.g. *Jersey City* cost £320,300 or around five times the price charged a few years later:-

ASLAUG HAALAND	4655/20	J.E. Neelands Rederi
CYCLE	4676/20	Howard Smith & Co. Ltd, Australia
JERSEY CITY	6322/20	Reardon Smith, Cardiff
AGE	4718/21	Howard Smith & Co. Ltd, Australia
STAKESBY	4762/22	Headlam & Rowland, Whitby
YORK CITY	6397/22	Reardon Smith, Cardiff

as well as the tankers *British Lord* 6098/22, *British Lady* 6098/23 and *British Duchess* 5973/24. However the post-WWI boom was followed by an equally dramatic slump in 1920/21 with many orders cancelled, and the construction of the Australian colliers *Cycle* and *Age* was considerably delayed by strikes at the yard, with management unwilling to give way as the yard would soon run out of work. There was very little activity at the yard in 1923, however orders were taken in 1924 for two small ships for Howard Jones Ltd, two tramps and four motor-driven cargo-liners for the new Silver Line Ltd, whose managers Stanley and John Thompson belonged to the Thompson yard family, and naturally favoured the yard with orders for eight ships up to 1930:- *Silveray* 4535/25, *Silverash* 5299/26, *Silverbeech* 5311/26, *Silverbelle* 5302/27, *Silverhazel* 5302/27, *Silverpalm* 6373/29, *Silverwillow* 6373/29 and *Silveryew* 6373/29.

Tramps completed at the yard during the 1920s included *Cragness* 4809/24 for Reardon Smith of Cardiff, *Fylingdale* 3918/24 for Headlam & Rowland of Whitby, *Thistlebrae* 4647/28 for the local Albyn Line, and *Helmstrath* 4214/28 and *Helmspey* 4637/29 for S.C. Downing. Cunard Line placed orders for four small Mediterranean cargo-liners of 3510 dwt and completed in 1928 as *Bosnia, Bactria, Bothnia* and

Bantria all 2407/28; and Eagle Oil ordered two 'Mosquito' shallow-draft tankers for use on Lake Maracaibo, *San Camilo* 2450/27 and *San Castro* 2455/28.

The Depression following the Wall Street crash of October,1929 meant the yard ran out of work in 1930 after the completion of the Headlam & Son tramp *Runswick* 3970/30 and the Dutch tanker *Vigdis* 6094/30 for Brunn & van der Lippe. Grass grew on the slipways for the next five long years, however the yard's designers were hard at work during this period at the Teddington test tank. They produced the most efficient hull shape with a Maierform bow, fine stern with streamlined rudder for a 9100 dwt Economy steam tramp. Construction of the first of these started in 1935 while a contract to re-engine two Silver Line ships afloat was being carried out. *Silverlarch* and *Silverpine* had been built by Swan,Hunter & Wigham Richardson Ltd in 1924 on the Tyne, but had been laid-up since 1932 as they were uneconomical to run. This pair had their engines in the three-quarters aft position with four holds forward of the engineroom and only one aft, so it was simpler to cut the whole of the stern down to the waterline to remove the old engine and insert the new one. The stern was completed reshaped, thus lengthening the pair by three feet in the process, which had never been done before by shipbuilders or repairers with a vessel afloat.

Embassage for Hall Brothers of Newcastle was the first Thompson Economy steam tramp completed in September,1935, and she left the river with coal for her maiden voyage to Algiers later that month. Her coal fuel consumption was remarkably lower than earlier steam tramps of the same size, and 17 more examples of the type were completed by the yard up to the outbreak of WWII :-

The Thompson Economy steam tramp EMBASSAGE of 1935.

ST. ESSYLT going down the Thompson ways on 23rd May,1940 for the South American Saint Line.

DORINGTON COURT of 1939, the prototype of the 'Empire' standard tramp of World War II.

ST. HELENA	4313/36	South American Saint Line \31
ST. MARGARET	4312/36	"
ST. CLEARS	4312/36	"
ST. ROSARIO	4312/37	"
ST. ELWYN	4940/38	"
STARCROSS	4662/36	Anning Bros.,Cardiff 249
NEWTON MOORE	5673/36	Bespian S.S. Co. Ltd,London 182
LOCH DEE	5252/37	Maclay & McIntyre,Glasgow 198
LOCH DON	5249/37	"
CORABELLA	5682/37	Australasian United S.N. Co. Ltd
ROYAL SCEPTRE	4853/37	Hall Brothers,Newcastle 152
WELSH TRADER	4974/38	Trader Navigation,London 210
LERWICK	5626/38	Wallem & Co. 250
SIRE	5664/38	Sire S.S. Co. Ltd,London 251
SCOTTISH TRADER	4016/38	Trader Navigation,LOndon 210
BRETWALDA	4906/39	Hall Brothers,Newcastle 152
DORINGTON COURT	5281/39	Court Line,London 26

The first quartet for the South American Saint Line were built under the Scrap & Build Scheme of 1935, but were powered by the dual coal/oil-fired White steam engine, which was a twin high-speed compound engine geared to a low pressure turbine. *Starcross* was also built under Scrap & Build for her Cardiff owners. Two cargo-liners were also completed, the motor ship *Port Saint John* of 5688 grt in January,1938 for Port Line, and the turbine-propelled *Silverlaurel* of 6162 grt of March,1939 for Silver Line. The motor tanker *Sandanger* 9432/38 of 14500 dwt was launched in 1938 for Westfal-Larsen of Bergen and watched by crowds of several thousands as she was the biggest ship launched on the river since 1914. However Sir Norman Thompson speaking at another yard launch at the end of 1938 pointed out that four Wear yards were closed due to lack of orders, and another four were at starvation level, and asked for further Government assistance, which came in the form of the Shipping Loan scheme for shipowners in 1939.

The yard produced a magnificent output of 40 ships of 277,697 grt during World War II. The motor cargo-liner *Port Quebec* 5800/39 was completed first in November,1939 for Port Line, but was requisitioned by the Admiralty and converted into a minelayer carrying 500 mines for barrage work. She served as a minelayer until 1943 when she became an aircraft repair ship and finally started commercial service in 1947. Seven more Economy type followed:- *Argyll* 4897/39 and *Inverness* 4897/39 for B.J. Sutherland, *Royal Emblem* 4900/39 for Hall Brothers, *Confield* 4956/40 for E.J. Sutton & Co. Ltd,Newcastle, *Graiglas* 4312/40 for Graig Shipping Co. Ltd,Cardiff, *Thistlegorm* 4898/40 for the local Albyn Line and the motor-driven *St. Essylt* 5634/40 for the South American Saint Line. The yard was then switched in

The Shell 'mosquito' tanker GYROTOMA of 1950 (above), and the BRITISH NAVIGATOR of 1951 (below) owned by BP. (A. Duncan)

early 1940 to building the first of 23 standard *'Empire'* tramps, of which 13 were based on the same plans as those of the Thompson-built *Dorington Court* of 1939, capable of carrying 10,000 tons of cargo at 11 knots powered by a modest 2500 horse power engine.

More significantly, these plans were taken to North America in September,1940 by Cyril Thompson, Managing Director of the yard. He was accompanied by Harry Hunter of the North Eastern Marine Eng. Co. Ltd, and after talks with the United States Maritime Commission and visits to yards owned by Henry Kaiser, an option for 60 of these ships, known as *'Ocean's*, was taken. However before the contract could be signed, Cyril Thompson returned to Britain in December on the *Western Prince* of Prince Line. She was unfortunately torpedoed and sunk at dawn on the 14th, and Mr. Thompson and 153 survivors were in lifeboats for nine hours before rescue by another ship. He returned by air to America via Lisbon, Portuguese West Africa, Brazil and Trinidad to sign the contract on 20th December. The British mission then went on to Canada, where an initial order for 20 of the same type, known there as *'Fort's*, eventually led to 300 being built in Canada. When the U.S.M.C. decided to build an emergency tramp programme, the New York consultant naval architects Gibbs & Cox again used the *Dorington Court* plans for the famous *'Liberty'* ship, of which over 2700 were built.

Seven more tramps were built for private owners by Thompson during WWII as well as two cargo-liners, *Chinese Prince* 9485/43 and *Silveroak* 6957/44, and four 'Intermediate' type tankers of 5000 dwt. Much damage was done to the yard by bombs during two heavy air raids in the Spring of 1943. One bomb wrecked the offices and Board room, necessitating a complete rebuild, another damaged a ship on the stocks, and the tramp *Denewood* fitting-out at Manor Quay was sunk at her berth. *Chinese Prince*, also fitting-out alongside, was damaged, and more bombs did heavy damage to the shops and plant of the yard. However morale at the yard was lifted by the visit of King George VI and Queen Elizabeth on 14th March,1943. After repairs to the damaged yard, three fast cargo-liners powered by two steam turbines were then completed to Government order during 1944/45.

A return to tanker building was made in 1946, and some 38 tankers were built over the next 20 years, the rapidly increasing sizes being shown in the following deadweight table:-

GALEOMMA	8264/46	Anglo-Saxon/Shell
GANESELLA	8265/46	"
GOMPHINA	8254/48	"
GEMMA	8214/49	"
GYROTOMA	7900/50	"
BRITISH ROSE	8396/46	British Tanker Co. Ltd

THe bridge amidships Newcastle tanker ROYAL CROWN of 1953 (above) photographed on trials (Turners Ltd); and the bridge-aft Shell tanker ARIANTA of 1959.

BRITISH VENTURE	8396/48	British Tanker Co. Ltd
BRITISH NAVIGATOR	8520/51	"
BRITISH ROVER	8420/51	"
BRITISH WARRIOR	8490/51	"
THORSHAVN	15185/49	Thor Dahl A/S,Norway
ATHELTEMPLAR	12800/51	Athel Line
HARWI	15135/52	Rudolf Wigand,Norway
SANDALWOOD	15300/51	John I. Jacobs
HOEGH RANGER	15135/52	Leif Hoegh A/S,Norway
HOEGH RIDER	15135/52	"
ROYAL CROWN	16400/53	Hall Brothers,Newcastle
SHEAF ROYAL	18600/53	W.A. Souter,Newcastle
TORVANGER	18678/54	Westfal-Larsen,Bergen
TIDERACE	19000/54	Admiralty
BRITISH VISION	16870/54	British Tanker Co. Ltd
SHEAF HOLME	18567/55	W.A. Souter,Newcastle
HAUKEFJELL	18600/55	Olsen & Ugelstad,Norway
BORDER TERRIER	16028/56	Lowland Tanker Co. Ltd
HATASIA	18500/56	Shell Tankers Ltd
BRITISH RENOWN	16672/57	British Tanker Co. Ltd
EASTGATE	18130/57	Turnbull,Scott
SPINANGER	19005/57	Westfal-Larsen,Bergen
BEECHWOOD	27300/58	John I. Jacobs
ALUCO	20120/59	Shell Tankers Ltd
ARIANTA	20120/59	"
NORDIC HERON	37100/60	Nordic Tankships,Denmark
LUXOR	19944/60	Moss Tankers Ltd,Liverpool
BUSIRIS	39426/61	Moss Hutchinson Line
BRITISH CAVALIER	54557/62	British Tanker Co. Ltd
BORGSTEN	91356/64	Fred Olsen,Norway
BRITISH COMMERCE	69579/65	British Tanker Co. Ltd
NORTH SANDS	69680/66	Doxford Group

In 1954 the yard became a subsidiary of Sunderland Shipbuilding,Dry Dock & Engineering Co. Ltd, which consisted of the Thompson,Laing and Crown yards and the repairer T. W. Greenwell. The title was changed to Doxford & Sunderland Shipbuilding & Engineering Co. Ltd in 1961 when the Doxford yard joined, but it was not until 1st April,1966 that a full merger of the yards occurred with each losing its identity. A multi-million reorganisation of the North Sands yard was completed in 1960 on land formerly occupied by the neighbouring Crown yard, which was purchased in 1946. A giant new berth was sited at right angles to the existing berths to allow the much longer supertankers and bulk carriers up to 100,000 dwt to be launched across the inner harbour, with in addition new prefabrication sheds.

One interesting conversion to a bulker carried out in 1962 by the yard was to the 'Half-crown' ship *Rondefjell*, owned by Olsen & Ugelstad and so-called because

Two giant tankers built by Thompson in the 1960s, BRITISH CAVALIER of 1962 (above) and the Norwegian BORGSTEN of 1964 (below).

she had been built in two halves by the neigbouring John Crown & Sons Ltd yard in 1951 as a 22,400 dwt tanker. The Thompson yard built a new midships section, and she was lengthened,deepened and strengthened for heavy cargoes and emerged as a 26310 dwt bulker with seven holds forward of her bridge and still powered by a 6800 bhp Doxford oil engine. The old midships section was scrapped by Thos. Young & Sons Ltd at Sunderland.

Silver Line had lost eleven cargo-liners to enemy action during World War II, and ordered six turbine-powered replacements in 1946 from the Thompson yard. Their last two cargo-liners from the yard had been turbine-propelled, and the new sextet were to be similar but distinguished by twin funnels, the forward funnel being a dummy. The beautiful *Silverbriar* and *Silverplane* of 10160 dwt were completed in 1948 for the Round the World service of Silver Line, however the company had been sold to new owners in 1947 and the direction of the company was changed from a liner company to tramping and time-charter trading. The remaining quartet were thus surplus to requirements, and three of them were sold to Blue Funnel Line and the last one to the Indo-China Steam Navigation Co. Ltd, all four then being completed with single funnels only. A full list of all cargo-liners completed by the yard from 1946 to 1966 is now given:-

BIR HAKEIM	9074/46	French Government
BENCRUACHAN	8047/46	Ben Line
EGYPTIAN	3607/47	Ellerman Line
IONIAN	3596/47	"
PATRICIAN	3604/47	"
VENETIAN	3604/47	"
SILVERBRIAR	7242/48	Silver Line
SILVERPLANE	7242/48	"
ULYSSES	8969/49	Blue Funnel Line
TEIRESIAS	8910/50	"
TEUCER	8922/50	"
EASTERN GLORY	6491/49	Indo-China S.N. Co. Ltd
BENAVON	8079/49	Ben Line
BRANDANGER	7392/49	Westfal-Larsen,Bergen
CITY OF MANCHESTER	7585/50	Ellerman Line
ST. ESSYLT	6855/48	South American Saint Line
ST. THOMAS	6855/48	"
ST. JOHN	6889/54	"
ST. ROSARIO	9183/61	"
TROUTPOOL	7989/56	Ropner
EASTERN ROVER	4407/61	Indo-China S.N. Co. Ltd
EASTERN RANGER	4407/61	"

ST. ROSARIO being launched for the South American Saint Line in early 1961 (above); and SILVERLEAF of 1963 (below) of Silver Line.

The quartet built for the South American Saint Line featured very streamlined bridge structures and funnels, and the first was launched on 15th September,1947 as *St. Essylt* by Lady Howard de Walden and Seaford. Her sister *St. Thomas* was launched six months later, and the almost identical *St. John* followed in 1954, all with accomodation for 12 passengers on their service to South America. They had deep tanks for the carriage of edible oils, and were powered by five-cylinder Doxford oil engines of 5300 bhp to give a service speed of 15 knots. The larger *St. Rosario* was completed in June,1961 at a cost of £987,000. *Troutpool* had been ordered by Ropner for their liner service to the Gulf of Mexico, but by the time she was delivered in early 1956 they had given up the service, and she went tramping instead.

The ore-carrier *Lindisfarne* of 18280 dwt was delivered in 1960 to the Bamburgh Shipping Co. Ltd managed by W.A. Souter & Co. Ltd,Newcastle. Two cargo ships of 15050 dwt had been delivered to Norwegian owners in 1958, *Sunheim* to Hjalamar Bjorge and *Gjendefjell* to Olsen & Ugelstad.   Silver Line ordered two of 15500 dwt, completed as *Silverweir* of 1961 and *Silverleaf* of 1963 at a time when owners were still debating as to whether to have an all-aft bridge and machinery design. Unusually *Silverweir* was completed as all-aft, but the later *Silverleaf* was completed with bridge amidships. The 24800 dwt bulker *Silksworth* was completed in 1964 for R.S. Dalgleish Ltd, followed by the 34400 dwt *Sheaf Mount* for W. A. Souter & Co. Ltd in 1965 and by *Kirriemoor* of 38300 dwt for W. Runciman & Co. Ltd in 1965, all Newcastle shipowners.

The 70150 dwt tankers *Daphnella* and *Donacilla* were delivered to Shell Tankers Ltd in June and November,1966 after Thompson's had become the North Sands yard of the Doxford & Sunderland Group, and another sister of 70,000 dwt was completed for Greek shipowner Economou for Liberian registration in 1967 as *Trident*. In the five years of 1966 to 1971, the yard completed eleven bulk carriers in the range 32,300 dwt to 70,000 dwt, the latter Panamax size being the largest to be able to use the Panama Canal. The Norwegian shipowner Fearnley & Eger took *Fernriver* and *Fernspring* of 50800 dwt in 1967, and a sister was delivered to the Greek fleet as *G.M. Livanos* for the shipowner of the same name in 1968, and another to the Liberian fleet of Greek shipowner Economou in 1968 as *Argonaut*. The 52500 dwt bulker *Sheaf Tyne* was delivered in July,1967 to Newcastle shipowner W.A. Souter & Co. Ltd; while the 59100 dwt sisters *Amber Pacific* and *August Pacific* were delivered in 1969 to Pacific Bulk Carriers Ltd,London. The 69100 dwt bulker *Iron Endeavour* was delivered in 1969 to the Nile S.S. Co. Ltd,London on long-term charter as an iron ore carrier to the Broken Hill Pty. Co. Ltd of Australia and managed by Denholm Ship Management of Glasgow. Three of the

The Bibby Line bulker CHESHIRE of 1970 on charter to Wallenius of Sweden (top); and the giant ORENDA of 1971 owned by Houlder Brothers. (Houlder Brothers)

smaller bulkers of 32300 dwt were delivered to Bibby Bulk Carriers Ltd,Liverpool in 1970/71 as *Berkshire, Cheshire* and *Oxfordshire.*

The yard in 1971 then began the steelwork-intensive construction of four very large bulk carriers, the largest possible to be launched in the inner harbour of Sunderland. The slipways had been specially extended and the first of these giants was launched as *Orenda* of 137,500 dwt on 3rd November,1971 for Ore Carriers

Ltd, managed by Houlder Brothers and completed in March,1972 as *Orenda Bridge* on charter to the Seabridge consortium. She was fitted with the largest Doxford oil engine ever manufactured, a 9-cylinder version of 22,500 bhp. Two ore-bulk-oil sisters of 161,800 dwt were then built for the Naess Group of Norway, the first launched as *Naess Crusader* and completed as *Nordic Crusader* in 1973 and the second as *Nordic Chieftain* in 1974 and managed by Denholm Ship Management,Glasgow. The final big splash from the North Sands yard took place on 25th June,1975 when the 154,500 dwt *Aurora* was launched for P & O Bulk Carriers Ltd and watched by large crowds around the harbour. All four giants were forced to make a stern-first exit through the Sunderland Piers when they sailed for dry-docking and trials.

The yard then completed two of a five ship order for Panamax bulk carriers of 70500 dwt placed by Jugoslavenska Oceanska Plovidba. *Kosmaj* and *Kordun* were launched at North Sands and the other three at the Deptford yard. Two smaller B30 bulkers were then completed in 1978 for Consolidated Goldfields Ltd,London and managed by coaster owners Comben,Longstaff Ltd as *Durhambrook* and *Devonbrook*. The final launch at the North Sands yard took place on 24th May,1979 when the container carrying cargo-liner *Badagry Palm* was put into the water for Palm Line Ltd. She was of 16525 dwt and of all-aft design and her Doxford 4-cylinder oil engine was one of the last manufactured and gave over 17 knots on trials. She was completed in November,1979 and the fierce international competition in shipbuilding existing at this time is shown by her owners having subsequent ships of the same design built in Japanese and Polish shipyards. The North Sands yard was placed on a 'care and maintenance basis' with the steelworking facilities intact and the Manor Quay outfitting-berth in use for ships launched by the other two yards in the Group.

However this was not quite the end of the story for ships built at the North Sands, for the yard was reactivated in 1986 for the construction of an enormous crane barge capable of lifting 2000 tons for use in North Sea oilfields and elsewhere. She had been ordered by I.T.M. Offshore Ltd of Middlesbrough and was launched in November,1986 as *I.T.M. Challenger* without ceremony as her owners had gone into receivership shortly before the launch. The diesel-electric twin screw crane barge was however completed and lifting trials conducted in the inner harbour for most of 1987 until a new American buyer was found and she was renamed *McDermott DB50*. The yard has since been demolished and levelled for housing and redevelopment. So ended the centuries old tradition of shipbuilding at North Sands.

Last ships from North Sands, the Palm Line cargo-liner BADAGRY PALM of 1979 (above), and the crane ship I.T.M. CHALLENGER of 1986 (below). (Author).

37 **SIR JAMES LAING & SONS LTD.**

The famous Laing shipbuilding family came from a Fifeshire farming community, and Philip and his brother John started shipbuilding at Sunderland in 1793, helped by David, son of John. Their first ship *Horta* was completed in 1794 on the harbour sands, but David unfortunately died in 1796. The two brothers subsequently used a number of sites including the Bridge Dock near the Monkwearmouth Bridge and at Southwick. John left the partnership in 1818, allowing Philip to start his own yard at Deptford in the same year, and his first ship from there was *Anne*. Philip built himself a house within the Deptford yard, and his son James was born there in 1823.

In 1844 James Laing took control of the Deptford yard and his first ship was launched on 19th January,1844 as *Agincourt* for Duncan Dunbar, the Limehouse millionaire for whom thirty magnificent sailing ships were built over the next twenty years. James Laing was the first Wear shipbuilder to build in iron in 1853 with the steamer *Amity*. Several of the subsequent iron steamers were used as transports in the Crimean War. In 1866 construction of wooden ships ceased altogether with the launch of *Parramatta*, although composite ships continued to be built until 1875. The most famous sailing ship ever built at Deptford was the composite full-rigger *Torrens*, launched in 1875, and in which writer Joseph Conrad later sailed as Second Mate in the Australian trade between 1891/93.

In 1873 two ships building for the Ryde Line were acquired by the prestigious P & O and completed as their passenger/cargo ships *Khiva* and *Kashgar*. The yard then built a series of cargo-liners for well known companies such as Bullard,King for the South African trade, taking 14 ships starting with *Umlazi* 1793/88 and ending with *Umvuma* 4399/14. The British India Steam Navigation Co. Ltd had nine ships built for Indian and African passenger services, starting with *Mombasa* 4662/88 and ending with the large *Yamuna* 10606/03 of length 505 feet. However at the end of her maiden voyage *Yamuna* was sold to the famous Cunard Steamship Co. Ltd and renamed *Slavonia* for Transatlantic services.

The Union Steamship Co. Ltd took two high-class passenger liners for their services to South Africa, *Durban* 2875/77 and *Mexican* 4668/82, but by the time their next ship was ordered from the yard they had merged with competitor Castle Line to form the Union-Castle Line, for whom *York Castle* of 5310 grt was then completed in 1901. The French liner company Cie Havraise Peninsulaire with world-wide services had twelve ships built, starting with *Ville de Strasbourg* 2312/82 and ending with *Ville de Majunga* 3657/00 and *Havraise* 4646/03. The famous Hamburg-Amerika Line had three ships built:- *Galicia* 2860/89, *Dortmund* 5065/00 and *Hoerde* 4974/00, while the Pacific Steam Navigation Co. Ltd took four cargo-liners for their service to the West coast of South America:- *Bogota* 4603/05, *Duendes* 4602/05, *Esmeraldas* 4491/06 and *Flamenco* 4540/06. Companhia Mexican de Navegacao had the liner *Victoria* built in 1884, and she won first prize at an exhibition for passenger/mail steamers. Local owners W. & T.W. Pinkney had 26 steamers built for their Neptune Steam Navigation Co. Ltd for services between Rotterdam and Baltimore with a call at the Tyne for bunkers. Their names all ended in 'O' and the first built by the yard had been *Yesso* 2104/80 and the last was *Moreno* 6350/01. Huddart,Parker & Company had the liner *Westralia* built in 1896 of 2884 grt, and four passenger ships were delivered to the Russian Volunteer Fleet in 1896: *Yalta, Batoum,Novorossisk* and *Sevastopol* with all four of 1325 grt and capable of carrying troops in times of war. Five cargo-liners were delivered to Bucknall Brothers between 1892 and 1900, *Basuto, Bloemfontein, Pondo, Manica* and *Barotse*.

The Swedish passenger liner *Rex* delivered to Capt. Wallenborg in 1897 was of high standard for carrying passengers to the Norwegian fjords, as were two very fine twin-funnelled passenger ships for Nippon Yusen of Japan, *Nippon Maru* and *Hong Kong Maru*. Other passenger/cargo ships were delivered to Konink. Nederlandsche, *Minerva* and *Mars* in 1880; Thomas Hogan & Sons,New York *Montauk* of 1887 and *Mineola* and *Mohawk* both 4765/00; the Deutsche-Australische Line with *Sonneburg* of 1894; Donaldson Line of Glasgow with *Orthia* 4225/96; Cairn Line of Newcastle with *Cairnross* 1509/94; while fellow Newcastle shipowner William Milburn had his *Port Douglas* of 1890 arrested by the yard for non-payment of the staged payments for his ship. Liverpool owners T. & J. Harrison took *Navigator* 2571/86, and Saint Line of Liverpool managed by Rankin,Gilmour took *Saint Marnock* 2969/89, *Saint Hubert* 3046/90 and *Saint Irene* 3877/94, with fellow Mersey shipowner Frederick Leyland & Company taking *Belgian* 3657/00 for their Transatlantic services.

The Laing family were shipowners too and had the two-masted auxiliary-powered sailing ship *Hiogo* of 738 grt launched on 19th December,1865 for their own account. Unfortunately she was wrecked on her maiden voyage, but other ships were built to the ownership of the builder including eight tramps for their Laing Steamship Co. Ltd between 1886 and 1905:- *Glendale, Edendale, Carradale, Clydesdale, Wensleydale, Langdale , Nidderdale* and the 'Turret' *Hopedale* 1746/95 built by Doxford. Tramps were also built for a large number of other owners including John Morrison of North Shields who took a dozen steam tramps between 1871 and 1889 starting with *Ben Lomond* 1171/71 and ending with *Ben Corlic* 2061/89. He also purchased the spar-decked screw brig *Tweed* in 1875 and built at

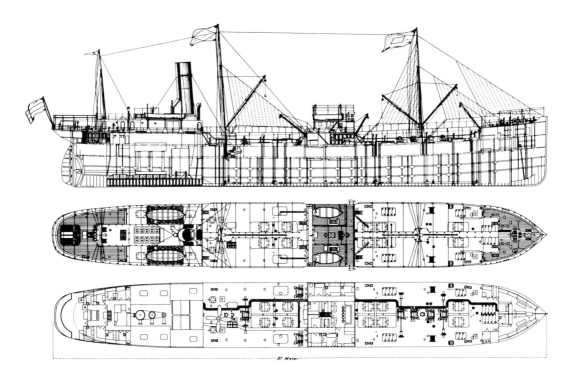

Plan and elevation of Royal Dutch tanker SULTAN VAN LANGKAT of 1897, and she is also pictured moored in a Sumatran river (below). (Dutch Shell).

the yard for James Laing in 1870, as well as the similar Laing-built *Samson* of 1860 purchased from the then Member of Parliament for Sunderland, Edward Temperley Gourley, elected in 1868 and holding his seat until his retirement in 1900. James Laing built the majority of the Gourley ships and also took a half-share in most with a majority of the 64 shares in several others.

James Laing was married twice and three of his four sons worked at the Deptford yard. Philip Laing of 1849 served as an apprentice in the Austin & Mills shipyard before joining the family yard. James Laing Jnr. of 1862 spent two and a half years as an apprentice at Deptford, followed by 18 months at the Denny yard at Dumbarton and on his return was engaged in yard management until six months before his death in 1895, having suffered from ill-health for some years. Hugh Laing of 1871 was educated at Wellington College and Cambridge University, and served his apprenticeship at the North Eastern Marine Engineering Co. Ltd engine works at South Dock before becoming a director of the yard. He came into prominence with the construction of the first oil tanker at the yard in 1892 for Marcus Samuel, founder of the famous Shell company. *Turbo* was designed to carry 5500 tons of Russian oil in bulk from the Black Sea ports of Baku and Batoum through the Suez Canal to ten different ports in the Far East where Marcus Samuel had erected tanks. The snag was that the Suez Canal Company viewed kerosene as an extremely dangerous cargo and turned away all oil cargoes. However Samuel submitted plans for a new safe design with twin cofferdams at each end of the tanker and finally won their approval. His first tanker *Murex* built at the Gray shipyard at West Hartlepool made her first passage with oil through the canal on 24th August,1892 for Singapore, and *Turbo* from the Deptford yard was his third tanker when completed in December of that year. She was followed by sisters *Trocas* in March,1893 and *Spondilus* in April,1893, and by several others for Bessler,Waechter & Company of London but managed by Stephens & Mawson of Newcastle, and for Alfred Suart of London, and Lane & Macandrews of London, and the Anglo-American Oil Co. Ltd, which was the British arm of Standard Oil of the U.S.A. founded by John Rockefeller in 1870 and later known as Esso. Some early tankers from Deptford were:-

TURBO	4134/92	Anglo-Saxon/Shell
TROCAS	4129/93	"
SPONDILUS	4129/93	"
BATOUM	4054/93	Alfred Suart
SURAM	3629/93	Stephens & Mawson
VEDRA	4057/93	Alfred Suart
MEXICANO	1973/93	Northern Transport Ltd
SULTAN VAN LANGKAT	2336/97	Royal Netherlands Petroleum
TUSCARORA	6117/98	Anglo-American Oil Co. Ltd

The liner BERMUDIAN of 1904 pictured as FORT HAMILTON when owned by Furness Line (above); and the Silver Line cargo-liner SILVERMAPLE of 1927. (A. Duncan).

TEREK	3710/99	Lane & Macandrews
BALAKANI	3696/99	"
CAUCASIAN	4656/08	Lane & Macandrews
SERVIAN	4997/08	"
LUTETIAN	4757/08	"
TURBO	4782/12	Anglo-Saxon/Shell
LUCELLUM	5179/12	H.E. Moss
LUCELLUM	5184/13	"
SHABONEE	5167 /13	Tank Storage & Carriage Co. Ltd
TEUTONIAN	4824/14	Lane & Macandrews

James Laing was knighted in early 1897, and at the beginning of 1898 the title of the yard was changed to Sir James Laing & Sons Ltd. The cargo-liner *Anatolia* for the Papayanni Steamship Co. Ltd, later part of Ellerman Lines, was the first ship built under the new title, and she was followed by her sister *Adalia* later in the year. The yard was head of the river in terms of tonnage in 1900 with 40,307 tons. Sir James died in 1901 having controlled the destiny of the Deptford yard for 58 years, and having taken a leading role in the changes from building wooden sailing ships to building large iron and steel steamers. He had been Chairman of the River Wear Commissioners for 32 years and first Chairman of Hendon Docks, and first Chairman of the Wear Shipbuilders Association for the very long period of 48 years from 1853 to 1901, President of the Chamber of Shipping for the U.K., Vice President of Lloyds Load Line and Bulkhead committees and also sat on the Council of the Royal Institute of Naval Architects, a Director of the Suez Canal Company as well as several local railway and water companies.

Management remained with Philip Laing and his brother Hugh Laing, but after the death of Philip in 1907 the yard got into financial difficulties. The conversion of H.M.S. *Cyclops* into a repair ship showed a loss of £100,000, and there was a similar loss on three Italian emigrant liners built in 1907. Two of these twin-funnelled liners had been ordered by James Knott for his Prince Line, however the Italian Government nationalised the emigrant service to the U.S.A. and they were completed as *Re D'Italia* 6237/07 and *Regina D'Italia* 5204/07 and *Prince de Piedmonte* 5204/07, all for Lloyd Sabaudo. Two more emigrant liners completed that year were *San Giorgio* 6392/07 and *San Giovanni* 6592/07, both capable of 14 knots on the service to New York of Sicula Oceanica Societa di Navigazione owned by the Fratelli family. The liners *Bermudian* 5530/04 and *Guiana* 3657/07 were completed for the Quebec Steamship Co. Ltd, which was purchased in 1919 by Furness,Withy & Co. Ltd, who also purchased in 1911 two refrigerated meat carriers built by the yard for the Anglo-Argentine Shipping Co. Ltd as *La Blanca* 6813/06 and *El Argentino* 6809/07. Sir Christopher Furness also purchased the remaining three tramps owned by the Laing Steamship Co. Ltd, *Langdale, Swaledale and Wensleydale*, sold in 1909 to raise money to overcome the financial difficulties of the yard.

Sir James Marr was appointed to the Board of Sir James Laing & Sons Ltd in 1909 to overcome the financial difficulties faced by the yard as not a single ship had been launched that year. He had first worked in the Thompson yard at North Sands in 1876 and had been appointed Managing Director there in 1901. The success of his work is shown by the fact that the yard had an output of 26,000 tons in 1912, including the twin-funnelled Greek emigrant liner *Macedonia* of 6333 grt, and some of these vessels built up to the start of World War I were:-

MEXICANO	3694/11	W. Wilhelmsen, Norway
RAWSON	3101/11	N. Michanovitch
DETMOLD	4431/11	Holzapfel,Newcastle
MACEDONIA	6333/12	National Greek Line
EASTWELL	4666/12	Tyzack & Branfoot,Sunderland
BOWES CASTLE	4650/12	James Chambers & Co.,Liverpool
CLAN MACBETH	4647/13	Clan Line,Glasgow
NOVGOROD	5285/13	Russian Volunteer Fleet
SAN JOAQUIN	6987/13	W. Wilhelmsen,Norway
LA HABRA	7021/13	"
BELRIDGE	7027/14	"
STOCKWELL	5643/14	Tyzack & Branfoot,Sunderland
CALORIC	7013/14	W. Jebsen,Bergen

The yard now had five building berths and a graving dock arranged around the inner side of a sinuous bend of the river at Deptford, and had the highest tonnage of any Wear yard over the four years 1914 to 1918 with 18 ships of 109,924 tons as well as six small naval craft.   Companies controlled by Furness,Withy & Co. Ltd received three cargo-liners:- *Bay State*   6824/15 for the Warren Line, *Start Point* 6560/15 for the Norfolk & North American Steamship Co. Ltd and *Rexmore* 5277/18 for Johnston Line, as well as managing two cargo ships ordered by W. Wilhelmsen of Norway at the beginning of the war and completed for the British flag, *Glastonbury* 6031/17 and *Appleby* 6030/17.   The Clan Line Steamers Ltd took delivery of *Clan Matheson* of 5960 grt in 1916. Amongst valuable tankers built for the war effort were *Lumina* 6281/15 for H. E. Moss of Liverpool, *Winnebago* 4666/15 and *Tuscarora* 7106/17 for the Anglo-American Oil Co. Ltd, and five tankers ordered by Norwegian owners at the start of the war but completed for the British fleet and managed by H.E. Moss of Liverpool. Four of these had been ordered by W. Wilhelmsen in 1919/20:- *Mirita* 5830/16, *Mendocino* 6973/17, *Mirlo* 6978/18 and *Montana* 6970/18; and *Meline* 6983/18 had been ordered by Thor.

Berg of Tonsberg. All except *Mirlo*, which had been torpedoed and sunk by submarine, were returned to their rightful owners in 1919/20. In addition twelve 'WAR' standard ships, seven of them tankers, were ordered by the Shipping Controller, but only three of these had been completed by the end of war.

King George V and Queen Mary visited the yard and several other Wear yards on 15th June,1917 to give encouragement to the workers in their vital task of rebuilding the British fleet during the black year of 1917 when the U-boat had ravaged the merchant fleet. Their subsequent conferment of a Baronetcy on Sir James Marr, Managing Director of Laings as well as Thompsons and Sunderland Forge & Engineering, was a great honour for a Wear shipbuilder whose services had greatly benefitted his country. Standard ships that were still building at the Deptford yard in November,1918 were quickly bought by private shipping companies and completed for them during 1919/20 e.g. *Barrymore* 5415/20 for Johnston Line. The initial post-war boom also brought a flood of orders for new tonnage especially tankers for the rapidly expanding British Tanker Co. Ltd set-up during the war in 1915. These and other tankers completed during the 1920s were:-

BRITISH COLONEL	6999/21	British Tanker Co. Ltd
BRITISH JUDGE	6735/21	"
BRITISH CHANCELLOR	7085/21	"
BRITISH COUNCILLOR	7048/22	"
BRITISH ADVOCATE	6994/22	"
BRITISH STATESMAN	6991/23	"
BRITISH AMBASSADOR	6940/24	"
BRITISH CONSUL	6940/24	"
BRITISH RENOWN	6997/28	"
BRITISH GLORY	6993/28	"
MALMANGER	7078/20	Westfal-Larsen,Bergen
SCOTTISH AMERICAN	6999/20	Tankers Ltd,Glasgow
SYLVAFIELD	5709/25	Hunting & Son,Newcastle
TYNEFIELD	5856/25	"
MASIMPUR	5586/27	Burmah Oil,London
SCHUYLKILL	8964/28	Anglo-American Oil Co. Ltd
PAQUITA	2618/28	Shell B.V.
THORSHOLM	6748/30	Thor Dahl A/S,Norway
THORSHAVN	6749/30	"
LONGWOOD	9463/30	John I. Jacobs,London

The large cargo-liner *Moena* 9286/23 was built for the Nederland Stoomv. Maats of Holland, and two cargo-liners for the new Silver Line, *Silverguava* 5294/27 and *Silvermaple* 5302/27. Tramps *Saltwick* 3775/29 and *Glaisdale* 3777/29 were built for Headlam & Son of Whitby, and *Kirkpool* 4840/28 for Ropner of West Hartlepool, as well as three for local owners Albyn Line managed by Allan,Black &

Co. Ltd, *Thistleford* 4764/28, *Thistleglen* 4750/29 and *Thistlegarth* 4750/29 all of 8350 tons dwt with the last two engined at the quay of the Scotia Engine Works, originally owned by Sir William Allan, on the south bank of the river opposite Manor Quay. In addition two colliers of 3300 dwt, *Clanwood* and *Kentwood*, and another pair of 2900 dwt, *Fernwood* and *Moonwood*, were completed in 1924 for William France,Fenwick & Co. Ltd. After completion of the tanker *Longwood* in 1930 the yard closed down and the workforce was paid-off except for the indentured apprentices, who later began the slow and painful process of building the cargo ship *Dore* by themselves as a speculation.

After the Government introduced the Scrap & Build Scheme in 1935 the yard finally received orders for two cargo ships for Liverpool owners in 1936. This pair were for the Lancashire Shipping Co. Ltd managed by James Chambers & Co. Ltd, and *Lowther Castle* was launched on 12th December,1936 and completed in February,1937 with her sister *Lancaster Castle* completing in March,1937. They were of 9250 tons dwt and of coventional split superstructure appearance with five holds, and had triple expansion reheater steam engines by the North Eastern Marine Engineering Co. Ltd. Fellow Liverpool owner Charles G. Dunn kept the yard in work with an order for another similar ship *Haughton Hall* in 1937, together with a collier for Burnett, *Wallsend* 3157/37. Tramp building restarted with *Baron Elphinstone* 4635/37 and *Baron Minto* 4637/37 for Hogarth of Glasgow, *Gemstone* 4986/37 for the Minster Steamship Co. Ltd,London, *Ael-y-Bryn* 4986/38 for Ambrose,Davies & Matthews of Swansea and *Grayburn* 6342/38 for Wallem & Company. The design of tankers *Eidanger* 9432/38 and *Alar* 9444/38 of 14500 dwt for Norwegian owners was very significant for they formed the basis of the standard 'Norwegian' class of tankers built by the yard and the Furness yard at Haverton Hill during the war. The 12000 dwt tanker *British Prudence* was delivered to the British Tanker Co. Ltd in 1939 before the outbreak of war.

The Depford yard had a magnificent record of output during World War II, with 41 ships of which 32 were tankers, completed between 1939 and 1946. Fifteen tankers to their 'Norwegian' design of 14700 dwt, eight to the 'Intermediate' design of 5000 dwt, and five to the 'Fast Oiler' type of 12000 dwt were completed to Government order. In addition to private order were *Athelcrest* for Athel Line in 1940, *Wearfield* and *Thamesfield* of 'Norwegian' class design in 1943 for Hunting & Son, and *Beechwood* of 'Fast Oiler' design in 1945 for John I. Jacobs. In addition, eight tramps were built, one to Government order and the other seven for private owners: *Beechwood* and *Glenwood* for John I. Jacobs; *Bolton Castle* for James Chambers; *Charlton Hall* for Charles G. Dunn; *Wandby* and *Fishpool* for Ropner; and *Tynemouth* for Burnett. The fast cargo-liner *Empire Paragon* 9892/44 was powered by three steam turbines to give a speed of 15 knots, and she joined the P & O fleet in 1946 as *Pinjarra*. There were five building berths in operation at the yard for ships up to 550 feet at the end of the war.

The reputation for tanker building at the Depford yard was now second to none, and this was reinforced in a speech by Princess Elizabeth at the launch of *British Princess* on 30th April,1946 at the yard. In it she paid tribute to the great shipbuilding yard of Sir James Laing & Sons Ltd and its men who had inherited all those gifts and traditions which made British shipyards pre-eminent and who had given years of patient and devoted work to the construction of tankers. Full order books for tankers were customary throughout the twenty years from 1946, and their escalating size is clearly shown in the following deadweight table:-

BRITISH PRINCESS	12354/46	British Tanker Co. Ltd
BRITISH HOLLY	12310/47	"
BRITISH FERN	12310/47	"
ROSEWOOD	14794/47	John I. Jacobs
MATADI PALM	9210/48	Palm Line
ATHELKNIGHT	12840/48	Athel Line
ATHELDUKE	12840/49	"
HOEGH ROVER	15400/48	Leif Hoegh A/S,Norway
BJORN STANGE	15482/49	Harald Stange A/S,Norway
STEINGRIN STANGE	15482/49	"
BRITISH RELIANCE	16687/50	British Tanker Co. Ltd
MARIETTA	15314/50	Thor Berg,Tonsberg
HOEGH ARROW	22808/50	Leif Hoegh A/S,Norway
HOLLYWOOD	17720/51	John I. Jacobs
HOEGH EAGLE	22808/51	Leif Hoegh A/S,Norway
BRITISH BIRCH	12270/51	British Tanker Co. Ltd
BRITISH MAPLE	12160/51	"
LONDON GLORY	15347/51	London & Overseas Freighters Ltd
LONDON ENDURANCE	15347/51	"
LONDON SPIRIT	15330/52	"
MERCHANT KNIGHT	15330/52	Drake Shipping Co. Ltd
MARICOPA	17440/53	Thor Berg,Tonsberg
ALVA STAR	18340/53	Alva S.S. Co. Ltd
HUNTFIELD	16820/54	Hunting & Son
LAURELWOOD	18560/53	John I. Jacobs
MORGENEN	18410/55	Thor Berg,Tonsberg
THORNABY	18270/55	Ropner
BORDER REIVER	16182/55	Lowland Tanker Co. Ltd
O.B. SORENSEN	27400/56	Smith Sorensen Tank A/S,Norway
TIDERANGE	20000/56	Admiralty Oiler
BRITISH VIGILANCE	16672/57	British Tanker Co. Ltd
THIRLBY	20070/58	Ropner
CORHAMPTON	20700/60	W. Cory & Sons Ltd
MONTANA	20700/61	Thor. Berg,Tonsberg

Tanker BRITISH PRINCESS (above) was launched by Princess Elizabeth on 30th April,1946; and tanker ATHELDUKE of 1949 (below) of Athel Line. (Real Photos).

The Newcastle ore-carrier SHEAF WEAR of 1959 (above); and the tanker BRITISH BEECH of 1964 (below).

| BRITISH BEECH | 20750/64 | British Tanker Co. Ltd |
| BRITISH WILLOW | 20750/64 | British Tanker Co. Ltd |

7 Cunard Line were among the first shipowners to order replacements for their fleet in 1946, and the yard won orders for two fast turbine-propelled, partly-refrigerated cargo-liners of 11150 dwt for Transatlantic services, *Asia* 8723/46 and *Arabia* 8720/46. Furness, Withy & Co. Ltd ordered a turbine cargo-liner of similar size of 11750 dwt for their service to the Pacific coast of the U.S.A. and Canada. *Pacific Unity* 9511/48 had complete 'tween decks, the lower of which was fully insulated for the carriage of fruit homewards. All three cargo-liners could carry 12 passengers, as was also the case with a trio built for Ropner of West Hartlepool, who had started a liner service to the Gulf of Mexico from U.K. and European ports in 1946. *Daleby* 5171/50 was ready for launching at the Deptford yard in the Spring of 1960 resplendent in a fresh coat of bottle green paint, the first company ship to wear the new hull colour. She and her sister *Deerpool* 5169/50 could carry 7846 tons of cargo and 12 passengers on their 12 day voyage to Gulf and Mississippi ports and were equipped with mechanical heating and ventilation. A four-cylinder Doford oil engine gave a service speed of 13.5 knots and was economical to run with a fuel consumption of 10 tons/day of diesel oil. *Dalepool* left Sunderland on her maiden voyage under the command of Capt. John Kenny, and *Deerpool* under the command of Capt. C.H. Churchill, and they were joined on the Gulf service in 1954 by the larger Laing-built *Somersby* 5893/54.

In 1955 the yard then began building a series of ten ore-carriers of between 15500 dwt and 19500 dwt for completion over the next six years for the following shipowners:-

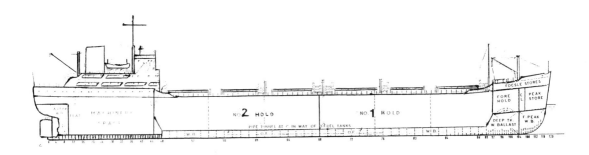

KNOB LAKE	12721/56	Iron Ore Transport Ltd, Canada
TRITONICA	12714/56	Nordstrom & Thulin A/B, Sweden
ATOMENA	12721/57	"
SILVERSAND	10887/58	Silver Line, London

SILVERCRAG	10887/58	Silver Line
SHEAF FIELD	10867/59	W.A. Souter & Co. Ltd,Newcastle
SHEAF WEAR	10867/59	"
BISHOPSGATE	12718/60	Bishopsgate Shpg. Co. Ltd,London
ALDERSGATE	12718/60	"
MOGEN	12618/61	Victor Jensens A/S,Norway

with usually two or three holds for carrying ore, each of which was served by a similar number of hatches, and the earlier examples had a small flying bridge amidships but this had soon moved aft to join the Doxford oil engine which gave a service speed of 14 knots. The engines and bridge structure of ordinary tramps had been moving aft since 1957, and in that year the yard had built one all-aft pair of 14480 dwt for Ropner, *Rushpool* and *Romanby*, while another pair of 11675 dwt for Silver Line kept to traditional design, *Silverforce* and *Silverlake*.

Around 1960, the economics of transporting bulk cargoes demanded ever larger ships and led to the development of a special type, the bulk carrier. Under Managing Director Allan Marr the yard was given larger berths and new prefabrication sheds to launch these larger bulk carriers downstream of the old berths, starting with a pair of 24500 dwt for Swedish owners in 1961/62, *Atomena* for Nordstrom & Thulin A/B and *Barbara* for Dore Ulff A/B. The similar *Barlby* of 24870 dwt for Ropner of West Hartlepool was completed later in 1962, and was followed by *Silverhow* of 37280 dwt for Silver Line in 1965 for operation in the Seabridge consortium, and by *Oakwood* of 35000 dwt in 1965 for John I. Jacobs. The latter owners had also placed orders for two conventional cargo ships several years earlier with the yard, *Teakwood* of 12850 dwt and *Rosewood* of 15575 dwt.

The Laing yard became the Deptford yard of the Doxford & Sunderland Group on 1st April,1966. However the first of two cargo-liners of 14830 dwt for Navrom, the Roumanian shipping company of Constantza, was delivered under the Laing name just before this date in March as *Sinaia*, whereas her sister *Predeal* was delivered in June,1966. An engines-aft tramp of 15000 dwt, *Sheaf Crest*, was then built for W.A. Souter of Newcastle, however the main thrust of the Doxford & Sunderland Group building programme at the Deptford and North Sands yards over the next ten years was to be bulk carriers up to Panamax size of 70,000 dwt. The yard built a total of 17 bulk carriers ranging from 21000 dwt to Panamax size. The Greek shipowner Chandris took delivery of a pair of 21000 dwt in 1969, *Federal Lakes* and *Federal Seaway*, while a trio of 51500 dwt had earlier been built during 1967/68:- *Roslagen* for Nordstrom & Thulin A/B,Sweden and *Mylla* for Inter-essenskaper A/S,Norway and *Orotava* for Ore Carriers Ltd,London managed by Houlder Brothers. A quartet of bulk carriers of 35000 dwt was completed for Greek owners between 1971/73 as *Flisvos, Pindar, John Lyras* and *Fidias*, and then the first of the Panamax size was completed in 1974 as the Greek *Thetis* and was followed over the next three years by seven more, with *Melete, Naiad* and *Nikitas Roussos* for Greek shipowners; *Jadran,Sutjeska* and *Orgen* for Yugoslavenska Oceanica Plovidba; and *Mersey Bridge* for Bibby Bulk Carriers Ltd,Liverpool. The yard was also given four cargo-liners to build for Bank Line in 1973, transferred from the Pallion yard where a new shipbuilding hall was being built and completed as *Fleetbank,Cloverbank, Birchbank* and *Beaverbank*. Three tankers had also been built of 25500 dwt, two for John I. Jacobs as *Laurelwood* and *Hollywood*, and *Sea Griffin* for Destiny Tankers Ltd.

The Panamax bulk carrier WELSH CITY of 1977. (Skyfotos Ltd)

After the yard was nationalised on 1st July,1977 five more bulkers of Panamax size were built with *Orient City* and *Welsh City* for Reardon Smith of Cardiff, *Benhope* for Ben Line of Leith although ordered by W.A. Souter of Newcastle, and *La Pampa* and *La Chacra* for Buries Markes Ltd,London. The yard shared in the building of the last six cargo-liners for Bank Line in 1979, transferred from the long series built for this owner at Pallion, and similarly an order for six cargo-liners of 16170 dwt for the Shipping Corporation of India was split between

Two Panamax bulk carriers, **LA PAMPA** of 1982 owned by Buries Markes Ltd (above), and **BENHOPE** of 1978 owned by Ben Line (below).

the Deptford and Pallion yards. A B30 bulker was completed in 1981 for Indian owners Chellaram Maritime as *Darya Kamal* although managed and registered at Hong Kong. Two of B35 size followed for Lyras Brothers of Greece in 1983, *Markos Lyras* and *George Lyras*, and one of B45 size for John Swire & Sons Ltd of Hong Kong, *Hupeh* of 1984. The final pair of a similar size of 46,700 dwt were completed for Transportacion Maritima Mexicana SA of Mexico in 1985 as *Colima* and *Mitla*, with the latter being the last ever launch by the yard on 3rd May, 1985.

Mitla was also the last large ship built by the Doxford & Sunderland Group as the Pallion yard had just completed the last of their B30 bulkers. The Deptford yard was never used for shipbuilding again, although hopes were raised of building a replica of the full-rigger *Torrens* of 1875. The site has since been used by a number of engineering companies including Wear Dock Engineering Ltd.

The last launch, the Mexican owned MITLA is checked by drag chains on 3rd May, 1985. (Author)

SHORT BROTHERS LTD *SP*

This medium-sized yard was known as the 'local' yard because it built more ships for local ownership than any other in Sunderland. It was founded in 1850 at Hylton by George Short, who had previously been foreman at John Watson's yard where many Wear shipbuilders had learnt their trade. The yard built small wooden sailing ships e.g. *Breeze* of 216 tons in August,1859 for John Reed, and also traded as timber merchants. His four sons, George, John Young, Thomas and Joseph had all entered the yard by the time it had been transferred down-river in 1869 to Pallion to a site beside Pallion Hall. Iron construction was adopted at this time with the first iron ship being *High Stretfield* of 1871 for J.S. Barwick of Sunderland. The yard became known as Short Brothers in 1871.

John Y. Short was an able designer of ships in the 1870s and his outstanding designs for cargo ships with better lines and greater beam to give more stability and seaworthiness brought him much acclaim. He received full recognition in 1877 when he received a gold medal in London for the best designed steamer, and at the Paris exhibition in 1878. The shipyard was awarded two medals for steamer models at an exhibition held by the Worshipful Company of Shipwrights in 1882. A number of long associations were made with local owners and the reputation of the yard was established as a builder of quality ships. Such associations provided financial stability for the yard, and were not uncommon at this period when, if the owner was satisfied, repeat orders were placed without the present-day practice of competitive tendering. Most of the ships built for long standing customers were developments of the previous vessel and not exact sisters, allowing full rein to the designing ability of John Y. Short.

James Westoll of Sunderland had some 40 cargo ships built at the yard, the last three being *Roker* 3499/98, *Coniscliffe* 3920/01 and *Salient* 3879/05. *Coniscliffe* was named after his country residence at High Coniscliffe Hall, five miles west of Darlington, and where both he and his wife Lavinia were buried. Other regular Sunderland customers were John S. Barwick with 21 vessels with local names such as *Bede* 2134/86 and whose last ship from the yard was *Ella* of 1122 grt in June,1894; Taylor & Sanderson with 24 ships starting with *Cyprus* of 1888 grt completed in December,1878, with more having been built before 1878 for the Taylor family. One of their ships was named in honour of *Lady Joicey* in 1898, wife of the local colliery owner and shipowner. The local Member of Parliament, Edward Temperley Gourley, had his *Florence* of 2492 grt completed by the yard in October,1889 as well as *Constance* of 3930 grt in November,1892. However the

Short Brothers built for local owners such as Westoll with COGENT of 1883 pictured; and for Prince Line with KAFFIR PRINCE of 1891 (below).

latter ship was sold soon after completion to Christopher Furness of West Hartlepool and then early in 1893 to Houlder Brothers. Other local owners who had ships built by the yard were W. & T.W. Pinkney with *Chicago* 2617/90 for his Neptune Steam Navigation Co. Ltd, and Bulman & Dixon Ltd with *Oakdene* 1681/84.

The association between James Knott of North Shields and the yard resulted in 37 cargo-liners being built for his Prince Line between 1883 and 1918. *Highland Prince* of 1516 grt was completed first in December,1883 and was followed by exact sisters *Ocean Prince* and *Royal Prince* of 1737 grt in 1885. All had Prince names except *Bea Bellido* of 1914 grt launched on 16th February,1893 and completed in April of that year, although she later acquired a Prince name. She was the first of a quartet built during 1893 for Prince Line, the others being *Italian Prince, Creole Prince* and *Carib Prince*. The four ship contract showed a return on capital employed to the yard of only 6.3%, and Shorts costings were so exact that on contracts for other owners they showed small losses.

	CONTRACT	COST	PROFIT
BEA BELLIDO	£23,355	£22,361	£994
ITALIAN PRINCE	£32,644	£30,582	£2062
CREOLE PRINCE	£25,069	£23,600	£1469
CARIB PRINCE	£25,069	£23,212	£1857
TOTALS	£106,137	£99,755	£6382

Another long association with the yard was provided by Colonel John Thomas North and his Nitrate Producers Steamship Co. Ltd, managed by Lawther,Latta. John Young Short took a fair sized shareholding in the company, formed on 4th March,1895 to ship nitrates from the Atacama desert in Chile to Europe for use as fertilizers. The first ship built for the company by the yard was *Col. J.T. North* completed in May,1895 at a cost of £27,350 with a profit of £3170 to the yard. Subsequent ships had names with the prefix 'Anglo' e.g. *Anglo-Peruvian* 5494/05, and the yard had a complete monopoly of ships for this company with all thirty built by the yard, the last being *Anglo-Indian* 5609/38.

Newcastle shipowners were also prolific customers, with Common Brothers having 22 tramps built by the yard between 1895 and 1941. Their Hindustan Steam Shipping Co. Ltd had been formed in Sunderland in 1893 with the keel of *Kurdistan* of 3036 grt laid at the yard on 6th October,1894, and launched on 25th March,1895 and completed on 23rd May,1895. A further eight tramps were built for this company up to the outbreak of WWI:- *Afghanistan* 3427/99, *Daghestan* 3466/00, *Hindustan*

SYRIAN PRINCE of 1893 was one of 37 ships built for Prince Line (above); and the Newcastle tramp HARTSIDE of 1909 (below).   (York Collection).

3756/02, *Sagami* 4212/02, *Laristan* 3675/10, *Hindustan* 3692/12, *Daghestan* 3691/12 and *Kurdistan* 3730/14. *Sagami* had been ordered by the New York & Oriental Steamship Co. Ltd (Barber & Co.),Liverpool for whom *Shimosa* 4221/02 was actually delivered. The Cairn Line of Steamships Ltd managed by Cairns,Noble had four cargo-liners built by the yard:- *Cairnloch* 1546/95, *Cairnisla* 1597/96, *Cairnavon* 1591/05 and *Cairnnevis* 1587/05. The Dene Steam Shipping Co. Ltd managed by John T. Lunn placed an order in 1890 for three steam tramps of 4000 dwt with triple expansion engines by William Allan & Sons Ltd and George Clark Ltd. These were completed as *Aloedene* 2411/90, *Beechdene* 2508/90 and *Ferndene* 2637/91, and were followed by *Myrtledene* of 4500 dwt in 1892. Newcastle shipbuilder John Wigham Richardson subcontracted a ship to the yard in 1896, and she was completed as *Wingrove* in October,1896. The Charlton Steam Shipping Co. Ltd managed by Charlton,McAllum had eight tramps built by the yard, with a quartet ordered before WWI, *Hollinside* 2682/05, *Hartside* 2740/09, *Heatherside* 2767/09 and *Hesleyside* 3994/12, and a quartet ordered in the inter-war years: *Homeside* 4617/24, *Hazelside* 4646/28, *Hollinside* 4172/30 and *Hazelside* 5297/40.

Leonidas Embiricos and his family of Greece were good customers ordering seven tramps between 1897 and 1914 and more in the inter-war years, starting with *Leonidas* 2751/97. One completed in September,1914 was named in honour of *Dorothy T. Short*, wife of Joseph Short. Sir Christopher Furness ordered two tramps from the yard for his subsidiary, British Maritime Trust Ltd, and completed as *Gloriana* 2768/98 and *Cebriana* 4221/99; and Owen Cosby Philipps, later Lord Kylsant, ordered four tramps and completed as *King David* 2555/95, *King Edgar* 2552/96, *King Frederick* 2577/97, and *King Frederick* 3756/06.

John Y. Short died in his office on 24th January,1900 at the age of 56 years when the shipyard had a workforce of 1500 workers. He had introduced the eight hour working day at the yard in 1892 and set-up an Institute for his workers. He had been Chairman of the Sunderland Shipowners Association in 1898, a River Wear Commissioner since 1885, and a founder member of the Royal Institute of Naval Architects. He left £385,000 in his will and his brother Joseph took over the management of the yard, turning the partnership into a limited liability company, Short Brothers Ltd, later in 1900. In 1899 the neighbouring yard of the North of England Shipbuilding Co. Ltd had been taken over, and output in 1900 reached 26,017 tons.

New customers such as James Chambers of Liverpool then ordered *Kendal Castle* 3885/10 for his Lancashire Shipping Co. Ltd, and Glen & Company of Glasgow *Lissa* 3882/11, which was completed in six months from keel laying. In

the year before the outbreak of war, the yard launched the last two ships for Prince
Line to the order of Sir James Knott, who sold his company to Furness,Withy & Co.
Ltd early in 1917. These were *Moorish Prince* launched on 26th February,1914 and
completed in May, and *British Prince*, launched on 8th May,1914 and completed in
August,1914, and two more came from the Doxford yard. The contribution that Sir
James Knott had made to the Wear yards and Short Brothers in particular is shown
by the fact that the wages bill of all his Wear-built ships had topped £2M.

The output of the yard during World War I was 17 ships of 86,391 tons, and
14 barges for the Admiralty. Those built to private order were *Ferrona* 4591/14 for
William Lowden & Company, *Rose Castle* 7546/15 for Lewis Steamship Co. Ltd (T.
Lewis),Liverpool,   *Murcia* 4871/15 and *Adra* 4860/17 for C.T. Bowring & Co. Ltd,
Anglo-Chilean 6987/16 for Nitrate Producers Steamship Co. Ltd.   The tanker
Birchleaf was built in 1916 for the Admiralty and managed by Lane & Macandrews,
plus four small oilers *Creosol, Celerol, Sprucol* and *Teakol.* Some eight standard
WAR 'B' types were built, and *War Seagull* was launched in late December,1918 in
total darkness in the early hours of the morning to complete a record year for the
yard of 34,967 tons. Two cargo-liners of 9900 dwt were also completed for Prince
Line as *Gaelic Prince* and *Celtic Prince* in 1918.

In the ten years from 1920 to 1930 some 36 tramps and cargo-liners were
built by the yard, with eight for Chapmans of Newcastle, ten for Common Brothers of
Newcastle, three for Charlton,McAllum of Newcastle, and six for the Nitrate
Producers Steamship Co. Ltd.   Two cargo-liners for Union-Castle Line aroused
interest as they were the first turbine-propelled ships built for the company,
Sandown Castle 7607/21 and *Sandgate Castle* 7607/22, and three turbines were
single reduction coupled to a single screw to give a service speed of 14 knots. Two
cargo-liners were completed for the South American service of Donaldson Line of
Glasgow, *Corrientes* 6683/20 and *Cordillera* 6683/21. Three steam tramps were
completed for the Embiricos family of Greece, *Eugenie S. Embiricos* 4882/20,
George M. Embiricos 5728/21 and *Irene S. Embiricos* 4164/27. Strikes and near-
empty order books in 1923 and 1926 were signs of the times, and the last tramp
completed before the yard closed down due to a completely empty order book was
Harberton of 4558 grt in June,1930 for J. & C. Harrison of London.

In early 1933 the yard received the order to build the first of three new tramps
to the 'Arcform' hull shape, designed by Sir Joseph Isherwood. Her cross-section was
shaped like a wine cask standing on end, her widest beam being just below the
waterline and some 10% greater than a normal tramp. Higher speed and lower fuel
consumption were claimed by the designer, and the keel of *Arcwear* was laid on 4th
May,1933, she was launched on 2nd November,1933 and completed on 11th

January,1934. On her maiden voyage the economic fuel consumption was not in doubt, she was indeed faster and more economical, but her sudden rolling with a jerky motion in calm weather and heavy rolling in heavy weather with seas halfway up her hatches and putting the whole foredeck under water put the design in doubt. Several 'Arcform' tramps were built, including *Arctees* at the Furness yard on the Tees and *Arcgow* at Lithgows yard on the Clyde, both in 1934, and some 'Arcform' tankers but the design was not very successful.

The Scrap & Build Scheme of 1935 brought the yard orders for six ships, five of them colliers. The tramp was the more interesting, for she became the single-decker *Biddlestone* of 8000 dwt, fitted with the new White twin high-speed compound steam engine exhausting to a low pressure turbine. She was launched on 10th May,1937 for the White Shipping Co. Ltd,Newcastle managed by R.I. James, and completed in July,1937. The five colliers were built to the order of the Springwell Shipping Co. Ltd at a cost of around £27,500 each met by a 90% Government loan. *Springwear* was the first launched of these four-hatch colliers of 1600 dwt on 19th May,1936 and completed during June, and the other four, *Springwood, Springwave, Springtide* and *Springdale* followed over the next year.

There were seven more tramps completed by the yard between 1936 and the end of 1938, when the yard closed again due to lack of orders. *Stamatios G. Embiricos* 3941/36 was built for the Embiricos family of Greece, the motor vessel *Corinda* 3376/37 for the Australian United Steam Navigation Co. Ltd, and the 'Arcform' design *Anglo-Indian* 5609/38, last ship built for the Nitrate Producers Steamship Co. Ltd. The first of three Maierform design tramps of 8120 dwt for Chapman of Newcastle, *Generton* 4781/36, for which a half knot speed advantage over traditional designs was claimed, although her sharply raked stem would also have come in useful in cutting through the Spring ice in the St. Lawrence as she made her way up the estuary to load her first grain cargo of the season. London Greek owner Rethymnis & Kulukundis ordered three motor tramps of 9500 dwt, and completed in 1938 as *Elias G. Kulukundis, Helene Kulukundis* and *Master Elias Kulukundis*.

The remaining two Maierform hull tramps for Chapmans of Newcastle were built when the yard opened again in the summer of 1939, *Hermiston* and *Scorton*. Output during World War II was 28 tramps and two small motor tankers for Far East service and a tank landing craft for the Admiralty. The Goverment ordered 24 of the tramps, most of which were built to Shorts own prototype, but towards the end of 1944 partially-prefabricated 'C' types were delivered. Two were completed for the Admiralty as the hull repair ship *Dullisk Cove* and the aircraft engine repair ship *Solway Firth*. The four tramps built to private order were *Barnby* 4813/40, *Hazelside*

The 'Arcform' hull designed ANGLO INDIAN of 1938 (above); and the Newcastle tramp RIPLEY
of 1953 (below).

5297/40, and the motor tramps *Hindustan* 5245/40 and *Newbrough* 5255/40 for Common Brothers of Newcastle. There were three berths and a workforce of around 900 workers at the end of the war.

In 1946 the management of the family yard was in the hands of Chairman John H. Short, and he was joined on the Board that year by the great-grandson of the founder, H.S. Short. The yard had only completed seven tankers in its history of nearly one hundred years when an order was taken from O. Wallenius of Sweden for a steam tanker of 10,000 dwt for delivery in April,1950, completed as *Soya-Christina*. A flood of orders for steam and motor replacement tramps for overseas owners was received in 1946, with British, Norwegian, Swedish, Danish, Dutch and Greek tramp owners then ordering more ships for delivery throughout the 1950s up to 1960. The Greek *Stamos* was typical of these ships, being a shelterdecker of 11840 tons dwt on a mean summer draft of 28.5 feet. She had five holds, three in front of the bridge and engine room and two aft, with a deep tank suitable for water ballast in nos. 3 and 5 holds. Her 7-cylinder B & W oil engine burnt heavy oil and developed 5000 bhp at 110 rpm and was built at Greenock by Kincaid to give the tramp a service speed of 13.5 knots. She was followed by some of the last ships built by the yard:-

STAMOS	8789/56	Fafalios,Greece
RODSLEY	8357/56	Stephens,Sutton Ltd,Newcastle
DORINGTON COURT	6223/57	Court Line,London
ATNA	6055/56	D/S A/S Sverre,Norway
LYNTON	6140/57	Chapman & Willan,Newcastle
SCORTON	6150/57	"
GRAINTON	6149/58	"
CLARKAVON	6860/58	H. Clarkson,London
CLARKEDEN	6860/58	"
NICETO DE LARRINAGA	6778/59	Larrinaga S.S. Co. Ltd,Liverpool
AMBERTON	6073/59	Chapman & Willan,Newcastle
NORTON	6073/59	"
CLEARTON	6073/60	"
BRIGHTON	6073/60	"

Clarkavon and *Clarkeden* were Port Talbot type ore-carriers of 9200 dwt completed for charter to the British Iron & Steel Corporation, and managed by Denholm of Glasgow. The three years from 1961 to the end of 1963 were the last years of production at the yard. Three cargo ships of 14800 dwt were then completed, two for D/S A/S Sverre of Norway, *Aramis* 9869/62 and *Arna* 9383/63, with *Radley* 9746/63 for Stephens,Sutton Ltd of Newcastle. The larger six-hold engines-aft cargo ship *Virana* of 18700 dwt was completed in 1961, and then two bulk carriers, *World Explorer* of 21900 dwt for Niarchos of Greece and *Carlton* of 20500 dwt for Chapman & Willan Ltd,Newcastle. The latter was of a type called a Universal Bulk Ship designed by the hatch cover manufacturers Macgregor, her principal difference being the provision of four upper holds at the junctions of the five main holds and having separate hatches and further divided longitudinally into three compartments. A total of seventeen cargo spaces made the bulker eminently suitable for parcels of grain cargoes especially from the Plate. Shorts launched their ships stern-first up the Wear, and *Carlton* was the last such launch on 17th October,1963.

Unfortunately the Short family were unwilling to undertake the necessary expenditure to extend the berths of the yard to build bigger bulk carriers, and it closed with the loss of 300 jobs in January,1964 on the completion of *Carlton*. The yard was subsequently demolished, but the fitting-out quay was purchased by Bartram & Sons Ltd later in 1964 and was in use for fitting-out work until the 1980s.

The Chapman tramp SCORTON of 1957 at anchor.

W. PICKERSGILL & SONS LTD.   1838 - 1958 132
AUSTIN & PICKERSGILL LTD.   1958 - 1986 224

William Pickersgill began shipbuilding in 1838 in the North Dock area of Sunderland in partnership with Miller, but transferred up-river to Southwick in 1851. The partnership was dissolved soon afterwards and the business became exclusively a family affair.   Barques,brigs and snows of around 400 grt were the main products, with one of these having an interesting launch when she demolished the outer wall of a riverside house on the other side of the river.   The last of 46 wooden ships, *Coppename*, was launched in 1880 and construction was immediately started on the first iron ship, *Camargo*. However during the building of the second iron ship, *Stuart*, William Pickersgill was killed and his son William John then took over in 1887. The full-rigger *Margarita* was launched in July,1893, the last of her breed from Sunderland, with Pickersgill having also built the full-riggers *Andorinha* of 3400 grt, and *Margarita, Chepica, Inca, Charla, Samanco, Mowhan* and *Drumalis* of 3000 grt.

The slipways of the three berths at the Southwick yard were lengthened with the passage of time to take the main products of the yard - tramps, cargo-liners and colliers. The Queen Alexandra bridge was built next to the yard in 1909 and ships were launched directly under the bridge. Main customers of the yard up to World War I included James Chambers of Liverpool and his Lancashire Shipping Co. Ltd which took eleven ships starting with the sailing ship *Naworth Castle* 1895/92 and ending with *Skipton Castle* 3823/07. Saint Line also of Liverpool took seven ships e.g. *Saint Bede* 3575/99; Morel of Cardiff with five tramps e.g. *Lyndhurst* 2025/88; Rowland & Marwood of Whitby with *Kildale* 3830/06 and *Erlesburgh* 3809/11; Strick Line with *Arabistan* 2891/01; and Stag Line of North Shields with *Photinia* 4584/13.

William J. Pickersgill incorporated the yard as William Pickersgill & Sons Ltd in 1907, but the lack of orders following the slump in freight rates up to 1910 forced the yard into building colliers e.g. *West Quarter* 1548/10 for J. Ridley,Son & Tully of Newcastle.   Output during the Great War was a dozen ships of 54,715 grt and included *Beemah* 4750/15 and *Sneaton* 3470/16 for Headlam & Rowland of Whitby as well as five standard *WAR* 'A' and 'B' types of tramp, and in addition a number of small naval vessels.   Two cargo-liners were completed for Prince Line as *Persian Prince* 5685/18 and *Arabian Prince* 5764/19, with three more built by the yard also going to Furness companies, *Maplemore* 4330/16, *Cottesmore* 4240/17 and *Linmore* 4274/17 for the Johnston Line Ltd,Liverpool. The post-war boom in freight rates in 1919/20 was followed by an equally dramatic slump in 1920/21 with shipowners frantically cancelling all shipyard orders. Pickersgill and five other

The Newcastle 'corrugated' tramp NEWTON BEECH of 1925 (above); and CAIRNESK of 1926 (below) of Cairn Line of Steamships Ltd, Newcastle pictured loading at her home port.

Sunderland yards consequently had no launches at all in 1923, with only a slow upturn from 1924 with the following tramps:-

THISTLEBEN	4589/24	Albyn Line,Sunderland	79
THISTLEROS	4615/25	"	
KILDALE	3877/24	Headlam & Rowland,Whitby	199
LARPOOL	3872/24	"	
SANDSEND	3612/25	"	
NEWTON ASH	4619/25	Tyneside Line Ltd,Newcastle	207
NEWTON BEECH	4644/25	"	
CAIRNESK	5007/26	Cairn Line,Newcastle	194
CAIRNGLEN	5019/26	"	
WINKLEIGH	5055/27	W.J. Tatem,Cardiff	58
FILLEIGH	4856/28	"	
SHEAF HOLME	4811/29	W.A. Souter,Newcastle	208
UFFINGTON COURT	4976/29	Court Line,London	26
WELLINGTON COURT	4979/30	"	
ALDINGTON COURT	4891/29	"	

Most of the above had triple expansion steam engines, however the Cairn Line pair were fitted with three Parsons turbines double reduction geared to a single screw shaft, and *Aldington Court* and *Sheaf Holme* had Doxford oil engines. The yard closed down later in 1930 as the Depression began to bite with only a few men employed making mantelpieces and kitchen boilers and did not re-open until the latter part of 1935. In the next four years ten new tramps were built, with one of these, *Hylton* 5197/37, being financed with a 100% Government loan for her construction cost of £95,937 under the Scrap & Build Scheme of 1935. Her owners, the Hebburn Steamship Co. Ltd of Newcastle managed by W.A. Souter & Co. Ltd provided three old tramps for scrap, and *Hylton* started trading in January,1937 powered by an oil engine from North East Marine Eng. Co. Ltd,Newcastle. *Egton* for Headlam of Whitby was completed in April,1938 and fitted with a maierform hull with a soft-nosed bow to improve fuel economy, and her triple expansion engines were also adjusted for economy when fed with steam from two single-ended boilers and one auxiliary boiler. Tatem of Cardiff took four Pickersgill-built steam tramps at this time:- *Northleigh* 5450/37; *Chulmleigh* 5445/38; *Goodleigh* 5448/38 and *Winkleigh* 5468/40.

The first tramp launched by the yard after the outbreak of World War II was *Daydawn* on 9th December,1939 for the Claymore Shipping Co. Ltd,Cardiff. She was completed in January,1940 and sunk by U-boat ten months later in the North Atlantic. *Winkleigh* was completed next followed by eight tramps for the Stanhope Steamship Co. Ltd,London and two for Watts,Watts & Co. Ltd and eight built under Government order as standard *'Empire'* tramps. Two smaller tramps built under

Government order were completed as the Norwegian *Vindeggen* 4191/46, and *Hubert* 4251/46 for the Booth Steamship Co. Ltd,Liverpool. The defunct neighbouring Priestman yard was taken over during the war and with Admiralty assistance was laid out as the West Yard for the construction of frigates and landing craft. When peace returned William J. Pickersgill was still in control, and the East Yard soon received many orders for replacement ships over the next ten years, including:-

The launch of the Royal Mail Line BRITTANY in 1946.

HENDRIK	2269/46	Euxine Shipping Co. Ltd,London 2||
BRITANNY	6951/46	Royal Mail Line,London 3|
LORD GLANELY	5640/47	W.J. Tatem,Cardiff 58
MEMPHIS	3575/47	Moss Hutchinson Line,Liverpool 200
CHATEAU PALMER	2216/48	Worms et Cie,France
HENZEE	2372/48	Euxine Shipping Co. Ltd,London 2||
SEBAA	2226/48	G. Rastit,Marseilles
ALFA	2805/48	A. Falter,New York
NEFERTITI	2276/48	Egyptian Shpg. Co. Ltd,Alexandria
DUNSTAN	2993/48	Booth S. S. Co. Ltd,Liverpool 202
DENIS	2993/49	"
KYPROS	3499/50	Moss Hutchinson Line,Liverpool 200
ADMIRAL FRASER	2276/48	W.A. Phillips,Anderson,Australia
CAPT. LOUIS MALBERT	4259/50	Union Industrielle,France
SIDDONS	4459/52	Lamport & Holt,Liverpool 47
JERSEY DAWN	7842/53	Morel,Cardiff 209
BARON ARDROSSAN	5254/54	H. Hogarth,Glasgow 158
WELSH TRADER	5671/54	Trader Navigation,London 210

Two views of the yard from the Queen Alexandra Bridge, (above) on 10th September,1954 and
in 1957 (below) showing SUSSEX TRADER of Trader Navigation fitting-out.
(Newcastle Chronicle & Journal Ltd)

Prefabrication had not yet arrived at the Pickersgill yard in the mid-1950s, and the
five or six low capacity tower cranes arraned around each berth were used to
individually lift each plate, frame or section into their correct positions. The tower
cranes and fitting-out berth of the Short Brothers shipyard at Pallion are visible
at the upper left of both photographs.

DEERWOOD	6616/55	France Fenwick,London 212
DARTWOOD	6139/56	"
ROSSETTI	4693/56	Lamport & Holt,Liverpool 47
ANDRE MASSET	4159/56	Union Industrielle,France
STANWEAR	8108/56	Stanhope Shipping Co. Ltd 132
SUSSEX TRADER	6041/57	Trader Navigation,London 210

In addition, six colliers of 4600 dwt were delivered to the newly-created Central Electricity Generating Board in 1950/51: *Barford, Capt. J.M. Donaldson, Cliff Quay, Lord Citrine, Sir Archibald Page* and *W.J.H. Wood.* The yard also won three out of a ten-ship order for electricity colliers of 1600 dwt, completed in 1949 as *Poole Island, Poole Quay* and *Poole River.* A final electricity collier was completed in 1955 as *Sir Johnstone Wright* of 4530 dwt.

In September,1954 a merger between William Pickersgill & Sons Ltd and collier builders S.P. Austin & Son was announced as well as an ambitious reconstruction of the two berths of the West Yard at Southwick to be followed by the closure of the three berths of the East Yard. The maximum size of ship built was restricted to 450 feet and the machinery serving both yards was scattered and old-fashioned. In addition, the two yards were separated by a dominating ballast hill some 90 feet high and 600 feet long. The ballast hill material was chiefly sand and ashes and very suitable for filling in and compacting, and the main area of the yard at the head of the berths was raised by between 5 feet and 8 feet and the berths were graded to suit. This massive earth moving operation provided an additional 9.8 acres of land suitable for welding and assembly shops. In the East Yard, some 24,000 tons of material and 3,800 tons of rock were dug and removed to make the foundations of a new quay wall which was built to retain 65,000 tons of material from the ballast hill.

The new West Yard now had three realigned berths to handle ships of bigger length and beam with No. 1 Berth being 525 x 80 feet, No. 2 Berth being 575 x 84 feet, and No. 3 Berth being 525 x 83 feet; with No. 1 berth being a completely new one and cut out of land occupied by the ballast hill. The penultimate ship from the old East Yard was the ore-carrier *Naess Trader* 6853/57 for Norwegian shipowner Erling D. Naess and managed by J. & J. Denholm of Glasgow. The last ship from the East Yard was launched on 5th February,1958 as the ore-carrier *Needles* for the Clyde Shipping Co. Ltd,Glasgow, and the first ship launched from the new West Yard was *Essex Trader* for Trader Navigation in April,1958. The construction of the new fitting-out quay in the old East Yard then started and was completed during 1960. The total cost of the improvements to the yard was in excess of £2.5M and the new West Yard could build ships on a system of pre-welded units of 30 tons up to almost 30,000 dwt.

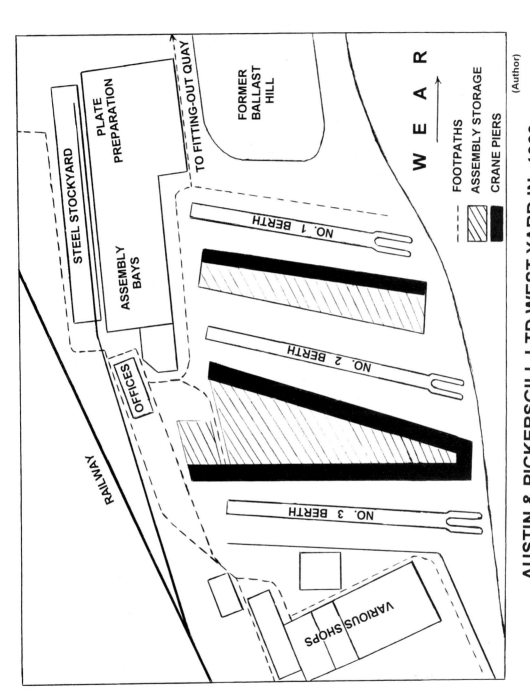

AUSTIN & PICKERSGILL LTD. WEST YARD IN 1960

FOOTPATHS
ASSEMBLY STORAGE
CRANE PIERS

W E A R

(Author)

General view of the Austin & Pickersgill Ltd yard in the early 1960s with a hull almost complete on No. 2 berth (above); and GLANELY of 1960 (below) for Tatem of Cardiff. (Skyfotos Ltd)

Under Managing Director Kenneth Douglas the new equipment dramatically reduced building times, with tramps *Baron Pentland* 8067/59 and *Baron Maclay* 5444/59 and *Baron Wemyss* 7746/60 for Hogarth being completed in 26 weeks instead of nearly 50 weeks for their sister of five years earlier. Two ore-carriers of 18,500 dwt for the Bamburgh Shipping Co. Ltd,Newcastle *Longstone* 13062/60 and *Cheviot* 13082/61 were completed in 22 weeks; while two ore-carriers of 16,000 dwt for charter to BISCO were completed in 28 weeks as *Iron Ore* 10950/59 and *Iron Barque* 10950/60. The Port Talbot class ore-carrier *Ravensworth* 6805/60 was completed in 25 weeks for R.S. Dalgleish Ltd,Newcastle, while the sugar carrier *Booker Venture* 9516/61 was completed in 21 weeks for Booker Line,Liverpool. The tramp *Torr Head* 7956/61 was completed in 24 weeks for Head Line,Belfast, while the ore-carrier *Finnamore Meadow* 13057/61 was completed in only 20 weeks for Greek shipowner Basil Mavroleon.

In 1957 the yard was acquired by a consortium led by London & Overseas Freighters Ltd, a London Greek shipping company headed by Basil Mavroleon, in association with another London shipowner Lambert Brothers Ltd, and merchant banker Philip Hill,Higginson Ltd. Later in 1970, London & Overseas Freighters Ltd took full control of the yard and some 26 ships were to be ordered by companies associated with Basil Mavroleon. The largest ore-carriers built by the yard were two of 28300 dwt completed for the British flag in 1963 - *Victore* 19543/63 and *Welsh Herald* 19547/63 - the latter being the first British ship to be fitted with comprehensive automatic alarm scanning and data logging systems. A feature of the 1960s at the yard was the building of varying sizes of bulkers up to 30,000 dwt, with the B25 size eventually being chosen as the more marketable ship :-

BRIDGEPOOL	B16	Ropner,West Hartlepool
TAMWORTH	B16	R.S. Dalgleish, Newcastle
SCOTTISH TRADER	B16	Trader Navigation,London
MIDDLESEX TRADER	B22	"
SURREY TRADER	B22	"
ESSEX TRADER	B23	"
IXIA	B26	Stag Line,North Shields
WEARFIELD	B30	Hunting & Son,Newcastle
BARON INVERFORTH	B30	Hogarth,Glasgow
MARGARITA CHANDRIS	B30	Chandris,Greece
MARI CHANDRIS	B30	"
ALESSANDRA	B25	Mavroleon,London
LAWRENTIAN	B25	Continental(London) Ltd
COUNTY CLARE	B25	Rethymnis & Kulukundis,London
HELENE	B25	"

An unusual method of building larger bulkers was tried with two of 53800 dwt completed in 1966/67 - they were built in two halves and later joined together in dry-dock to form *Sygna* 30503/66 and *Happy Dragon* 30815/67. The order book for the years 1963/65 had been slim and had been made worse by the cancellation of further options e.g. a third B30 for Chandris, and it was decided to attack an even larger market from 1965 in replacements for the twenty-year old 'Liberties' built during WWII in the U.S.A. A draft design for a five-hold shelterdecker of 14,000 dwt costing £900,000 was prepared in 1966, and orders were taken for five of these 'SD14's for Greek shipowners with deliveries starting in March,1968. However the design was deepened by six inches before the first from the Southwick yard, *Nicola* 8868/68, was completed to give a deadweight of 15,000 tons. This design was to prove a great world-wide success resulting in 211 of the type being built in modified 'Series II' to 'Series IV' production from the Southwick yard and six licencees. The total production of the design between 1968 and 1987 can be summarised by totals from the various participating yards:-

Austin & Pickersgill Ltd,Southwick	72	between	**1968 - 1983**
Austin & Pickersgill Ltd,South Dock	54	between	**1968 - 1978**
Hellenic Shipbuilders,Skaramanga,Greece	27	between	**1968 - 1972**
CCN - Maua, Rio de Janeiro	43	between	**1972 - 1982**
Robb - Caledon Shipbuilders Ltd,Dundee	3	between	**1976 - 1978**
AFNE, Ensenada,Argentina	6	between	**1977 - 1980**
Smiths Dock Co. Ltd,Middlesbrough	6	between	**1982 - 1987**
TOTAL	**211**		

however two from the Brazilian yard, Companhia Comercio e Navegacao, were launched in 1982 and laid-up for six years before completion in 1988. The choice of main engine for the basic design fell on the well-tried and proven Sulzer slow-speed diesel engine manufactured at Winterthur in Switzerland and by licencees throughout the world. This was considered preferable for a number of reasons to the medium-speed geared Pielstick engine fitted to the Japanese competitor, the *Freedom* design built by Ishikawajima- Harima Heavy Industries (IHI), of which 200 examples were built. The Sunderland and Greek-built SD14s were all powered by Sulzers, 153 in total, to give a service speed of 14 knots, except for six Greek-built liner types for Hellenic Lines, which had German M.A.N. diesels. The Brazilian-built ships all had M.A.N. diesels, and the Argentinean shipowner Empresa Lineas Maritimas Arentineas (ELMA) specified Doxford oil engines built at Sunderland for their nine ships built at Dundee and Ensenada in Argentina.

The initial great success of the SD14 was due in major part to Greek shipowners and the connection with Greek and London Greek shipowners provided by Chairman Basil Mavroleon. The subsequent international success of the design can be shown by an analysis of the flags of registration on completion:- Greek (62), British (41), Brazilian (34), Liberian (16), Singapore (10), Argentina (9), Germany (7), Panama (7), Cyprus (4), Dutch (4), Cuba (4), Vietnam (3), France (2), Mauritius (2), Chile (2), Norway (1) and Pakistan (1). As for British-flag shipowners, P & O ordered the most with six ships, followed by London & Overseas Freighters Ltd with four, Worldwide Shipping with four, Lamport & Holt Ltd with four, Jardine Matheson with four, Larrinaga S.S. Co. Ltd with three, Metcalfe Shipping Co. Ltd with three, Welsh Overseas Freighters Ltd (in which yard had a small shareholding) with three ships, Australind S.S. Co. Ltd with three ships, and John Swire & Sons Ltd with two ships.

The majority of the world-beating SD14 programme had been launched under Chairman and Managing Director Derek Kimber, and it was fitting that the last one should also be launched from the Southwick yard, *Sunderland Venture,* on 17th November,1983 while he was still in control. He had also seen some 21 standard bulk carriers in three sizes of B26, B30 and B35 completed since 1975 or under construction :-

CAIRNSMORE	B26	Jardine Shipping Ltd
ANNA M	B26	Interocean Navigation
LEON	B26	Leon Corporation
CAMILLA M	B26	Star Seas Transports
RIGHTEOUS	B26	Righteous Navigation
UPWEY GRANGE	B26	Houlder Bros.
LYNTON GRANGE	B26	"
WELSH VOYAGER	B26	Welsh Overseas Freighters Ltd
LONDON BARON	B26	London & Overseas Freighters Ltd
LONDON EARL	B26	"
LONDON BARON	B26	"
LONDON VISCOUNT	B26	"
EL CHALLENGER	B26	El Challenger S.A.
INGENIOUS	B26	Ingenious Navigation
CARRIANNA PEONY	B26	Carrianna Corporation
CARRIANNA PRIMROSE	B26	"
FAYROUZ 1	B30	Fereniki Lines,Greece
FAYROUZ 2	B30	"
FAYROUZ 3	B30	"
FAYROUZ 4	B30	"
CAIRNSMORE	B35	Jardine Shipping Ltd
POMORAC	B35	Jugoslavenska Oceanska Plovidba

B26 bulk carrier UPWEY GRANGE of 1976 on trials. (Houlder Bros.)

The switch to building bulkers in 1975 had conincided with the start of an ambitious reconstruction and expansion scheme at Southwick costing £27M, of which £9M was provided by the British Government and the remainder by owners London & Overseas Freighters Ltd. Phase One of the scheme called for the construction of a partially enclosed building berth with adjacent stern section and block assembly hall to launch ships down-river, while Phase Two called for identical facilities for launching ships up-river (See Shipyard Plan). In the event Phase Two was never built due to lack of construction capital and orders, but the Phase One work started on 3rd December,1975 and was completed to allow the keel of the first 'Series IV' SD14 to be laid in the summer of 1977 and she was launched unnamed on 10th November,1977 and later completed during 1978 as *Empros* for Greek shipowner Dracopoulos. Production of SD14s was then much speeded up for the new facilities allowed for a completed stern section to be slid across to the main building berth for construction of the forward half and subsequent launching. A total of six 60-ton overhead travelling cranes served the Phase One facility, and in addition, the existing steel shops were expanded to more than double their former size, and access roads were improved. The yard was now one of the most modern in Europe and comparable to the new Pallion facilities on the other side of the river, both allowing production line assembly of two ships simultaneously.

ENLARGED SOUTHWICK YARD

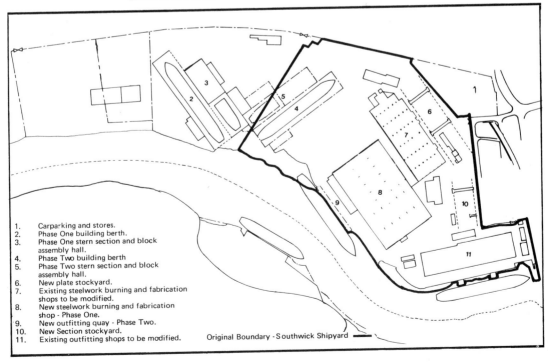

1. Carparking and stores.
2. Phase One building berth.
3. Phase One stern section and block assembly hall.
4. Phase Two building berth
5. Phase Two stern section and block assembly hall.
6. New plate stockyard.
7. Existing steelwork burning and fabrication shops to be modified.
8. New steelwork burning and fabrication shop - Phase One.
9. New outfitting quay - Phase Two.
10. New Section stockyard.
11. Existing outfitting shops to be modified.

Original Boundary - Southwick Shipyard ▬▬

New block assembly hall under construction in 1976

Some thirty Series IV 'SD14's and five bulkers had been built in the new Assembly Hall and the two outside berths then in use between 1978 and early 1983. Another standard design made an appearance in 1981 when three of the 'SD18' design were completed for the Pakistan National Shipping Corporation. *Murree,Kaghan* and *Ayubia* had three masts fitted with sets of Vele swinging derricks for handling containers, and other features were a swimming pool located on the aft side of the superstructure block, and Sulzer diesels capable of a service speed of 15 knots. The only other variation from the successful 'SD14' built by the yard had been a single 'SD15' *Armadale* 10325/70 completed for the Australind Steam Shipping Co. Ltd more than ten years earlier.

The launch of the first of a quartet of B30 bulkers for Fereniki Lines on 2nd February,1983 as *Fayrouz 1*, named after the grand-daughter of the owner, marked the start of the yard's problems. The other three were launched later in 1983, however after entry into service of the first the owner alleged extensive welding cracks to the main structure and refused to take delivery of the remaining three. Extensive and expensive repairs were necessary at the fitting-out quay to the welding defects, and the last of the quartet was not handed over until August,1984 with the finance package to the owner being restructured.

A new Managing Director was appointed from the start of 1984 in George Parker, and the next two ships launched from the Assembly Hall were two general purpose cargo-ships of 10500 dwt for Ethiopian National Line, *Abbay Wonz* 11292/84 and *Abyot* 10851/85. The last of the B35 bulkers, whose construction had been frozen in the stern section of the Assembly Hall for some time, was launched

Launch of 'SD14' FUTURE HOPE on 9th August,1979 for German owner Egon Oldendorff from the new block assembly hall (above); and a view of the fitting-out quay at the end of 1979 with the German-owned GLOBE TRADER and the British-owned BELLOC. (Author).

unnamed and without a buyer on 21st February,1985. However she was sold in May,1985 to Yugoslavenska Oceanska Plovidba and named *Pomorac*. The yard then tackled unsophisticated but steelwork-intensive flat-topped barges for the North Sea oilfields, and five were built for North Venture Shipping, Smit Internationale B.V. of Holland, and J.P. Knight of Rochester, and the last large barge for Knight involved widening the outside berth of the yard. The first of two bulker/container ships of 22500 dwt was launched for Egon Oldendorff of Lubeck on 26th March,1986, and she was commissioned and named *Dietrich Oldendorff* on 3rd November,1986, when her sister *Johanna Oldendorff* 15988/87 was also put into the water.

The yard became the Southwick yard of North East Shipbuilders Ltd on 1st April,1986, and shortly afterwards began construction of what proved to be its last type of ship - several red-painted Danish ferries to an unusual design without engine-room and powered by replacement generator units in yellow containers on deck. The Mark IV version of these *Superflex* ferries was constructed at Southwick, and the Mark III version at the Pallion yard of N.E.S.L. The last of the Mark IV version was launched at Southwick in December,1988 after the closure announcement was made by the British Government for political reasons of North East Shipbuilders Ltd on 7th December,1988. The yard including the most modern Assembly Hall in Europe was demolished in 1990 and the site levelled shortly afterwards for redevelopment.

Unsold Superflex ferries alongside Manor Quay with the Thompson shipyard in the background. (Author).

BARTRAM & SONS LTD [07

George Bartram founded a shipyard at Hylton in 1838 in partnership with John Lister. Bartram had been orphaned , and at the age of 11 years had started his apprenticeship in 1811 with Gales of Sunderland. He then went to sea as a ship's carpenter, but returned to the Wear and became manager for shipbuilder Dryden and then Reay at Biddick Ford and Hylton. The keel of the first ship was laid on 14th January,1838 and she was launched as *Crown* on 7th July,1838 for William Thompson, baker of Monkwearmouth. The second ship was *City of Rochester* for Benjamin Grainger of Whitby, and the yard went on to build 40 barques, schooners, snows,brigs and brigantines with the largest being *John and Mary* of over 100 feet in length and 400 gross tons before the partnership with Lister was dissolved in 1854. Bartram then continued in business with his son Robert Appleby Bartram, born 1835, until they transferred to a new yard at the South Docks facing the sea in 1871.

George Bartram retired at this point, and Robert A. Bartram formed a partnership with George Haswell under the style Bartram,Haswell & Company. The Haswells had also previously built ships at Hylton, and George Haswell had previously been with Sunderland shipbuilder William Pile for a number of years. The new yard went straight into iron shipbuilding, and launched their first ship, *Ardmore* for Hine Brothers, on 6th June,1872, and other early iron steamers were *Stag* 1558/74 for Stag Line of North Shields, and *Joseph Ferens* 1970/80 for Hunting & Pattinson of Newcastle, and the two-decked *Clan Monroe* 2158/81 and *Clan Mackay* 2171/82 for the newly-formed Clan Line of Charles Cayzer. However the sailing ship era was by no means over, and the yard built some very fine barques and full-rigged ships for Hine Brothers of Maryport for Australian trading. The last four-masted barque built was *Mercia* of 751 tons and she sailed away in 1876.

John Haswell retired in 1890 and the two sons of Robert A. Bartram - George and William - joined the partnership as Bartram & Sons, which became a limited liability company in 1922. Robert A. Bartram was later knighted in 1921 and lived to survive both of his sons until his death in 1925 at the age of 90 years. The management of the yard then passed to his grandsons, Robert A. Bartram and George H. Bartram, with the former as Colonel R.A. Bartram remaining in charge until the yard passed out of family hands in 1968 when taken over by Austin & Pickersgill Ltd. Colonel R.A. Bartram retired in 1971 and was the last of the Sunderland family shipbuilders at his death in 1981, having joined the yard as an apprentice in 1911.

The family yard was unusual as ships were launched straight into the North Sea at the old south entrance to the South Docks. Customers were well satisfied however with the yard products, with many shipowners placing repeat orders e.g. Ben Line of Leith had ten clipper-bowed cargo-liners built between 1902 and 1914; and Thomas Dunlop of Glasgow had seven tramps built for his Queen Line between 1891 and 1897; and John Mathias of Cardiff had a similar number of tramps built between 1911 and 1914 for his Cambrian Steam Navigation Co. Ltd. Six tramps were built to the order of George Pyman of Hartlepool between 1900 and 1905, and other customers included the local F. W. Ritson and his Nautilus Steam Shipping Co. Ltd; Crawford Brothers of Grangemouth; McFarlane & Lander of Cardiff; Watts,Watts of London; J. & C. Harrison of London; John Angel Gibbs of Cardiff; William J. Tatem of Cardiff; Stephens & Mawson of Newcastle, and Frederick Bolton of London.

The yard output at the turn of the century was 18,530 grt of ships, and during the four years of World War I some 12 ships of 41,658 grt were built, mostly to private order e.g. *Hindustan* 4990/17 for Common Brothers of Newcastle, and two small craft for the Admiralty. Ten standard *'WAR'* 'B' tramps were built with the last completing as *Stonewall* 5073/20. After the post-WWI boom had passed the yard continued building steam tramps as well as one tanker, *Malistan* 5553/24 and 8387 dwt for Common Brothers of Newcastle, with steam engines aft and divided longitudinally on the centre line into eight port and eight starboard tanks each of 27 feet in length. There were also small summer tanks in the top corner of each tank to give the extra carrying capacity to load down to summer marks. The deck crew lived in the foc's'tle with the engineers aft and the master and mate in the 'midships bridge accomodation. Some typical examples of steam tramps built during the 1920s were :-

RAMSAY	5053/21	Bolton Steam Shipping Co. Ltd *267*
BUCKLEIGH	5074/25	William J. Tatem,Cardiff *58*
CHULMLEIGH	5076/25	"
PETERSTON	4680/25	Evan Thomas Radcliffe,Cardiff *70*
FLIMSTON	4680/25	"
LLANDILO	4966/28	"
LLANFAIR	4966/28	"
LLANWERN	4966/28	"
LLANOVER	4959/28	"
LLANARTH	5053/29	"
LLANISHEN /	5053/29	"
BADJESTAN	5573/28	Common Brothers,Newcastle *67*
PUKKASTAN	5809/29	"
RAJAHSTAN	6391/29	"

HARPATHIAN	4708/30	J. & C. Harrison,London	268
HARPENDEN	4678/30	"	
SOUTH WALES	5619/29	Gibbs & Co.,Cardiff	235

However the onset of the Depression soon saw the yard run out of orders in 1930 and most men were idle for six years. The yard laid down a ship 'on speculation', the only ship built between 1930 and 1936, and incorporated all the latest advances in economical design e.g. superheated steam engine, streamlined rudder and fins. Her construction was slow as only a small number of men were employed building her, but she was finally completed as *Eskdene* in October,1934 of 6640 dwt for the Dene Shipmanagement Co. Ltd headed by Walter S. Hinde. However a few of the boilermakers and fitters were kept on breaking up several submarines, and a few of the out-fitting trades built caravans for motorists. When the upturn in trade came in 1935 Evan Thomas Radcliffe of Cardiff ordered two tramps of 700 dwt at a cost of £80,000 each, which were completed as *Llanashe* in November,1936 and *Llandaff* in May,1937. The yard gained four orders from the Scrap & Build Scheme of 1935, all from Evans & Reid of Cardiff for delivery at the end of 1936 and throughout 1937 at a total cost of £300,000. They were given triple expansion steam engines boosted by a low pressure exhaust turbine, and the first to be launched was *Nailsea Court* on 9th June,1936. She sailed from Sunderland on 17th August,1936 under the command of Capt. P. Brooks on charter to the Kawasaki Steamship Co. Ltd of Japan, and was followed to the Pacific by *Nailsea Meadow* in February,1937 under the command of Capt. W. Cheeseman for the same charterer. Their sisters, *Nailsea Moor* and *Nailsea Manor* left Sunderland with coal on their maiden voyages on 24th September,1937 and 5th January,1938 respectively.

Some eleven tramps were completed between 1936 and the outbreak of war in September,1939, although the yard was closed down briefly at the beginning of 1939 due to shortage of orders. World War II production, however, was huge at 24 ships with two tramps for J. & C. Harrison Ltd of London and two for Counties Ship Management Co. Ltd, headed by London Greeks Rethymnis & Kulukundis. Nine were built to Government account to a standard Bartram design, with *Jersey City* 6686/42 for Reardon Smith of Cardiff also being to this design. Five to the *Empire* 'B' design were then built, followed by four to the 'C' type design plus one hull completed as a repair ship for naval service in the Far East. Their best year was 1943 when five tramps were launched, and they also carried out conversion work on four ships to fit them for the Russian convoys. A new berth was built to cope with the orders and a new platers shed and welding shed, and new 15-ton electric travelling jib cranes were installed. The yard could also boast to having the first woman welder to be admitted to the boilermaker's union, Mrs. Collard, who worked until the end of the war.

Peace brought a flood of orders from British and foreign shipowners for replacement ships lost during the war. The Portuguese company Sociedade Geral de Comercio Industria & Transportes placed orders for seven ships completed in 1948/49:- *Aquitaine, Alcobaca, Almerim, Ambrizete, Andulo, Arraiolos* and *Alenquer* all of 5500 grt; with *Rovuma* and *Mocamedes* also being built for this flag for Nacional de Navegacao, who also took delivery of the cargo-liners *India* and *Timor* with accomodation for 96 passengers in 1950/51. The Argentinean Government ordered a number of tramps from Wear yards with *Rio Tercero* and *Rio Chico* coming from Bartrams. The Norwegian shipowner Fearnley & Eger took delivery of *Fernland*, and Swedish shipowner Wallenius of *Boheme* and *Tosca* in 1953. Maersk Line of Denmark took *Lexa Maersk* and *Hulda Maersk* in 1950, and Van Ommeren took *Kieldrecht* in 1950, with *Tjibantjet* in 1952 for Java-China Packet Line N.V. for the Dutch flag. Two Polish tankers were built in 1952 , *Beskidy* and *Tatry*, and Greek shipowners took delivery of the tramps *George Lyras, Anna, Ayia Markella, Despina C, Theomanna Odigitria, Costis, Maria C, Ermis* and *Ermoupolis* up to 1958.

Aerial view of the Bartram yard and its three berths with South Dock at top.

Two five-hold motortramps of 1953/54, the Newcastle-owned NORTH CORNWALL (above) and the London-owned LA CHACRA (below)   (A. Duncan)

In 1952 the area of the yard was increased by one-fifth, and one berth was extended by 30 feet with a suitable extension to the crane rails to take larger ships. The yard was the first in the field with a number of innovations, notably x-ray examination of welding, optical lofting procedures, shot-blasting of all steel, and the use of paint primer. British liner shipowners began to need cargo-liners to new designs, and the Vestey Group placed orders for eight cargo-liners in the 1950s and 1960s for Blue Star Line and Lamport & Holt Ltd; with P & O following with orders for four twenty-knot cargo-liners fitted with Hallen cargo gear for their subsidiary, New Zealand Shipping Co. Ltd:-

RAPHAEL	7971/53	Lamport & Holt Ltd 47
RONSARD	7840/57	"
CANTERBURY STAR	7539/60	Blue Star Line 5
MONTREAL STAR	7483/62	"
AMERICA STAR	7899/63	"
HALIFAX STAR	7879/64	"
NEW YORK STAR	7887/65	"
TIMARU STAR	8366/67	"
AUSTRALIND	8451/61	Australind S.S. Co. Ltd 87
TURAKINA	7707/60	New Zealand Shipping Co. Ltd 6
TAUPO	8219/66	"
TEKOA	8226/66	"
TONGARIRO 4	8233/67	"

These sophisticated reefer ships had automated machinery, and/or bridge control of the main engine with full data logging of propulsion and auxiliary machinery and cargo refrigerating machinery. British tramp owners placed many orders with the yard e.g.

LA CHACRA 1	6072/53	Buries Markes Ltd,London 247
LA FALDA	8525/58	"
LA MAREA	10112/58	"
LA LOMA	10251/59	"
LA LAGUNA	9306/60	"
SILVERPOINT	8833/57	Silver Line Ltd,London 181
SILVERBECK	9542/60	"
HANNINGTON COURT 2	6266/54	Court Line Ltd,London 26
JEVINGTON COURT	6248/56	"
ARLINGTON COURT	9571/62	"
FILLEIGH 2	5668/57	Tatem S.N. Co. Ltd,Cardiff 45 56
LANDWADE	7856/61	"
RUNSWICK	8482/56	Headlam & Son,Whitby 199
EGTON	9958/62	"
NORTH CORNWALL 2	5570/54	North Shpg. Co. Ltd,Newcastle 174
NORTH DEVON 2	5770/58	"
LLANTRISANT	6140/52	Evan Thomas Radcliffe,Cardiff 70

Court Line of London and Tatem of Cardiff were good customers in the 1950s and early 1960s, pictured is HANNINGTON COURT of 1954 (above) and FILLEIGH of 1957 (below). (F.W.Hawks)

LLANTRISANT	6171/58	Evan Thomas Radcliffe,Cardiff 70
LLANWERN	9229/62	"
BRITISH MONARCH	5806/54	Monarch S.S. Co. Ltd,Glasgow 269
CELTIC MONARCH	7777/57	"
SCOTTISH MONARCH	9466/59	"
WARKWORTH	9721/62	R.S. Dalgleish Ltd,Newcastle 270
WANDBY	11545/59	Ropner Shpg. Co. Ltd,Hartlepool 29
AVISFAITH	7797/62	Aviation & Shpg. Co. Ltd,London 271
LONDONER	6951/61	Continental (London) Ltd 272
LUTETIAN	10475/67	"

Altogether a total of 85 ships were built by the yard between 1946 and 1967, or an average of four ships/year. The first to have engines and bridge moved aft was *La Marea*, launched on 3rd July,1958 on the same day that her engines amidships sister *La Falda* was delivered. Other examples of this type were *Wandby* of 17445 dwt and *Lutetian* of 16060 dwt, however the restricted slipways of the yard could not be extended to build the bigger bulk carriers of this type. The narrow width of the lock entrance to the yard's out-fitting berth in the South Dock meant that most ships in the 1950s had to be sent to the Tyne to be engined and fitted-out, involving much travelling and extra expense. After the closure of Short Brothers yard at Pallion in 1964, Bartram acquired their fitting-out quay, and from that date all new ships were towed directly after launch up-river to the Short quay.

In the wake of the Geddes Report of 1965, the yard was acquired by Austin & Pickersgill Ltd of Southwick in November,1968 and commenced building 'SD14' general cargo ships. The Southwick yard had recently completed the installation of three main engines for the Bartram yard, and this was a contributory factor in the merger. The design of the 'SD14' was similar to that of *Arlington Court* of 14400 dwt, completed for Court Line Ltd in 1962 with engines in the 'three-quarters aft' position with four holds forward of the bridge and one aft. In the event the deadweight of the 'SD14' moved up to 15,000 tons as the draft of the prototype was increased by six inches. The keel of the first 'SD14' was laid at the Bartram yard on 8th June,1967 and launched on 1st December,1967 as *Mimis N. Papalios,*nearly one month ahead of the first of the type from the Southwick Yard. However faster fitting-out at Southwick gave this yard the honour of completing the first ship, *Nicola* for Mavroleon, one day ahead of *Mimis N. Papalios* for Greek shipowner Papalios on 14th February,1968.

The second 'SD14' launched at the Bartram yard was *George N. Papalios* on 29th February,1968, and the yard went on to complete a total of 54 examples of the type until the yard was closed after the launch of *Australind* on 23rd March,1978. *Australind* was towed up-river to the fitting-out quay of the former Short Brothers yard to be completed, and she sailed from the river in July,1978 on her maiden

Silver Line had SILVERBECK completed in 1960 (above); and R.S. Dalgleish of Newcastle had WARKWORTH completed in 1962 (below). (G.R. Scott).

Two launches from Bartrams, LLANWERN in July,1962 for Cardiff owners

and VIRTUS on 27th August,1969 for Liberian owners. (Sunderland Echo).

voyage to Australia and the Pacific for the liner services of her owners, Australind Steam Shipping Co. Ltd managed by Trinder,Anderson of London. The concept of the 'SD14' had initially been that of a general purpose tramp, but in the later stages of the series production, many shipowners such as Lamport & Holt Ltd used them as cargo-liners with useful deck areas for carrying around 30 containers.

Many of the Bartram-built examples of the 'SD14' were for foreign flag shipowners e.g. Greek, French, Pakistan, Dutch, Norwegian etc., and the South Dock workforce continued building more examples after they were all moved to the Southwick Yard and integrated into the Austin & Pickersgill Ltd workforce. The yard was subsequently demolished and used as container storage areas by the Port of Sunderland.

Last ship from the Bartram yard, AUSTRALIND of 1978 for the Australind Steam Shipping Co. Ltd of London. (Author).

ROBERT THOMPSON & SONS LTD.

The Thompson family yard at North Sands has already been described in the section on Joseph L. Thompson & Sons Ltd. Robert Thompson Junior left this yard in 1854 to move to Southwick to commence business under his own name. He had in fact left his father's yard in 1850, but was persuaded to return and offered a partnership in 1853 and represented the North Sands yard on the first meetings of the Wear Shipbuilders Association. However on 8th August,1854 he purchased the patent slipway and shipbuilding yard of John Candlish at Southwick. The first wooden barque built was *Graces* of 449 tons for Thomas Coxon of North Shields, and there followed 21 wooden ships until the first composite ship was built in 1864. He built many fine composite ships and was then early into iron construction in 1868 with the launch of the full-rigged *Ireshope*. His first iron steamer was *Canadian* of 512 tons in 1870 for J. Culliford & Company, Sunderland.

Joseph L. Thompson sent two of his sons to his brother's Southwick yard to learn iron construction, and the North Sands yard commenced building in iron in 1871. The Southwick yard then turned out many iron steamers e.g. the first tramp owned by Stephens,Mawson & Kendrick of Newcastle *Rayner* 1269/74; as well as the iron steamers *Orsino* 2048/80 for the North Shipping Co. Ltd, Newcastle managed by Hugh Roberts; *Daylesford* 1403/82 for Thompson & Wrightson, Sunderland;and *Cambodia* 2929/82 for Crow,Bogart & Rudolf, Liverpool. Steel had replaced iron in both Thompson yards by 1888, and examples of steel tramps then built at Southwick were *Obi* 3046/92 for Mercantile Steamship Co. Ltd,London; *King Bleddyn* 2351/94 for King Line Ltd; *Eversley* 2871/96 for H. Scholefield & Son,Newcastle and *Lynton* 3232/99 for Liver Shipping Co. Ltd,Liverpool.

The yard became Robert Thompson & Sons in 1881 when he took two of his sons into partnership, and from the four berths launched no less than 12 ships to give the yard the third highest output on the river. In the same year the Bridge Dockyard on the north bank of the river at Monkwearmouth bridge was purchased, largely for repair work. Later this yard was used for shipbuilding but because of the narrowness of the site ships were launched broadside e.g. *Lewis* in August,1897, *Frennington* in 1899 and *Protector* in 1900. Output of both yards in 1900 was 15,260 tons of ships including *Durham* 2626/00 for local owner Viginty T. Thompson, and *Hesleyside* 2631/00 for Charlton & McAllum of Newcastle. The Southwick yard was extended and modernised in 1901, and the business incorporated as a limited liability company in 1906. The larger *Evangeline* 3344/01 for the Anglo-Grecian Steamship Co. Ltd (Mango,Doresa), London was an example of the medium-sized tramps then built up to the death of Robert Thompson in 1910.

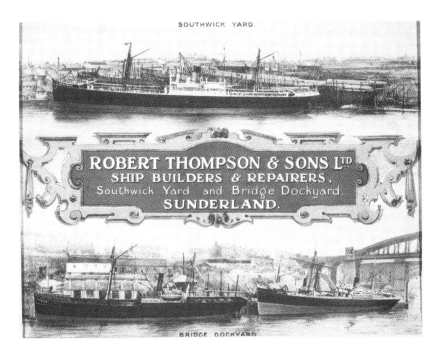

SOUTHWICK YARD.

ROBERT THOMPSON & SONS L^TD
SHIP BUILDERS & REPAIRERS,
Southwick Yard and Bridge Dockyard.
SUNDERLAND.

BRIDGE DOCKYARD

He had been very active as a Wear Commissioner for 23 years, and philanthropic to Southwick people and to Southwick local council, to whom he donated the council offices. After his death, medium-sized tramps continued to be built up to the Great War e.g.

HORNGARTH	3609/11	Turnbull Bros.,Cardiff
IOSSIFOGLU	3559/13	Socrates Iossifoglu,PIraeus
EVANGELOS	3572/13	Ambatielos Bros.,Argostoli
BERTRAND	3613/13	Turnbull Bros.,Cardiff
ELLERDALE	3720/13	T. Smailes & Sons,Whitby
KELTIER	2468/13	Antwerpsche Geevaart Maats
BIARRITZ	2452/14	Plisson & Cie,Bayonne
KONGSFOS	3197/14	Thor. Thoresen,Oslo
EGGESFORD	4414/14	W. Tatem, Cardiff

Output during World War I was ten ships of 31,702 tons and nine barges and two patrol vessels for the Admiralty. Tramps built to private order included *Rocio* 3721/15 for Orders,Handford & Co.,Newport; *Leikanger* 3544/16 for Westfal-Larsen,Bergen; *Capelcastle* 3872/17 for A. Capel & Co.,Newport; *Sunray* 3173/17 for Scarisbrick Steamship Co. Ltd,Cardiff and *Notanda* 3338/18 for the Gordon Steamship Co. Ltd,London. The Shipping Controller ordered six standard *WAR* types: three 'A' completed as *Aymeric* 5196/19 for Bank Line, *Lahore* 5201/19 for P & O, and *Barracoo* 5284/19 for Elder,Dempster; and three 'C' including *Matadi* 3096/19 for Elder,Dempster.

Some 28 tramps and colliers were then completed during the next ten years from 1920 before the yard closed down in 1930:-

RONALEE	3194/20	P. Samuel & Co.,London	273
IGNAZIO FLORIO	5386/20	J.V. Florio,Palermo	
LAHORE	5251/20	P & O, London	8
ROMULUS	3707/21	A.O. Lindvig,Oslo	
ELLASTON	3708/22	William S. Miller,Glasgow	274
EIRINI KYRIAKIDES	3780/22	N.G. Kyriakides,Piraeus	
SCORESBY	3843/22	Rowland & Headlam,Whitby	275
AKENSIDE	1894/23	Quayside Shpg. Co. Ltd,Newcastle	276
BRIAN	1063/24	J.J. Robson,Sunderland	277
GWENTLAND	1821/23	Mordey Jones,Newport	278
GOATHLAND	3821/24	Rowland & Headlam,Whitby	275
MERVYN	3401/24	Mervyn S.S. Co. Ltd,Newport	279
BEECHTREE	1552/24	Tree S.S. Co. Ltd,London	280
DAYBREAK	4113/25	Claymore Shpg. Co. Ltd,Cardiff	281
SNEATON	3677/25	Rowland & Headlam,Whitby	275
IDDESLEIGH	5205/27	Tatem S.N.,Cardiff	58
MONKLEIGH	5203/27	"	
GOODLEIGH	3845/28	Tatem S.N., Cardiff	58
GEORGE N. LIVANOS	3831/28	Stavros G. Livanos,Chios	
FAIRWATER	4108/28	Fairwater Shpg. Co. Ltd,Cardiff	282
DAYROSE	4118/28	Claymore Shpg. Co. Ltd,Cardiff	281
MONSELET	3379/29	Soc des Chargeur de l'Ouest,Nantes	
VEGO	2922/29	Boe & Pedersen,Bergen	
SANDO	2922/29	"	
DUNSLEY	3862/29	Headlam & Son,Whitby	l99
BELOS	2830/29	O. Hillerstrom,Helsingborg	
HARMATTAN	4558/30	J. & C. Harrison,London	268
HARMONIC	4558/30	"	

The yard re-opened briefly in 1931 to build two Portuguese trawlers, *Descobridor* and *Corte Real* launched in April and May,1931 of 1550 tons. Unfortunately the owners defaulted on payment just before completion, and the sister trawlers languished for a long time in the river before eventually being sold to French owners. The Bridge Dockyard continued with repair work until 1933 when the business was wound up, the Southwick yard having built 341 ships under the Thompson name. The yard was acquired by National Shipbuilders Security Ltd and demolished.

SIR JOHN PRIESTMAN & COMPANY 93

John Priestman was born at Bishop Auckland in 1855 the son of a baker. He made his first visit to Sunderland at the age of 13 years, and in his next year became apprenticed to the Blumer shipyard. He later gained a place in their drawing office, and then became Chief Draughtsman for Pickersgill, which was the last Wear yard to change to building in iron. He designed their first iron steamer at the yard in 1880, and then left in 1882 to open his own shipyard at Southwick to the west of the Pickersgill yard.

He launched his first ship, *Troutbeck* of 817 tons, in the summer of 1882, with *Acaster* and *Caerloch* following later in 1882. *Isle of Cyprus* of 1064 tons was completed in early 1883 for Dixon,Robson & Company, Newcastle with a sister completed as *Isle of Dursey* in June,1883. After building ten iron ships the yard was closed for nearly five years before the first steel ship *Gemini* of 938 tons was completed in October,1888. Early customers included Plymouth shipowners Pearse & Haswell with *Sir John Hawkins* 2693/92 and *Sir Richard Grenville* 2715/92; Sir Christopher Furness of West Hartlepool with *Antwerp City* 3229/94; and Walter Runciman of Newcastle with *Glenmoor* 3075/94; Woods,Taylor & Brown with *Rosefield* 3089/96; and Rickmers Rhederei of Hamburg with *Deike Rickmers* 3438/96; and De Freitas of Hamburg with *Karthago* 2863/96. The latter shipowner also ordered the passenger/cargo-liner *Pontos* 5703/00 but she was completed for the prestigious Hamburg-Amerika Line along with her sisters *Granada* 5125/99 and *Sevilla* 5135/00. The white-hulled Greek passenger ship *Moraitis* of 6045 grt was completed in June,1907 for the Greek emigrant trade to New York. She had two funnels and two masts, and triple expansion engines drove twin propellers to give a service speed of 13 knots.

The yard built 120 steel ships in the thirty year period up to the start of the Great War or an average of four ships/year, and is best remembered for its 'Tower-deck' self-trimming tramps of a type similar to the Doxford 'Turret' and the Ropner 'Trunk-decker'. The difference of the Priestman 'Tower' was that the plating from the top of the tower deck sloped diagonally to the side of the hull. *Enfield* of 2124 grt was the first completed in November,1897 to the order of W. Ormston of Newcastle. Two more examples were built, *Universe* 2535/98 for A/S Universe (H. Roed), Tonsberg and *Kilmaho* 2155/98, for John Cory of Cardiff, who subsequently purchased *Enfield* in 1922 after *Kilmaho* had become a war loss.

The yard produced 20,362 tons of ships in 1900 and continued to build tramps for well-known customers such as Wilhelm Wilhelmsen of Norway with *Thode Fagelund* 4352/04, and Edward Haslehurst of London with *Claverburn*

The Priestman 'Tower - deck' tramp ENFIELD of 1897 (above); and the Priestman-owned EASTLEA of 1924 (below).   (York & Solomon Collections).

4501/03 and *Claverdale* 4523/04. However the slump in freight rates after 1907 was felt in the years 1908/09 when only four ships were launched. Regular Wear customers such as Sir James Knott and his Prince Line then came forward with orders for two cargo-liners for the Brazilian trade, *Eastern Prince* and *Asiatic Prince* completed in 1910. Their design was typical of the period with four holds, two forward of the engine room and two to the rear. The bunker hold for the triple expansion engines was immediately forward of the engine and could hold 314 tons of coal. The two masts had ample cargo derricks and could each carry two trysails. This pair were two of twenty ships completed in the years leading up to the Great War with tramps *Haworth* 4456/12 and *Wentworth* 3828/13 for R.S. Dalgleish of Newcastle, and *Hannington Court* 5166/12 for Court Line of London and others for Greek owners.

The yard output during World War I was 15 ships of 67,255 tons, and two were completed for companies controlled by Furness,Withy & Co. Ltd: *Malvern Range* 4524/15 for the Neptune Steam Navigation Co. Ltd and *Modesta* 3832/17 for Gulf Line Ltd. Two tramps were completed for the Maindy Shipping Co. Ltd,Cardiff, *Maindy Court* 3792/17 and *Maindy Manor* 3791/17, and another Cardiff owner Jones & Company with *Uskmouth* 2320/16. *Cliffside* 3726/17 was built to the order of the shipbuilder for his Cliffside Shipping Co. Ltd, and the Government ordered one *WAR* 'A' standard type and five 'C' types, although three of the latter were not completed until 1919 and another was completed in 1920 as *Muristan* 3204/20 for Frank C. Strick.

The post-WWI boom in freight rates in 1919 soon led to an equally dramatic slump in 1920/21, with one Norwegian owner H.J. Hansen having to sell *Stornes* 4265/21 back to the yard shortly after completion. She was then traded by Sir John Priestman, who had been knighted in 1921, and was managed for him by John Morrison & Son of North Shields. In the 1920s with orders scarce, Sir John then built a dozen big tramps as a speculation for management by Morrison. Sir John was a shrewd investor and the shipyard profits were used to purchase shares in South African gold mines, which made him a vast fortune out of which he was able to fund the 'on-spec' tramps. One was named after his only daughter, *Barbara Marie* 4223/28 and the others were:- *Nestlea* 4274/21, *Barbara* 4290/23, *Eastlea* 4267/24, *Westlea* 4218/24, *Fernlea* 4212/25, *Cheldale* 4218/25, *Holmelea* 4223/28, *Farndale* 4222/28, *Ashlea* 4222/29, *Thornlea* 4261/29 and *Glenlea* 4252/30.

The Priestman tramps were traded with soft timber from Swedish Baltic ports to South Africa, then homewards via West Africa with palm kernels, groundnuts and logs on charter to the United Africa Co. Ltd (later Palm Line Ltd), as well as world-

Two Priestman-owned and built tramps, CHELDALE of 1925 (above) and BARBARA MARIE of 1928 (below), the latter named after the only daughter of Sir John Priestman. (F.W. Hawks & Solomon)

wide tramping. They all had five holds with no. 3 hold between bridge and engineer's accomodation doubling as a cross-bunker hold and full of coal for the long voyage to South Africa. The outturn of timber was always tallied, occupying much expense and time, and eventually a much simpler system was arrived at with the consignees accepting delivery of the timber without tallying if the Master had given a declaration that all of the timber loaded in the Baltic had been delivered and that none had been lost or unloaded elsewhere en route.

A dozen tramps were built for other owners between 1920 and 1930 including *Frances Massey* 4212/27 for W.A. Massey & Sons Ltd,Hull and *Knight of the Cross* 3857/29, *Knight of the Rose* 3865/29 and *Knight of the Realm* 3865/30 for Pardoe-Thomas & Co. Ltd,Newport. Two more ships were completed in 1930 before the workforce were paid off as these were the last orders, *Glenlea* in August and *Finland* in June. A further ship was left on the stocks after her Norwegian owner had failed to make the staged payments, but she was completed ready for launching. In February,1931 she was put up for auction after prospective buyers had inspected her on the stocks. However the top bid was only £20,000 and she was withdrawn from sale and was to linger on the stocks for another two years until launched in May,1933. Sir John Priestman during these idle years used to play tennis in the yard with his Yard Manager much to the amusement of those watching on the other side of the river. His last ship was sold in September,1934 and left the river as *Rio Novo* 2450/37.

The yard was closed in 1933 but the facilities remained intact until with Admiralty assistance in 1944 William Pickersgill & Sons Ltd took it over for naval construction as their West yard. Sir John Priestman had received a Baronetcy in 1934 and died in 1941 in his 87th year. He had been Sunderland's greatest philanthropist, giving away more than £500,000 to charitable, hospital and religious causes. He left over £1.5M in his will with a large sum in Trust for further charitable use. Some of his bequests were £100,000 to Haig homes, £50,000 to Sunderland Eye Infirmary and £20,000 for a library for Sunderland Technical College. He was a keen organist and had donated many organs to local churches, and in 1907 had built St. Andrew's church at Roker in memory of his mother. This had many architectural features such as towers with beautiful stained glass windows, and also had a large organ. He also rebuilt St. Michael's church in Bishopwearmouth between 1933 and 1935.

JOHN BLUMER & COMPANY

John Blumer commenced wooden shipbuilding on the North Sands in 1859 but transferred to the extreme eastern end in 1864 when William Pile wished to extend in area and develop iron shipbuilding. His first ship was the wooden *Avon* of 276 tons, and then he built iron steamers e.g. *Contest* of 486 tons and *Maria Fidela* of 646 tons. A wide range of ships was built from tramps to colliers to coastal packets e.g. *Adria* 1225/73 was built for the prestigious P & O China service. *Pioneer* was built for the Admiralty in 1874 for service on African rivers and was of composite teak/iron construction.

Colliers were built for customers such as Lambert Brothers of London with *Terlings* 576/71, *Kenley* 667/77 and *Vernon* 982/78; and for William France, Fenwick & Co. Ltd with *Hawkwood* 1155/99, *Monkwood* 1141/00 and *Cornwood* 2152/11, the latter costing £25,350. Regular tramp customers included Moor Line Ltd managed by Walter Runciman & Co. Ltd,Newcastle with 14 ships starting with *Arranmoor* 1897/97 and ending with *Spennymoor* 3992/15; Miller & Richards Ltd, London with ten ships starting with *Carisbrook* 2170/97 and ending with *Dorisbrook* 3431/15; and the Moss Steamship Co. Ltd,Liverpool with ten ships starting with *Busiris* 2720/04 and ending with *Hatasu* 3198/21 and including *Hathor* 3823/14. Three ships were built around 1890 for the Persian Gulf Steamship Co. Ltd,London as *Tigris* 2412/90, *Amara* 2454/91 and *Shatt el Arab* 2605/92.

Output in 1900 was six ships of 18,679 tons with three big tramps completed, the largest to date, *Drumcruil* 3938/00, *Pennmanor* 3835/00 and *Cymodocee* 3820/00. This size of 6500 dwt tramp was never exceeded by the yard even during the Great War. The aptly named *Weardale* 2728/03 was built for the Weardale Steam Shipping Co. Ltd, Sunderland and more distant customers included the Greek Embiricos and Stathatos families. However the freight rate slump starting in 1906 reduced output greatly in 1908/09 to only three ships, rising again in 1910 to bring orders for 25 tramps and colliers between 1910 and the start of the Great War. New tramp customers included Common Brothers of Newcastle with *Tynehome* 3157/13, named after the Sunderland home of the Common family for their Home Shipping Co. Ltd; Evan Thomas Radcliffe,Cardiff with *Euston* 2841/10 and *Boverton* 2958/10; and William E. Hinde,Cardiff with *Portloe* 3187/12; and a ship named in honour of the builder *John Blumer* 2350/14.

Some 14 ships of 48,456 tons were completed during World War I and five Admiralty lighters. Eight standard *WAR* 'C' types were ordered by the Shipping Controller with five being completed after the end of the war. Those built to private order during the war and shortly afterwards were:-

ARRANMOOR	3815/15	W. Runciman,Newcastle 33
DORISBROOK	3431/15	Miller & Richards Ltd,London 283
SARAGOSSA	3541/16	Harris & Dixon Ltd,London 243
PORTRUSH	3814/16	W.E. Hinde,Cardiff 284
HUDWORTH	3966/16	Trechmann Bros,Hartlepool 285
AYLESTONE	3380/17	Alexander Bros,Newcastle 286
CLIFFTOWER	3509/17	Hansen Bros,Cardiff 287
HATASU	3193/17	Moss S.S. Co. Ltd,Liverpool 288
LUXOR	3571/17	"
WULSTY CASTLE	3566/18	J. Chambers,Liverpool 289
DAYBEAM	3023/20	Claymore Shipping Co. Ltd,Cardiff 281
MATHILDA	3669/20	J. Christensen,Bergen
RYGJA	3543/20	J. Ludwig Mowinckels,Bergen
JACOB CHRISTENSEN	3594/20	J. Christensen,Bergen
HATASU 2	3198/21	Moss S.S. Co. Ltd,Liverpool 288
WILLIAM BLUMER	3604/20	C.H. Sorensen,Arendal
IXIA 2	2985/22	Stag Line,North Shields 25

However scarcity of orders led to the closure of the yard after the completion of the Stag Line tramp in July,1922. Two more hulls lay unfinished on the stocks for four years, one for R.S. Dalgleish,Newcastle which became *Usworth* 3535/26, and another for Stag Line, which finally left for sea trials in January,1927 as *Cydonia*. The last yard to build at the North Dock was then dismantled, ending a long tradition of shipbuilding.

S.P. AUSTIN & SON LTD. 209

This yard had an impressive reputation for the building of colliers of all sizes at its Wear Dockyard on the south side of the river, just downstream of the Wearmouth bridge. However the business had been founded on the north side of the river at the North Sands in 1826 by Peter Austin. He built small wooden colliers for the London trade, and repaired them in a primitive way by allowing the tide to float them on to a ramp or ways, and then by means of capstans worked by horses and manual labour, hauled them up for repair. Peter Austin retired in 1846, and his son Samuel Peter Austin immediately moved over to the south side of the river at the Wear Dockyard. He had two berths for building ships up to 550 tons, and he also laid down the first patent slipway in 1856 on the river for repairs, which formed a major part of the business.

In August,1870 a graving dock was opened on the site of the slipway, capable of repairing iron vessels up to 300 feet in length. A son of the same name had joined as a partner in 1860, the yard then being known as S.P. Austin & Son. On his father's death in 1867, Samuel Peter II continued to manage the yard assisted by his brother Stanley, who died in 1900. Their last wooden ship was built in 1869, with no new ships then built for the next four years until iron construction began in 1874. A partnership of a few years duration was then formed with George Hunter, who left in 1878 to form a new more famous partnership at Wallsend with Charles S. Swan as C.S. Swan & Hunter.

View from the Wearmouth Bridge of the Wear Dockyard of S. P. Austin & Son.

In 1871 Austins acquired the next yard downstream, and over the next twenty years acquired all of the land up to the Scotia Engine Works of William Allan. Three slipways were laid down for the construction of steel colliers up to 3000 tons dwt. An engine repair shop and offices were erected on land purchased in 1897 almost directly under the Monkwearmouth bridge. A large pontoon dry-dock was then ordered from C.S. Swan & Hunter at Wallsend capable of repairing ships up to 400 feet in length and 7000 tons dwt and opened alongside this site in 1903. The new J. L. Thompson-built Cunarder *Brescia* was first ship into the dock for painting before handing over to her owners.

The yard built for all of the well-known collier operators with William Cory & Sons having 36 built between 1898 and 1944, with others having been built for the constituent companies that formed William Cory & Sons Ltd in 1896. *Corton* of 5320 dwt was launched on 23rd January,1913 for Cory and was their first collier with the prefix *'COR'*. William France,Fenwick & Co. Ltd had 28 colliers built at the Wear Dockyard between 1912 and 1956; and Stephenson Clarke Ltd had 30 colliers built there between 1892 and 1958; and the Pelton Steamship Co. Ltd,Newcastle had nine colliers built between 1906 and 1957.

Output during World War I was 13 colliers of 28,979 tons and five small naval craft. One Cory collier *Corsham* 2797/18 sailed only six miles from Roker pier on her maiden voyage on 8th March,1918 before being torpedoed and sunk. Another for Cory, *Buffs* 3431/17, was in Government service until the end of the war. The King of Denmark, Honorary Colonel of the Buffs regiment ,presented the ship with his portrait in 1920 when she was renamed *Corland*. The yard also built six colliers for the Shipping Controller to the standard 'D' and 'H' types, but in the slump in 1920 after the end of the war suffered greatly. Cory ordered one, *Corsea* 2764/21 and the Tanfield Steamship Co. Ltd,Newcastle another, *Hetton* 2659/24, but then colliers had to be built 'on-spec'. One such ship was launched on 4th March,1927 with engines amidships and was acquired soon afterwards by Cory and renamed *Corchester* 2374/27. She was a single-deck self-trimmer of 4500 dwt with four holds and hatches and her triple expansion engine supplied by George Clark Ltd,Sunderland gave 10 knots. She was followed by two smaller sisters of 2500 dwt, *Corbridge* 1703/28 and *Corminster* 1703/28.

The Depression reduced output in 1932 to only two colliers, and these were the only ships launched on the Wear that year. One was launched in July,1932, the first launch on the river for nine months, watched by thousands of unemployed people from the nearby Wearmouth bridge. *John Hopkinson* and her sister 'flat-iron' *Colonel Crompton* , launched later in the year were completed for the London Power Company , and a smaller collier was also completed as *Corhaven* of 991 grt in 1933. The yard then closed until February,1934 when construction of a trio of 2700 dwt colliers for Cory began, *Corfirth* 1803/ 34, *Corfleet* 1803/34 and *Corfell* 1802/34. William France,Fenwick also had a trio of colliers completed during 1934/35 by the yard, *Wychwood* 2794/34, *Hawkwood* 2024/34 and *Phylwood* 1013/35, and also placed orders for another trio in 1936 and completed as *Goodwood* 1796/37, *Gwynwood* 1177/37 and *Monkwood* 1591/38. Two large down-river colliers for the Gas, Light and Coke Co. Ltd were important orders, *Mr. Therm* 2974/36 of 4600 dwt and *Icemaid* 1964/36 of 2900 dwt, the design of the latter ship being used as the prototype for the war standard colliers of that size built during World War II. Flat-iron colliers for the private light and gas companies swelled the order book.

The yard built a magnificent 26 colliers of 65,916 tons during World War II as well as a corvette and a tank landing craft and two coasters. The colliers were of three standard types, flat-irons of 2250 dwt and down-river types of 3000 dwt and 4200 dwt, developed by the builder and all for private order. When the war ended the yard could build colliers up to 360 feet in length, and had repaired hundreds of badly damaged colliers and coasters in the 300 feet dry-dock and on the 390 feet pontoon dock. One such flat-iron collier was *Gasfire*, which had her entire stern replaced with a new keel, stern frame, tail shaft and propeller fitted.

A flood of orders was received in 1946 for replacement colliers and coasters. Three twin-screw motor coasters of 1450 dwt were built for the General Steam Navigation Co. Ltd,London *Laverock* 1209/47, *Seamew* 1220/47 and *Auk* 1238/49, with the later *Adjutant* 1366/54 being fitted with a tank for carrying sea-water for London Zoo. The water was pumped aboard as the vessel motored through the Bay of Biscay en-route to the Thames, where it was transferred to a barge to be transported to the zoo for use in the salt-water aquarium. A collier of 3400 dwt was built for A/S D/S Progress,Copenhagen as *Elisabeth Nielsen* 2441/49 and a similar pair for D/S Heimdal,Copenhagen as *Martin Carl* 2499/47 and *Poul Carl* 2499/47. The Australian coastal trade of J. & A. Brown & Abermain Collieries Ltd, Sydney was the destination of the collier *Wallarah* 1448/52, but the vast majority of up-river flat-iron colliers and down-river types up to 4600 dwt were destined for British owners, and thirty were built during the ten years from 1946. The flat-irons *Samuel Clegg* 1773/50 and *Thomas Livesey* 1779/53 were built for the North Thames Gas Board, and the yard won four out of a ten-ship order with Wear shipbuilders for electricity colliers of 1700 dwt: *Mendip, Polden, Bodmin Moor* and *Brent Knoll,* all delivered in 1950. The largest colliers built during this period were four of 4600 dwt: *Bearwood* for France,Fenwick in 1955; *John Orwell Phillips* and *Frederick John Evans* for the North Thames Gas Board in 1955; and *Arundel* for Stephenson Clarke Ltd in 1956.

The yard merged with the Southwick yard of William Pickersgill & Sons Ltd in September,1954 and yard output was then completed under the Austin & Pickersgill Ltd name. These included two coasters of 1180 dwt for the British Transport Commission service from Goole to Copenhagen, *Kirkham Abbey* 1372/56 and *Byland Abbey* 1372/57. However collier sizes were now increasing beyond the maximum possible size from the yard, and some of the last completed were *Rondo* 3432/57 for the Pelton Steamship Co. Ltd,Newcastle; *Lancing* 1035/58 for Stephenson Clarke Ltd; *Southwark* 3065/58 for the South Eastern Gas Board;

Greathope 2750/58 for E.R. Newbigin,Newcastle with *Greenland* of 3000 dwt for Shipping & Coal Ltd,London being the last launched on 19th June,1962. Three motor yachts were then built, *Radiant II* for Basil Mavroleon, owner of Austin & Pickersgill Ltd, and *Suniper* and *Bobbina* in 1962. The yard closed in 1964 after building three barges for the Admiralty in 1963, and was subsequently demolished with the pontoon dry-dock being towed away for further use in June,1966.

JOHN CROWN & SONS LTD. *LOS*

John Crown and his father Luke Crown acquired a yard in 1847 adjacent to and to the west of the Thompson yard at North Sands, on land previously occupied by John Candlish. In 1880 the title of the yard was changed to the Strand Slipway Company, with *Ferdinand Corvilain* being the first ship launched under that name. In 1901 the title became John Crown & Sons with *Gratia* being the first ship launched under that title, and the yard became a limited liability company in 1903 with *Porthcawl* the first ship launched under that title in 1903.

The output of the yard was almost exclusively colliers and coasters, with some lightships and hoppers as well. Collier customers included the well-known William France,Fenwick & Co. Ltd with *Whitwood* and *Deerwood*, both 1926/19 and standard World War I colliers; William Cory & Sons Ltd with *Corfen* 1848/40 and *Corflow* 2158/46; Stephenson Clarke Ltd with *Matching* 1321/24 and *Portsmouth* 1805/50; Witherington & Everett,Newcastle with 14 colliers built between 1905 and 1924, starting with *Skipjack* 1120/05 and ending with *Speedfast* 1898/24, and including two built with the name *Wear* in 1911/12; Furness,Withy & Co. Ltd with five colliers built between 1906 and 1909 with Durham place names e.g. *Tudhoe* 1286/06; the Pelton Steamship Co. Ltd,Newcastle with *Canto* 967/00, *Presto* 1143/07 and *Lesto* 1893/18; as well as flat-iron colliers for the private London light and gas companies.

John Crown had died in 1902 but the yard remained a family one by his three daughters serving on the Board. Four colliers were built during World War I including a standard 'D' type and two more standard colliers for France,Fenwick; and then some 16 colliers during the 1920s including *Borde* 2014/21 for Stephenson Clarke Ltd, which was used as a mine destructor vessel during the next World War. *Chartered* of 2950 dwt was completed in October,1921 for the Gas,Light & Coke Company with modern engines-aft design with navigating bridge amidships. Her four hatches were 25 feet wide and she carried no derricks on her two masts to allow fast loading and discharge. Her triple expansion engine by North Eastern Marine Eng. Co. Ltd gave a modest 10 knots loaded service speed. Other colliers included two for Walter Runciman & Co. Ltd, Newcastle, *Royalmoor* 1907/24 and *Silvermoor* 1906/25, and the larger engines-aft *John Charrington* 2750/29 for the Charrington Steamship Co. Ltd, London.

The yard ran out of orders at the beginning of the Depression after completing the 'flat-iron' *Horseferry* 951/30 for the Gas, Light & Coke Company, and two small hoppers. In early 1934 an order for a small pleasure steamer, *Royal Lady*, for trippers' use at Scarborough was obtained, but the yard then closed down again after her completion until 1938 when a repeat order was obtained for *New Royal Lady*. Three more small ships completed the yard output before the start of World War II, when four colliers, nine *'Empire'* tugs, seven *'Flower'* class corvettes, three *'Isles'* class trawlers, one *'River'* class frigate and two *'Castle'* class frigates were built. At the end of the war the yard, the smallest on the river, was able to build ships up to 300 feet in length.

In 1946 the yard was taken over by the adjacent yard of Joseph L. Thompson & Sons Ltd, but continued building under its own yard numbers until 1960. Several orders were received in 1946 for replacement colliers and cargo ships of 2500 dwt for Norwegian owners such as Olsen & Ugelstad A/S, Rolf Wigands Rederi A/S and Ora A/S. Shell placed orders for two tankers of 4500 dwt, *Felipes* 3052/50 and *Tanea* 3060/50, the latter for New Zealand coastal trading, and for a bitumen carrier of 3300 dwt, *Shellphalte* 2929/52 for the French flag. The yard shared in a ten-ship order to Wear shipbuilders for electricity colliers of 1700 dwt, completing three, *Poole Harbour*, *Poole Channel* and *Poole Sound*, all 1366/49. However the most interesting order was for a tanker of 22400 dwt for Olsen & Ugelstad to be built in two halves and known locally as the 'Half-Crown' ship. The two halves were joined together in dry-dock at Middle Docks, South Shields to form *Rondefjell* 15077/51.

The yard facilities were extended in 1954 to build tramps up to 12000 dwt, and seven were subsequently completed:-

THISTLEDHU	7790/55	Albyn Line, Sunderland 79
STANCROWN	8002/56	Stanhope Shpg. Co. Ltd, London 132
SILVERDENE	5657/56	Silver Line, London 181
SILVERFELL	7843/57	"
BRETWALDA	5656/58	Hall Bros., Newcastle 152
THISTLEROY	7919/60	Albyn Line, Sunderland 79
SILVERISLE	7744/60	Silver Line, London 181

Two Clyde tugs were also completed in 1960, and the yard was then swallowed up in the multi-million pound reorganisation by owners Joseph L. Thompson & Sons Ltd yard, including a giant new berth sited at right angles to the existing berths as well as new prefabricating sheds to allow tanker and bulk carrier construction up to 100,000 dwt.

OSBOURNE, GRAHAM & COMPANY 334

Wooden shipbuilding at up-river Hylton had a centuries old tradition in 1871 with 160 shipwrights still employed there, when this, the greatest of all the Hylton yards, opened for business on the north bank of the river. Iron shipbuilding began immediately of tramps, colliers, barques and full-riggers, with the yard eventually specialising in colliers. The iron tramp *Chillingham Castle* 1613/72 for Hall Brothers of Newcastle was one of four ships of 4542 tons completed that year. The warship *Wye* of 1873, and the sailing ships *Woollahra*, *Gwrtheyryn Castle* and *Celestial Empire* were other early examples from the yard. The narrowness of the river at Hylton imposed a length restriction and the biggest ships of the 1880s were under 2000 grt e.g. *Irthington* 1909/80 and *Kathleen* 1700/88. By 1892 however, tramps of nearly 4000 dwt were being built for local tramp owners such as the Hindustan 138 Steam Shipping Co. Ltd with *Hindustan* 2420/92 the first ship owned by Francis J. Common, and *Miramar* 2415/92 for Glasgow owners Raeburn & Verel. 477

At the turn of the century some of the largest tramps ever built at Hylton came from the yard with three tramps of 9370 tons having been built in 1900, and followed by *Heathford* 3767/01 and *Ras Issa* 3774/02, both of over 5000 dwt and for London owners. Engines-amidships colliers in the 2000 - 3000 dwt range became a speciality, Furness,Withy & Co. Ltd taking six between 1905 and 1909 e.g. *Collingwood* 1278/05; and William France,Fenwick & Co. Ltd ordering six sisters of 3115 dwt for delivery between 1904 and 1907 e.g. *Wychwood* 1985/07. These colliers were designed by the builders, and a slightly larger near sister of 3500 dwt was completed in 1910 for the same owners at a cost of £25,375, *Ladywood*. Others were built for owners such as the Hessler Shipping Co. Ltd,Hartlepool with *Norman* 1840/01 and George Gibson of Leith with *Heriot* 1239/05.

In 1909, the pioneer 'corrugated' tramp *Monitoria* 1904/09 for the Ericsson 480 Shipping Co. Ltd,Newcastle was launched to the design of A.H. Haver, Doxford's former naval architect and designer of the 'Turret'. These tramps had two or three horizontal bulges running the full length of the hull to give a better flow of water to the propeller and thus increased speed, and others were built by Osbourne, Graham e.g. *Hyltonia* 1902/11. Another Osbourne pioneer was the 'Arch-decker' *Edenor* 2018/11 for Rederi A/B Edenor (T. Persson), Helsingborg. The upper deck was arched from stem to stern to a design by Ayre & Ballard. This longitudinal arch gave extra strength and long, unobstructed holds as stringers and hold pillars were unnecessary. Several more examples were built by the Blyth Shipbuilding & Dry Dock Co. Ltd (q.v.).

A dozen ships of 26,442 tons including two standard 'D' type colliers and some small naval craft were built during World War I. Most were colliers with two of 3100 dwt being completed for the Hudson Steamship Co. Ltd, London: *Hornchurch* 2159/16, *Upminster* 2176/17 to be followed by three more standard colliers of 3300 dwt after the war, *Hornchurch* 2162/19, *Dagenham* 2178/19 and *Lolworth* 1969/20. Two colliers, *Allendale* 2153/17 and *Keighley* 2150/17, had been ordered by Fearnley & Eger of Norway but were taken over for the period of the war and managed by Furness, Withy & Co. Ltd. The last of the 'WAR' standard colliers was completed in May, 1920 as *Warora* 2334/20 for British India Line. Private orders were scarce in the subsequent freight rate slump, and the following were the last ships ever built at Hylton:-

CAROLUS	2218/19	Sir E.O. Ohlson, Hull
ERICUS	2218/20	"
S. B. LUND	1749/20	Jens Lund A/S, Tonsberg
ORIA	2127/20	Fearnley & Eger, Oslo
GAP	2160/20	Soc. National d'Affretments, Havre
P.L.M. 6	2654/21	"
P.L.M. 7	2710/22	"
PAPALERA	1870/22	Fearnley & Eger, Oslo
SNAKE	2655/22	Temple, Thomson & Clark, London
ST. ROCH	1745/22	Jens Lund A/S, Tonsberg
GLYNWEN	1110/24	Stone & Rolfe, Llanelly
ARKLESIDE	1567/24	Thomas Rose, Sunderland
LARCHWOOD	914/24	J. Constantine, Middlesbrough
COPSEWOOD	969/25	"

The yard and its four berths was then closed after the completion of *Copsewood* in April, 1925. In July, 1931 the yard was purchased by National Shipbuilders Security Ltd and demolished.

SUNDERLAND SHIPBUILDING CO. LTD.

This yard was known locally as the 'limited' yard as it was the first yard owned by a limited liability company on the river. The site was at South Dock where wooden sailing ships had been built by John Haswell in the 1860s. Iliff & Mounsey took over the yard in 1870 for iron construction and built the first iron steamer in 1871 for Stag Line,North Shields, *Stephanotis* 1042/71. A further trio followed for this owner with *Nymphaea* 1138/71, *Nuphar* 1137/72 and *Danae* 1157/73. In 1872 the yard output was five iron ships of 7297 tons, and in 1873 the partnership became Mounsey & Foster and they built several medium-sized clippers in the 1870s e.g. *Duchess of Edinburgh, Eastern Monarch, Roderick Dhu, Senator* and *Kingdom of Sweden*. After Mounsey retired in 1880 Robert Foster continued under his own name for a short while until he set-up a limited liability company with the Sunderland name.

The prestigious Hansa Line of Hamburg ordered five cargo-liners in the 1880s and completed as *Drachenfels* 2251/82, *Trifels* 2766/88, *Gutenfels* 2673/89, *Rheinfels* 2717/89 and *Hochheimer* 2869/89. Steel colliers and tramps predominated however e.g. *Mount Park* 563/87 for J. & J. Denholm,Glasgow; and *Saxmundham* 2537/88 for Hunting & Son,Newcastle; and *Carlisle* 1035/89 for Livingston,Connor & Company,West Hartlepool. *Truro City* of 1006 grt was completed for Christopher Furness in 1889, and two colliers were built for Witherington & Everett,Newcastle in 1894, *Sprightly* and *Swiftsure*, both of 823 grt. Marquis of Scicluna 1599/83 was built by the yard and converted at Hebburn in 1886 by Andrew Leslie into a tanker by building a longitudinal fore-and-aft bulkhead subdivided by four transverse bulkheads. She then carried oil between the Black Sea port of Batum and the Adriatic ports of Fiume and Trieste. One of the largest ships built in the 1890s was the passenger/cargo-liner *Warrigal* of 4338 grt completed in August,1893 for the Australian immigrant service of Blue Anchor Line (W. Lund). The output in 1900 of 16,388 tons of ships made the yard the ninth largest on the Wear and included the big cargo-liner *St. George* 4149/00 for Saint Line of Liverpool.

A contract was transferred in 1903 to the Bridge Dockyard of Robert Thompson (q.v.) and launched broadside as *Admiral l'Hermite* and was one of the largest ships ever built there, making a fine spectacle when launched. Walter Cockerline & Co. Ltd of Hull then ordered four tramps for delivery in 1906/07 including *Gothic* 2648/06, and other tramps built by the South Dock yard up to World War I included :-

ALLANTON	4253/01	W.R. Rea,Glasgow 298
77 CHEVIOT RANGE	3458/03	Neptune S.N. Co. Ltd,Sunderland 299
TUDOR PRINCE	4208/03	Prince Line,North Shields 300
77 KINGSLAND	2848/05	S.R. Ruston & Co.,Cardiff 301
BRETWALDA	4037/11	Hall Bros.,Newcastle 152 302 152
SIAMESE PRINCE	4847/11	Prince Line,North Shields 300
GERALD TURNBULL	3177/12	Turnbull Bros.,Cardiff 223
TIARA	4068/13	Hall Bros.,Newcastle 302 152
HARPATHIAN	4588/13	J. & C. Harrison,London 268
HARBURY	4572/13	"

Output during World War I was eleven ships of 42,979 tons and no fewer than 19 small naval craft. Two of these were gunboats, *Mantis* and *Moth*, built outside the yard on the beach and were launched broadside into the open sea, as they were of shallow draft and designed for river service. The large cargo-liner *Veendijk* 6874/14 was completed for the Holland-Amerika Line, and tramps built to private order included *Trident* 4317/17 for Hall Brothers,Newcastle and *Aberdeen* 5616/17 for Adam Steamship Co. Ltd,Aberdeen. The yard also built six *'WAR'* 'B' types with the last completed as *Gharinda* 5306/19 and *Goalpara* 5314/19 for British India Line; *Burutu* 5275/18 for Elder,Dempster; *Cairngowan* 5295/19 for Cairn Line of Steamships,Newcastle, which also took *Cairnmona* 4666/18 and *Cairnvalona* 4929/18; and *Bretwalda* 5293/19 for Hall Brothers, who also took *Diadem* 4528/20 from this yard. Orders were very scarce after the 1920/21 freight rate slump, and the last ships built by the yard were:-

VECHTDIJK	6869/20	Holland-Amerika Line
ENGGANO	5406/20	Nederland Stoomv. Maats.
SOLON	5260/21	Cie de Nav. d'Orbigny,France
ZENON	5379/21	"
CAIRNROSS 2	5494/21	Cairn Line of Steamships Ltd,Newcastle 194
CAIRNTORR	5387/22	"
ALASKA	5376/22	Cie Generale Transatlantique,France
EUPHORBIA	3380/24	Stag Line,North Shields 25
LINARIA 2	3385/25	"
ARIZONA	5398/26	Brown,Jenkinson & Co. Ltd,London 303

Cairnross was powered by three Parsons turbines DR geared to a single screw shaft, whereas her sister *Cairntorr* had conventional triple expansion engines. No launches had taken place during 1923, and the South Dock yard passed quietly out of existence, and had been demolished before the Depression years further reduced Wear shipbuilding capacity.

45s

WILLIAM GRAY & CO. LTD EGIS YARD

The EGIS Shipbuilding Company was formed in 1917 to acquire a 15 acre site on the south side of the river at Pallion just to the west of Short Brothers yard and on the site of the former Kish,Boolds yard. The name was an acronym for Ellerman, Gray, Inchcape and Strick; with shipowners Sir John R. Ellerman, Lord Inchcape of P & O, and Frank C. Strick combining with West Hartlepool shipbuilder William Gray & Co. Ltd (q.v.).   Four berths of 440 feet in length were laid out together with a 460 feet long fitting-out quay. The first ship *Golconda* 5318/19 was a *WAR* 'B' standard type and launched in June,1919 for British India Line, a subsidiary of P & O., which took delivery of six more ships from the yard. Four were completed for Ellerman Lines up to 1925, the only ships being completed for other owners being *Siantar* 8439/21 for Ruys & Zonen, Rotterdam and *Platon* and *Solon*, both 4561/25 for Compagnie de D'Orbigny, France.

The yard had been absorbed into William Gray & Company (1918) Ltd, which in 1923 resumed the title William Gray & Co. Ltd. The yard was closed at the end of 1925 with no new ships completed in 1926, but when work resumed in 1927 only 19 more tramps were completed before the Depression took hold :-

RAMILLIES	4553/27	J. Cory,Cardiff 304
LEEDS CITY	4749/27	Reardon Smith,Cardiff 177
QUEBEC CITY	4754/27	"
NOHATA	4817/28	Hain S.S. Co. Ltd 78
THIRLBY	4888/28	Ropner,Hartlepool 29
KING CITY	4743/28	Reardon Smith,Cardiff 177
ALPHACCA	5546/28	Van Nievelt Goudriaan,Holland
ALPHERAT	5548/28	"
NEW WESTMINSTER CITY	4747/29	Reardon Smith,Cardiff 177
PRINCE RUPERT CITY	4749/29	"
TACOMA CITY	4738/29	"
VERNON CITY	4748/29	"
VICTORIA CITY	4739/29	"
GLENDENE	4412/29	W.S. Hinde,Cardiff 284
LADY PLYMOUTH	4732/29	Lewis Lougher,Cardiff 305
VEERHAVEN	5291/29	Van Udens Maats,Holland
DELFSHAVEN	5287/30	"
ATTHIS	4108/30	Mrs. Z. Nicolaou,Greece
THETIS	4123/30	E. Hadjilias,Greece

Grays decided to close the yard in 1930 after only 34 ships had been completed. In November, 1936 the yard was purchased by National Shipbuilders Security Ltd and the four berths were dismantled during 1938.

SWAN, HUNTER / SHIPBUILDING CORPORATION

Swan, Hunter & Wigham Richardson Ltd opened a four berth yard at Southwick in 1912 to the west of the Priestman yard to take up excess orders for colliers, coasters and Great Lakes steamers from their Tyne yards. Smaller floating docks were also built for customers such as Schiedam Docks and Portsmouth Dockyard. The yard helped the war effort with two standard 'D' type colliers and five standard coasters in 1919 of 1950 grt, *British Coast, Western Coast, Polo, Merganser* and *Sea Glory*. The yard closed in April, 1921 for two years and then shared in some of the fifty engines-aft, bridge-forward Great Lakes steamers of 2600 dwt built by the Swan, Hunter yards e.g. *Imari, Phenicia, Prescodoc* and *Starwell*. Some fifty ships had been completed by the start of the Depression in 1930, which extinguished the need for the yard as the owners had difficulty in finding enough work for their Tyne yards. The biggest ships built at the yard were the tramps *Hopecrag* 4007/29 and *Hopedene* 4010/29 of 6750 dwt, built on speculation and then traded by the Hopemount Shipping Co. Ltd, owned by Swan, Hunter; *Toftwood* 4302/28 of 7830 dwt for Joseph Constantine of Middlesbrough; and *Honved* 4250/28 of 7633 dwt for the Hungarian Levant Steamship Co. Ltd.

The last ship built by the yard under the Swan, Hunter name was the Stephenson Clarke collier *Flathouse* 1546/31 completed in December, 1931. A sister, *Sir Russell*, was completed at the Wallsend yard two years later, by which time the Southwick yard had been purchased by National Shipbuilders Security Ltd and was partly dismantled. In the second half of 1942, with ships being lost to U-boats at an alarming rate, workers from the Joseph L. Thompson yard began working on the derelict site. The only remaining features were the administration block and a large building which had been the joiners shop. Three berths were rebuilt and a large amount of equipment from the North Sands yard of Thompson was used to bring the old yard back to life.

The first launch from the National Shipbuilding Corporation (Wear) yard was the 'D' type standard ship *Empire Trail* in August, 1943 and she was completed in December, 1943. Unskilled and semi-skilled workers from the Thompson and other Sunderland yards were helped by a greater degree of prefabrication than usual, but only another four tramps had been completed by the end of the war. A total of ten

'Empire' tramps, and a few coastal tankers and barges for Burma had been completed by the beginning of 1947. This was the Government closing date for the yard, however there was still one ship left on the stocks due to a shortage of materials, and the yard was reprieved to launch her on 28th April,1947 as *Lagosian* for the United Africa Co. Ltd. She was completed in July,1947 and the yard then closed and was demolished in 1952.

Among the last ships from the EGIS yard and Swan,Hunter & Wigham Richardson Ltd yard were NEW WESTMINSTER CITY of 1929 (top) and HOPEDENE of 1929. (W.I.M.M.)

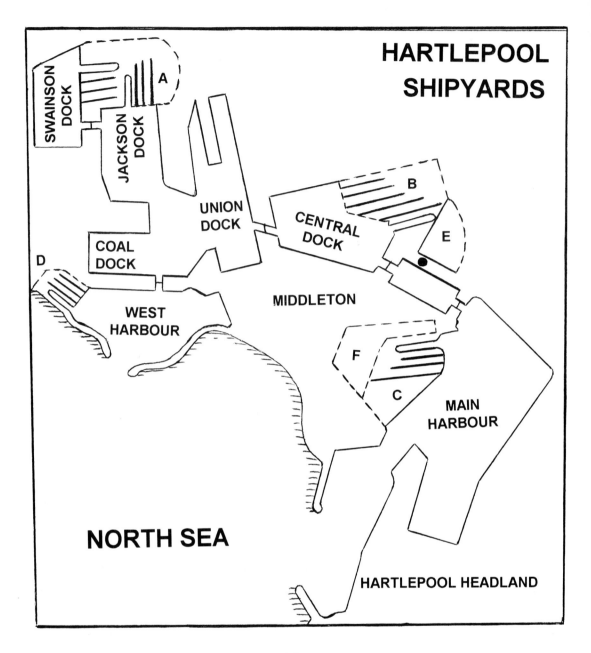

HARTLEPOOL SHIPYARDS

SWAINSON DOCK

JACKSON DOCK

A

UNION DOCK

COAL DOCK

D

WEST HARBOUR

CENTRAL DOCK

B

E

MIDDLETON

F

C

MAIN HARBOUR

NORTH SEA

HARTLEPOOL HEADLAND

A. WILLIAM GRAY DOCKYARD

B. WILLIAM GRAY CENTRAL YARD

C. FURNESS,WITHY & CO. LTD.

D. ROBERT IRVINE & CO. LTD.

E. CENTRAL MARINE ENGINE WORKS

F. THOMAS RICHARDSON ENGINE WORKS

WILLIAM GRAY & CO. LTD.

William Gray was born at Blyth in 1823 and established a drapery business in Hartlepool in 1843, and subsequently acquired shipping interests with the brig *Juanita* of 237 tons built in 1860 for the Mediterranean trade, and *Ravensbourne* and *Esperanza* of 1862, all built by John Punshon Denton at Hartlepool. In the following year Gray decided to form a shipbuilding partnership with Denton, and the first iron steamer *Dessouk* was launched in 1863 for the Pasha of Egypt, and the first iron steamer owned by William Gray was the *Golden Horn*, built by Denton,Gray & Company in 1865. The Dockyard of Pile,Spence at Jackson Dock, Hartlepool was acquired in 1869, and Denton,Gray & Company then built some 58 iron steamers up to 1874. One of their more impressive ships was the cable layer *Great Northern* 1422/70 for the Eastern and South African Telegraph Co. Ltd. After a dispute, the Denton family parted company with Gray, who launched his first ship for his own account in August,1874 as *Sexta*.

A dozen small steamers had been completed by William Gray up to the end of 1875, and the yard quickly captured the record output for a British yard in 1878 with 18 ships launched. In 1883, Gray acquired a ten acre site near the Central Dock to build a marine engine plant, and with quay space to lift the engines directly into the unfinished ships. The first engine of this Central Marine Engine Works was a triple expansion steam reciprocating engine fitted into the tramp *Enfield* 2158/85 owned by Pyman Brothers. In 1887 a three berth shipyard was opened in the adjacent Central Dock capable of building large ships of up to 450 feet in length, while the Dockyard at Jackson Dock continued to build smaller ships.

The cargo-liner *Missouri* of 2845 grt was the first ship launched from the new Central Dock yard in December,1888, the year in which the yard became a limited liability company as well as again having the record output of any British yard. The yard was also at the forefront of technology, having built the bulk oil tanker *Bakuin* in 1886, but as she was launched on 17th June,1886 one day after Armstrong's *Gluckauf* at Newcastle, she was always in the shadow of her contemporary. The British record output was achieved again in 1895, 1898 and 1900 with no fewer than twenty three large ships completed in 1900. The company entered the next century with five building berths and a dry-dock at their Central Dock shipyard, and another six berths and two dry-docks at the Dockyard at Jackson Dock. Some 3000 men were employed in the shipyards, and another 2000 men in the engine works.

William Gray was able to find plenty of customers for his yards because he was more than willing to help with their finance, sometimes taking only a deposit and purchasing some of the shares himself. This was particularly true for local shipowners, and also for the legendary Marcus Samuel, founder of the Shell oil company. His first bulk oil tanker *Murex* cost £47,000 to build but Samuel was only asked to pay £6350 and owned only four out of her 64ths, with Gray and Edward Pembroke jointly holding the other sixty. Similar arrangements were made for another five tankers at a total cost of nearly £300,000, and altogether eight Shell tankers were built between 1892 and 1895 at the yard: *Murex, Conch, Clam, Elax, Volute, Bullmouth, Pectan* and *Telena.*

Important local shipowners such as Robert Ropner had 53 tramps built between 1871 and 1937, while Christopher Furness had his first steamer *Chicago* launched at the yard in April,1878 and subsequently another twelve steamers up to 1905, including *Cambrian* 5626/96 for the Wilson,Furness Leyland Line. She was launched on 10th October,1896 and completed in December as the biggest ship yet built at Hartlepool with an overall length of 464 feet and had four impressive masts, and was propelled across the Atlantic by the the most powerful steam engine then constructed by the Central Marine Engine Works at 4,000 indicated horse power to give a service speed of 14 knots. Other local shipowners such as the Trechmann Brothers had eleven ships built between 1877 and 1911; the West Hartlepool Steam Navigation Co. Ltd another eleven ships between 1879 and 1937; John Coverdale & Company named one of their ships in honour of *Lady Gray* 2545/94; and others were built for Gladstone,Cornforth; Livingston,Connor; F. Herskind & Company, and the Hessler Shipping Co. Ltd, all of Hartlepool.

Sir William Gray was knighted in 1890, having been the first mayor of the new borough of West Hartlepool in 1887, and became High Sheriff of Durham County in 1892 as well as the President of the Chamber of Shipping for the U.K. He died on 12th September,1898 and left over £1.5M in his will to his wife and only surviving son William Cresswell Gray, born in 1867 and appointed a director in 1889. Under the direction of William C. Gray some 200 ships were built by the yards between 1900 and the outbreak of the Great War. Liner shipowners such as Ellerman Lines, British India, Furness,Withy & Co. Ltd were prominent as well as the majority of British tramp owners. Overseas customers included Greek, Danish, Dutch, German, Swedish, Norwegian, Australian, French, Austro-Hungarian, Spanish and Belgian owners. The tanker *Ricardo A. Mestres* 4468/14 was completed just before the outbreak of war for Consolidated Goldfields of South Africa Ltd with six oil-tight bulkheads and three water-tight bulkheads and cylindrical oil tanks. Her steam engines as well as her cargo pump, capable of discharging all of her 6240 tons of oil within 24 hours, came from the Central Marine Engine Works.

World War I output was 30 cargo-liners and tramps built to private order, 13 vessels built to Admiralty order and 30 standard *'WAR'* tramps built for the Shipping

The second Shell tanker, CONCH of 1892 (above) built by Gray, who also built for local owners such as Pyman, pictured is RUNSWICK of 1904 (below).

Controller. Ellerman Lines featured prominently among the private owners with ten cargo-liners completed for their Hall, City and Bucknall Lines, and tramp owners included John Cory of Cardiff, J. & C. Harrison of London, Turnbull of Whitby and Boltons of London.   The Admiralty orders were for four twin-screw shallow-draft gunboats, four patrol boats and five tankers, *Pearleaf* 5911/17, *Rapidol* 2648/17, *Montenol* 2646/17, *Oakol* 1144/17 and *Palmol* 1126/17, the last two also being the first diesel-engined ships ever built at the yard.   Their twin 4-cylinder Bolinders assembled by Perkins at Yeovil drove twin propellers and gave a service speed of around nine knots.   The standard *'WAR'* types completed for the Shipping Controller comprised 27 tramps (two 'A', eight 'B', eight 'C' , two 'D', two 'E' and five 'H' types) as well as three standard 'Z' tankers of 8460 dwt, *War Subadour, War Sikh* and *War Sepoy.*

In 1917 the morale of the workforce received a great boost with the visit of King George V and Queen Mary to the yard, and one of the noticeable features of the yard was a new 100-ton hammer head crane on the quay beside the Engine Works, which remained a Hartlepool landmark until demolished in the 1960s. After peace returned, Sir William C. Gray deceided to commemorate the safe return of his son, Capt. William Gray, by establishing and endowing a museum for the Town. The Gray Museum and Art Gallery opened on 5th November,1920 housed in 'The Willows', formerly the home of Hartlepool shipowner George Pyman as well as part of the Gray family. A new Wear yard known as the Egis yard was in the final stages of construction at the end of the war (See Sunderland section), and was absorbed into the Gray company as the reconstructed William Gray & Co.(1918) Ltd.   The company resumed its original title in 1923.

A boom in orders in 1919 was followed by a scarcity in the early 1920s due to the subsequent slump in freight rates, with yard output reduced to only three ships in 1922 and seven ships in 1923.   Several cargo-liners, however, were built at this time for Ellerman Lines, British India S.N., Strick Line, Ruys & Zonen of Holland and Union Steamship Co. Ltd, New Zealand. Sir William C. Gray died on 1st November,1924, having been in charge of the yard for 26 years as well as being a director of North-East steelworks and railway companies. He had introduced a profit-sharing scheme into the yard in March,1919 under which his workers got 20% of the net annual profit, but this was quickly shelved in 1921 with the slump.

A new repair yard was established at Graythorp near Seal Sands on the Tees in 1924 with a 500 foot dry-dock. *Serbino* of Ellerman Wilson Line had the honour of baptising the dock, which also boasted a long deep-water quay and four building berths. However the slump conditions of the 1920s with only four ships built at the Hartlepool yards in 1926, and the depressed conditions of the 1930s made the extra

WILLIAM GRAY
& CO. LTD.

74

Shipbuilders and Engineers

WEST HARTLEPOOL

BUILDERS OF

CARGO LINERS	TURBINES
TRAMPS	DIESEL ENGINES
TIMBER CARRIERS	RECIPROCATING ENGINES
COLLIERS	BOILERS

REPAIRERS AT

WEST HARTLEPOOL
3 GRAVING DOCKS

SEATON·ON·TEES
1 GRAVING DOCK

MIDDLESBROUGH
REPAIR SHOPS

Company advertisement of the 1930s

Greek-owned tramp DUKE OF SPARTA of 1940

building capacity unnecessary and it was never used. Concrete caissons were built in the dry-dock in 1944 for the Mulberry Harbour at Normandy, and repair work continued here until the early 1960s.

When Capt. William Gray (Sir William Gray III) took charge of the yards as Chairman in January,1925 the company was in a difficult financial position. The effects of the slump together with interest due on bank loans borrowed to develop the Tees yard had left the company with a substantial overdraft. Two tramps had been laid down 'on-spec' and were completed in 1924 as *Domira* and *Ingola* in 1925 , both of 6500 dwt and for Maclay & McIntyre of Glasgow. Several more ships were built 'on-spec' , with Sir William Gray entertaining as many shipowners as possible on his private yacht in the hope of obtaining more customers and orders.

The thousandth ship was completed at the Hartlepool yards in January,1929 as *City of Dieppe* 7958/29 for Ellerman Lines, which had taken twenty cargo-liners from the yards since the end of World War I. However the onset of the Depression at the end of 1929 caused many cancelled orders with one cancelled by C. Mathison of Bergen. The yard completed this tramp in 1930 in the hope that a buyer might materialise, and when this did not occur she was traded as *Josephine Gray* by the company and managed by Walter Stanley Hinde of Cardiff. After completing four barges for Tees Conservancy Commissioners later in 1930 the yard closed down, re-opening in 1932 to build a Tees pilot launch and six tramps: *Domby* for Ropner; *Hartington, Hartlepool* and *Hartismere* for J. & C. Harrison; and *Kepwickhall* and *Siltonhall* for West Hartlepool S. N. Co. Ltd, all completed in 1932. The yards then closed again but the Jackson Dockyard re-opened in 1934 to build two Humber paddle-driven ferries, *Wingfield Castle* and *Tattershall Castle,* both 556/34. *Wingfield Castle* has now been returned to Hartlepool and beautifully restored to the condition she was in when she left the builders yard. The Central yard re-opened in 1935 to complete a tramp laid-down 'on-spec' in 1933 and left on the stocks for two years. This was completed as *Boltonhall* for West Hartlepool S.N. Co. Ltd, and the only other ship completed during 1935 was the turbine-powered tramp *Clearpool* for Ropner, who were trying new forms of engine including diesels at this time in the search for economy.

The rise in freight rates brought orders in 1936, and some thirty tramps and cargo-liners, and two destroyers for the Admiralty, *Hazard* and *Gleaner,* were completed in the years before the outbreak of World War II for the following owners with courage and capital :-

CRESSDENE	4270/36	Dene Shipping Co. Ltd,London	306
EUGENIE LIVANOS	4816/36	Livanos Bros,Greece	
HAWNBY	5404/36	Ropner,Hartlepool	29

74

TORDENE	4254/36	Dene Shipping Co. Ltd,London 306
ATHINA LIVANOS	4824/36	Livanos Bros.,Greece
MELROSE ABBEY	2472/36	F. Jones,Cardiff 307
GERMANIC	5351/36	Walter Cockerline,Hull 308
OAKDENE	4255/36	Dene Shipping Co. Ltd,London 306
MALVERNIAN	3132/37	Ellerman Lines 34
BELGRAVIAN 2	3136/37	"
FELLDENE	4332/37	Dene Shipping Co. Ltd,London 306
THEOFANO LIVANOS	6636/37	Livanos Bros.,Greece
LINDENHALL	5247/37	West Hartlepool S.N. Co. Ltd 246
DANBY	4281/37	Ropner 29
G.S. LIVANOS	4835/37	Livanos Bros.,Greece
ITINDA	6648/37	British India S.N. 42
INDORA	6622/38	"
EVI LIVANOS	4839/37	Livanos Bros.,Greece
IONIAN	3114/38	Ellerman Lines 34
CORINTHIAN	3198/38	"
MICHAEL LIVANOS	4773/38	Livanos Bros.,Greece
MARGAM ABBEY	2470/38	F. Jones,Cardiff 307
ARIJON	4374/38	Cie d'Orbigny,France
PALERMO 2	2838/38	Ellerman Wilson Line,Hull 309
MARY LIVANOS	4771/38	Livanos Bros.,Greece
GEORGE M. LIVANOS	5481/38	"
TINTERN ABBEY	2479/39	F. Jones,Cardiff 307
CHIOS	5643/39	Livanos Bros.,Greece
FAUZON	4319/38	Cie d'Orbigny,France
NICHOLAS D.L.	5486/39	Lykiardopulo,London 310
ATLANTIC 2	5439/39	Walter Cockerline,Hull 308

Output during World War II by the two Hartlepool yards was a substantial 72 ships, with some 1750 ships repaired by the company dry-docks. Some thirty standard *Empire* tramps were launched with two of these sent to other yards for conversion into component repair yards for use by the Admiralty. Ten were built of a class of 4310 dwt engines-aft colliers with heavy lift derricks for use in the Far East, and 24 of the three-island Scandinavian type of 4700 dwt, and the total was completed by eight colliers of 4200 dwt for use on the trade from the North-East Coast to London. The output of the Central Marine Engine Works was equally substantial with engines built in three sizes for the standard classes of ship built in the company yards and elsewhere.

In the fourteen years from the end of World War II until 1959, some 105 cargo-liners, tramps and short-sea traders were built by the yards i.e. an average of 7.5 ships/year. In addition, three tankers were built, including the 12000 dwt sisters *Atlantic Duchess* 8631/50 for Livanos of Greece and *Bernhard Hanssen* 8739/51 for a Norwegian shipowner of the same name. The crew quarters of this pair were

CAIRNGOWAN of 1952 was built for the Canadian service of Cairn Line of Newcastle (above), Houlder Brothers ore-carrier ORELIA of 1954 (below).   (M. Donnelly)

heated and ventilated for world-wide trading and their Gray-Polar six-cylinder diesels gave them a service speed of 13.5 knots. The Greek shipowner Livanos went on to take the largest number of tramps from the yard, thirteen in total, with Irish Shipping Ltd following not far behind with eleven ships, including the steam tanker *Irish Holly* 2940/56 of 3350 dwt with engines supplied by Smiths Dock Co. Ltd at South Bank on the Tees.

Ten small shelterdeckers of 3400 dwt were completed in the immediate post-World War II years for Scandinavian owners such as P. Banck, C. Ostberg and A. Falkland of Norway; C.K. Hansen, M. Nielsen of Denmark; and C. Abrahamsen, O.M. Thore of Sweden. Ellerman Lines took fourteen small cargo-liners of up to 5300 dwt with eight for their Papayanni Line and six for their Wilson Line. The China Navigation Co. Ltd of John Swire & Sons took five small cargo-liners of 3650 dwt for their Far Eastern services. In addition, a trio of cargo-liners was completed for Elder,Dempster for their trade to West Africa, *Perang* 6177/54, *Degema* 8153/59 and *Dixcove* 8138/59, with a turbine-driven pair for Cairn Line of Steamships Ltd, Newcastle for their Canadian trade, *Cairngowan* 7503/52 and *Cairndhu* 7603/52, and another pair for British India S.N. Co. Ltd, *Urlana* 6835/46 and *Umaria* 6835/46. The Guinea Gulf Line of John Holt of Liverpool took delivery of the last Gray-built cargo-liner in June,1959, *Mary Holt* 7459/59. She was a turbine-driven ship of 8260 dwt with some 12,000 cu. feet of refrigerated space.

Houlder Brothers took delivery of six Port Talbot class ore-carriers of 9500 dwt between 1954/56, four of them fitted with twin five-cylinder Gray-Polar diesels and the last pair with five-cylinder Doxford oil engines, They were completed for Ore Carriers Ltd as *Orelia, Oreosa, Orepton, Oredian, Oregis* and *Oremina*; and a further pair of 9500 dwt ore-carriers was completed for Cia Sud-Americana de Vapores of Chile as *Tofo* 6861/51 and *Romeral* 6861/53. Tramps were supplied to many owners, including the last Hartlepool-built tramp for a Hartlepool shipowner, *Dunelmia* 4907/52 for the Metcalfe Shipping Co. Ltd, and the last tramp built by the yard was *Riverdore* 8080/59 for London Greek owner Michalinos & Company.

However the order book at the end of 1959 showed only two more ore-carriers for Houlder Brothers, and one bulk carrier each for Stephenson Clarke Ltd and Irish Shipping Ltd. The 17100 dwt ore-carriers *Joya McCance* 11871/60 and *Mabel Warwick* 11632/60 were completed as the largest vessels ever built at Hartlepool, their beam of 69 feet allowing just six inches clearance each side as they negotiated the locks out of Hartlepool. The bulker *Irish Sycamore* of 15550 dwt followed in 1961, and then the last ship completed by Gray, the bulker *Blanchland* of 12400 dwt completed in November,1961. The Central Marine Engine Works had supplied the majority of all steam and diesel engines for ships built at the

London Greek tramp RIVERDORE of 1959 (above), and restored paddle ferry WINGFIELD CASTLE alongside the Gray Dockyard.   (Hartlepool Council)

yard in post-World War II years, however the oil engine for *Blanchland* was manufactured by Doxford at Sunderland.

Sir William Gray III had remained as Chairman,but in 1955 his Managing Director F.C. Pyman had retired having served Grays since 1911. He was replaced by two Managing Directors in William T. Gray, and Stephen Furness, formerly in charge of the Furness family yard at Haverton Hill on Tees (q.v.) which had been sold in 1951 to London financier Charles Clore. Stephen Furness retired in 1958, and the Gray family then attempted to steer the business towards ship-repairing. Repair work continued in the Jackson dry-docks, and the Central Dock dry-dock and the Graythorp yard on the Tees until closure in March,1963 with the Dockyard at Jackson Dock having been occupied by Grays for nearly a century. A contract to convert four Norwegian tankers into bulk carriers had been carried out in 1961/62 for Olsen & Ugelstad A/S and Westfal-Larsen A/S of Bergen. The completion of the conversion of *Etnefjell* on 22nd October,1962 signalled the announcement of voluntary liquidation of the company.

The Graythorp repair yard was then acquired by Smiths Dock Co. Ltd in 1963, the contents of the Hartlepool yards having been auctioned in May,1963 and the yards then demolished. The Graythorp yard was used by Laing Offshore in 1974/75 to build two 400 feet high jacket structures for the B.P. Forties field in the North Sea. Sir William Gray III retired to his home at Eggleston Hall, where he lived until his death in 1978 at the age of 82 years, of which nearly 40 years had been spent as Chairman of the company. His son, William T. Gray was tragically killed in a car accident in 1972.

FURNESS,WITHY & CO. LTD.

The Middleton yard of Edward Withy situated in the main harbour at Hartlepool had been building ships under the Withy name since 1869 when local shipowner Christopher Furness acquired a controlling interest in 1884. Previously to 1869 the yard had been run in partnership by John Denton and William Gray (q.v.) before they vacated it to move to the Jackson Dockyard. Edward Withy and his partner Edward Alexander built thirty small steamers in a five year period, but Edward Alexander withdrew in late 1873 from the shipyard to move to Cardiff to join his cousin Capt. E.H. Capper in the new shipping company of Capper,Alexander & Company. Edward Withy continued building iron steamers under his own name, and built his first steel ship, *Cyanus* in 1880, for Steel,Young & Company of London, who had twenty five ships from the yard, and she was built on the longitudinal

The building berths and dry-dock of Furness, Withy & Co. Ltd. (Hartlepool Museum)

bracket system, invented and patented by himself and his employee, George W. Sivewright. However Edward Withy decided to emigrate to New Zealand in 1884.

Christopher Furness then appointed Henry Withy, brother of Edward, as Managing Director of the yard. The iron *Gothenburg City* was completed for Furness that year, followed by his first steel steamer *Washington City* in 1885. Tramps were then completed for many local owners such as Ropner; Herskind & Woods; Horsley; Sivewright, Bacon; and Hardy,Wilson. The passenger carrying *Wastwater* 2874/89 was launched by the wife of Henry Withy for the Australian coastal trades of James Huddart of Melbourne, and followed in the wake of *Era* 2379/88 which had been completed for Smith & Son of Australia. The last iron ship built by the yard was *Lydie* 1595/87 for Burdick,Cook of London, and then standard designs of steel single-deck tramps were built from 1887 and welldeck tramps with raised quarterdecks from 1890.

Christopher Furness then combined his Hartlepool shipbuilding yard with his shipowning interests into a limited liability company, Furness,Withy & Co. Ltd, incorporated on 16th September,1891 at Baltic Chambers, Surtees Street, West Hartlepool with a nominal capital of £700,000. There were 7,000 shares of £100 each of which all but £5,000 was paid-up. The directors were the three directors of the Withy yard, namely Christopher Furness, Henry Withy and Richard Vick; as well as Robert B. Stoker, George L. Wooley and Thomas King. George William Sivewright was appointed Manager of the yard and dry-dock under the Managing Director, Henry Withy.

The first ship completed by the Middleton yard under the new company title was the Greek *Marietta Ralli* 2339/91 for the Ralli Brothers. Christopher Furness used the inherent flexibility of the new company with its shipyard to good effect. Keels were laid down 'on-spec' and available for sale to other shipowners at any time during construction or 'off-the-peg' when completed. Any completed ship not sold at a good profit would then be traded by the company via its Chartering Department. The name *Calcutta City* was proposed for five steamers building at the yard, all of which were completed for other shipowners. He set-up subsidiary companies such as the Chesapeake & Ohio Steamship Co. Ltd in 1893 and built three steamers of 5000 dwt at his yard for the trade between Newport News and Liverpool and London, *Appomattox* 3338/93, *Chickahominy* 3332/93 and *Greenbrier* 3332/93. Seven more steamers were built for Gulf Line Ltd and the associated Manchester Liners Ltd between 1899 and 1904.

In 1896 extensive alterations were made to the Middleton yard by extending the three berths to 450, 550 and 700 feet in length, and by converting the yard to electrical power to handle large steel plates of 70 feet length and five feet width from the Consett Iron Company. A 380 feet long graving dock was built to dry-dock ships up to 7000 dwt with the total cost of these improvements in the region of £60,000. The yard capacity was now around 50,000 tons of ships/year.

Due to the alterations only three ships were completed in 1897, all to a standard design of spar-decked tramp of 3750 grt on dimensions of 340 feet by 47 feet, and a further sixteen examples of this design were built at the yard. The large passenger-cargo liner *Victoria* with accomodation for 120 passengers was launched in August,1897 by Lady Furness for the new Wilsons & Furness - Leyland Line Ltd service from London to Boston and New York. *Victoria* was the largest vessel built at Hartlepool at that time and was also impressive-looking with her four masts, and she could carry 8150 tons of cargo in her seven holds and 'tween decks, where 850 head of cattle and horses could be stabled. The similar *Chicago* 6438/98 was completed for Thomas Wilson to run on the new services with *Victoria* and other new Furness and Leyland ships. Transatlantic passenger/cargo-liners were built for other companies as well, with *Soestdijk* 6445/01, *Amsteldijk* 6435/01 and *Sloterdijk* 6498/01 for Holland America Line; *Marburg* 5967/00 and *Freiburg* 5178/00 for Norddeutscher Lloyd of Germany; and *Bodenia* 7649/02, *Frankenwald* 4026/08, *Westerwald* 4056/08 and *Spreewald* 3900/08 for Hamburg Amerika Line. The latter trio were the last ships to be built at the yard under the Furness,Withy name.

In 1909 Sir Christopher Furness amalgamated the Middleton yard with his Irvine's Harbour yard (q.v.), with both now trading as Irvine's Shipbuilding & Dry Dock Co. Ltd. This came about due to falling orders at the Middleton yard, and the realisation that more effective marketing would result from the use of a single yard name. He then introduced a profit-sharing scheme into the yards and six ships were ordered for Furness companies to set the scheme in motion, the first being the 4700 dwt *Asiana* launched in May,1909 by Lady Furness as the first ship from the Middleton yard under the new Irvine title. During the first nine months of the scheme the participants received some 9% interest on their shares. However it became obvious that the scheme had been deigned by Furness to improve output and efficiency at the Middleton yard, and it was then opposed by the trade unions, who held a ballot on the scheme which was voted out.

In 1911 Sir Christopher Furness took a 50% interest in Houlder Brothers and their managed companies, Empire Transport Co. Ltd and the British Empire Steam Navigation Co. Ltd. Some sixteen ships were then ordered for Houlder companies between 1911 and 1915 for trading to the Plate. These included the large refrigerated meat carriers for Houlder Line, *El Paraguayo* 8508/12 and *La Correntina* 8529/12, with two sets of triple expansion engines driving twin propellers at 15 knots. The completion of these Houlder orders in 1915 added yet another illustrious shipping company name to the yard's list of customers e.g. Hapag Lloyd, Holland America Line, Donaldson, Leyland, Wilson, Elder Dempster, Allan Line, Clan Line and the various Furness,Withy companies.

Output during World War I included the tankers *Palmleaf* 5489/16 and *Belgol* 2648/17, the tramp *Thistlemore* 5019/17 for Albyn Line of Sunderland, and two large cargo-liners for Manchester Liners Ltd, *Manchester Brigade* 6042/18 and *Manchester Division* 6048/18 as well as the refrigerated meat carrier *Duquesa* 8663/18 for Houlder Line. Six standard 'B' type tramps and one standard 'Z' tanker were also built, in addition to two Flower class sloops and six 'X' class motorised barges. The 'B' types were all completed in 1919 for private owners, four for Elder,Dempster *Boutry, Bereby, Badagry* and *Bonny*; and two for Leyland Line *Bolivian* and *Emlynian*.

The two yards under the Irvine title i.e. the Middleton yard and the Harbour yard, were sold by Furness,Withy & Co. Ltd in 1917 for £347,500 to a syndicate acting through the Commercial Bank of London. This syndicate included R.A. Workman of Workman,Clark & Co. Ltd, the Belfast shipbuilder, shipowner John Esplen, London financiers Clarence Hatry, P. Haig Thomas and S.W. Lund. A new company was formed with the same Irvine name and the capital structure was increased allowing the yard to prosper in the immediate post-World War I boom. The Middleton yard received three orders from Furness,Withy & Co. Ltd, the former owners, and completed as *Aviemore* 4060/20 for Johnston Line, and *Parisiana* 6640/21 and *Cynthiana* 6629/22 for the parent company.

However with the serious freight slump in 1920, the last year that the Irvine company showed a profit was 1921. Dividends on ordinary shares were not paid after 1920, and on preference shares after 1922. The last ships to be built in both the Middleton yard and Harbour yard went into the water in 1924. The final ships from the Middleton yard were :-

PENCARROW	4841/21	R. Chellew, Cardiff
WALLSEND	2851/22	Burnett S.S. Co. Ltd,Newcastle
PENDEEN	4231/23	R. Chellew, Cardiff
SALMONPOOL	4803/24	Ropner, Hartlepool
CORINTHIC	4823/24	Walter Cockerline,Hull

Both yards then remained idle until 1930 when liquidation was decided upon, and the Harbour yard was sold for scrap. The Middleton yard was reprieved by a local syndicate of businessmen, who intended to use the old yard for repair work but as there was so little available during the Depression they turned to shipbreaking. The Capper,Alexander tramp *Shrewsbury* built by Gray as *Coniston* in 1901 was broken up in 1932. Finally in 1938 National Shipbuilders Security Ltd purchased the yard and dismantled the berths, but left the dry-dock and fitting-out quay intact to be put to good use during World War II.

IRVINE'S SHIPBUILDING & DRY DOCKS CO. LTD

The Harbour yard of Robert Irvine referred to in the previous section was located on the south side of the West Harbour at Hartlepool. This harbour gave access to the much-used Coal Dock when Robert Irvine, a native of Glasgow, first began building ships in 1864 with his partner Alexander Currie. The partnership was dissolved in 1866 and the shallow-draft steamer *Ogmore* of 149 tons was the first ship built under the Robert Irvine name in 1866. A dry-dock of 315 feet in length was ready later that year and only repair work was undertaken until 1870. Some of his ships were built 'on-spec' and he traded six of these unsold steamers on his own account. By 1882 Robert Irvine had built colliers and small tramps for many local owners e.g. George Pyman, and following the death of his wife later that year the day-to-day running of the yard was left to his sons, particularly Robert Irvine Jnr.

During the years 1885 and 1886 no ships were constructed at the yard, which was modernised to build steel steamers beginning in 1887. Christopher Furness first appeared as a customer of Irvine in 1891, with the launch of his *Welldeck* 2697/91, which as the name implies was a well-deck steamer and was sold on to Hamilton,Fraser & Company,Liverpool before completion as *Inchdune*. Tramps were completed for many British and Greek owners e.g. Evan Thomas Radcliffe of Cardiff, Orders & Handford of Newport, and Michalinos of Greece. The tramp *Jacob Bright* of 4159 grt was launched in December,1896 for J. Bright of Manchester, and the yard was then closed for modernisation and expansion. While the work was being carried out, Christopher Furness and Furness,Withy & Co. Ltd gained control of the yard, which was renamed Irvine's Shipbuilding & Dry Docks Co. Ltd.

When the yard re-opened in 1898 it had three berths with the longest 390 feet in length, and the dry-dock had been extended from 315 feet to 380 feet. David G. Irvine, second son of the founder, became Managing Director with Sir Christopher Furness as Chairman and Henry Withy, Richard Vick and Stephen W. Furness on the Board. The former capacity of the yard at 20,000 tons of ships/year was more than doubled by the use of larger 70 feet long plates and the installation of 20-ton travelling cranes to lift them. The first ship launched after the modernisation was *Edenhall* for West Hartlepool Steam Navigation Co. Ltd, control of which was also gained in the same year by Sir Christopher Furness. *Edenhall* had been launched by Miss Anne Guthe, and Furness merged the Guthe tramp fleet into the West Hartlepool Steam Navigation Co. Ltd, now with a capital of £500,000 to expand the fleet. Seven tramps were built by the yard to the order of this company between 1899 and 1902, with *Lindenhall* of 1900 the first of a standard design of spar-decker tramp of 4000 grt of dimensions 345 feet by 48 feet of which a dozen were built by the yard. Another standard design of spar-decker tramp had dimensions of 325 feet by 47 feet and was of 3000 grt and twenty examples were built by the yard from 1903, although some were strengthened as two-deckers and some were completed as single-deckers. A standard design of collier was also produced of 1800 grt and measured 280 feet by 40 feet, starting with *Charleston* 1866/08, *Portinglis* 1867/08 and *Rouen* 1868/08 for Furness, Withy & Co. Ltd, and a further dozen examples were built before the outbreak of World War I. All of these standard designs of tramps and colliers were three-island types with engines amidships.

Robert Irvine had died in 1903 following the deaths of two of his sons, Robert Irvine Jnr. and William Charles Irvine. Robert Irvine Jnr. had managed the shipping side of the business after the Furness take-over in 1897 and his biggest ship had been completed at the yard in 1899 as *Robert Irvine*. Among other customers for cargo-liners were Elder, Dempster with *Palma* 2981/07, *Shonga* 3044/09 and *Winneba* 3040/09; Dampf. Union A.G., Germany with *Siegmund* 3034/05, *Sieglinde* 2887/05, *Gunther* 3037/06, and *Gurtrune* 3039/06 for North and South American services. Strick Line had the four-hold *Nigaristan* 4505/11 built at the yard, and the cargo-liner *Digby* 3960/13 was the most impressive of over twenty ships built for Furness companies since the take-over in 1897. She was built for the Warren Line service between Liverpool and North America. She had four holds with seven watertight bulkheads, two masts with 12 derricks, a long bridge structure with two decks for passengers above the weather deck and a fine counter stern. Her triple expansion engines gave a speed of 12.5 knots on 42 tons of coal/day. Her hull was strengthened forward for ice, and she was a real pioneer of cargo handling for she possessed a side-loading port! Her holds were ventilated for the carriage of fruit and dairy produce, and she had accomodation for 58 first-class and 32 second-class passengers.

The yard was busy on the outbreak of World War I with orders for Furness companies, and for companies managed by Houlder Brothers, half-owned by Furness since 1911. The yard was allowed to complete these ships before embarking on work for the war effort in 1915. This consisted of three 'Flower' class sloops of 1250 tons displacement, and six motorised barges of 100 tons dwt, and eight standard 'C' type tramps of 5060 dwt. A number of the latter were still under construction at the end of the war, and were purchased by tramp owners such as Tatem of Cardiff. The yard together with the former Withy yard was sold by Furness,Withy & Co. Ltd for £347,500 in 1917 as described in the previous section.

The new owners received orders for six ships from the previous owners of the yards, and *Dromore* 4096/20 and *Incemore* 4098/21 were completed for Johnston Line and *Peruviana* 4099/21 for the Furness parent company by the Harbour yard. The yard was to construct only five more ships before scarcity of orders forced closure in 1924 :-

EVANGER	3869/20	Westfal-Larsen,Bergen
BARON VERNON	2743/22	H. Hogarth,Glasgow 158
BENGORE HEAD	2609/22	Head Line,Belfast 34
KILNSEA	5415/23	Brown Atkinson,Hull 216
HEWORTH	2855/24	Burnett S.S. Co. Ltd,Newcastle 226

In addition the Spanish ship *Zabalbide* was fitted out and completed at the yard in 1922, after being towed down from the Tyne where she had been launched by the Newcastle Shipbuilding Co. Ltd (q.v.). After the launch of the collier *Heworth* in February,1924 the yard remained idle until 1930 when it was sold for dismantling with the dry-dock filled in. The site of the yard is now occupied by the clubhouse and boat compound of the Tees Sailing Club.

VAUXHALL of 1900 was built for local owners by Robert Irvine.

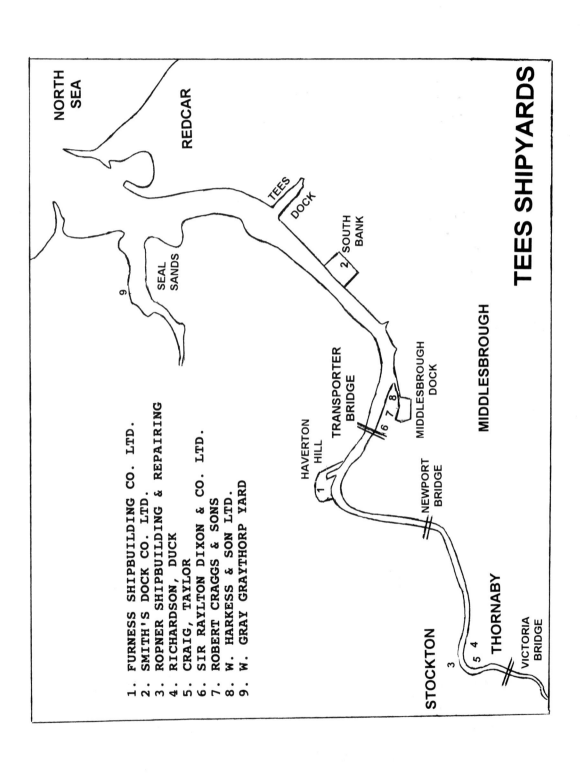

TEES SHIPYARDS

1. FURNESS SHIPBUILDING CO. LTD.
2. SMITH'S DOCK CO. LTD.
3. ROPNER SHIPBUILDING & REPAIRING
4. RICHARDSON, DUCK
5. CRAIG, TAYLOR
6. SIR RAYLTON DIXON & CO. LTD.
7. ROBERT CRAGGS & SONS
8. W. HARKESS & SON LTD.
9. W. GRAY GRAYTHORP YARD

NORTH SEA

REDCAR

SEAL SANDS

TEES DOCK

SOUTH BANK

MIDDLESBROUGH DOCK

MIDDLESBROUGH

TRANSPORTER BRIDGE

HAVERTON HILL

NEWPORT BRIDGE

STOCKTON

THORNABY

VICTORIA BRIDGE

FURNESS SHIPBUILDING CO. LTD.

This yard was the largest on the Tees in terms of size of ship built and steel output. It had been built as an emergency World War I shipyard as a subsidiary of Furness, Withy & Co. Ltd. At the end of 1917 approval was given by the Government to Marmaduke Furness, only son of Sir Christopher Furness (died 1912), to transform a ninety acre greenfield site at Haverton Hill on the north bank of the Tees. At the western end of the site was a cement works but the land was below river level at high water, necessitating the reclaiming of the land by dumping a million tons of rubble and sand to raise the 85 acres by some twelve to fifteen feet. The fitting-out basin was created at the eastern end, and was completed with an overhead crane and shops for engineers and out-fitting trades. The eight-berth yard could build ships of between 450 and 700 feet and had high tower cranes of 4 and 6-ton capacity on the berths. It was 'tooled-up' during 1918 and the first keel was laid only three months after the construction had started, with the workforce at full strength at the end of the war when manpower was more plentiful.

Eight standard 'N1' type prefabricated single deck shelterdeckers were ordered by the Government, with the first launched as *War Energy* on 29th April, 1919 and completed as *Danier* for Lloyd Royal Belge in October, 1919. The remainder of the Government order was also completed for Belgian and Italian owners during 1920, and the first commercially-placed order was completed for the Swedish East Asiatic Company as *Benares* 5762/20 in September, 1920. She was a single deck shelterdecker and seven more sisters were completed in 1920/21 with three for Cia Nav Sota y Aznar, Spain as *Abodi Mendi* 5873/21, *Arola Mendi* 5853/21 and *Altobizka Mendi* 5954/21 and the others as *Citta di Messina* 5879/20, *Rigi* 5810/21 and *Liss* 5853/21, with the last sister completed as *La Crescenta* 5873/23 for the Crescent Navigation Co. Ltd, London.

During August and September, 1919 the Furness family relinquished their shareholdings in Furness, Withy & Co. Ltd with Marmaduke, Walter, Ethelbert, Einar and John Furness resigning from the Board and taking no further interest in shipowning. A 'management buyout' had been mounted for their company and involved the purchase of all Furness family shares in return for £6M of orders for the new Furness shipyard. Some 18 two-deck shelterdeckers and two colliers were completed between 1921 and 1925 for Furness, Withy & Co. Ltd and its many subsidiaries. Two more two-deck shelterdeckers were laid down for Furness but completed for W. Wilhelmsen as *Delaware* 4501/20 and *Louisiana* 4497/21.

Some sixteen colliers of around 2000 dwt were then completed during 1923/24 for collier operators Broomhill Collieries Ltd, H. Harrison(Shipping) Ltd,

Vale Shipping Co. Ltd, E.J. Lindley and the local T.H. Donkin. One unusual completion during April,1924 was the two-masted schooner *Princess* for Sir James Knott, founder of the Prince Line who had sold out to Furness,Withy & Co. Ltd at the end of 1916. She was used to cruise the Mediterranean from a base at Monte Carlo and had dimensions of 185 feet length, 30 feet beam and 16 feet depth to the upper deck. The first of several tramps was also completed at the yard in 1925 :-

ENTON	4310/25	Avenue Shipping Co. Ltd
ASHLEIGH	4853/25	W.J. Tatem,Cardiff
TYNEBRIDGE	4442/25	Crosby,McGee & Co.,Hartlepool
LEVENBRIDGE	4342/28	"
OUSEBRIDGE	5601/29	"
APPLEDORE	5218/29	W.J. Tatem,Cardiff
EVERLEIGH	5222/30	"
HADLEIGH	5222/30	"

as well as five deep-sea tankers, with *Java* also sold to Athel Line in 1933 to become *Athelviking*:-

JAVA	8779/26	J. Ludwig Mowinckels,Bergen
ATHELPRINCE	8800/26	Athel Line,London
ATHELQUEEN	8780/28	"
ATHELCROWN	11999/29	"
ATHELREGENT	8881/30	"

A feature in the outfitting-basin between 1926 and 1930 were many bridge-forward engines-aft Great Lakes grain traders and gypsum rock carriers for customers such as Steamships Ltd,Montreal; Toronto Vessel Agency; Canada Cement Transport Co. Ltd; United States Gypsum Company,Chicago; Coal Carriers Corporation,Montreal; Imperial Oil Company of Canada and Frontenac Oil Co. Ltd, Montreal. One of these, *Cementkarrier*, was one of the first diesel-electric ships built in the North East, having two Polar single-acting two stroke cycle airless-injection engines each coupled to a direct-current generator, which supplied a propulsion motor. Four shallow-draft 'Mosquito' tankers were built for Gulf Oil for use in transporting oil from Lake Maracaibo to the refineries on the Dutch offshore islands.

However the best-looking ships from the yard at this time were a pair of twin-funnelled passenger/cargo-liners for Grace Line of the United States. *Santa Maria* was launched first on 15th August,1927 and her sister *Santa Barbara* followed her into the Tees on 8th December,1927. They were completed in April and August,1928 as handsome twin-screw motorships and they made a fine sight as

The Furness yard built ALLEGHANY of 1922 (above) for Furness,Withy & Co. Ltd; and
ASHLEIGH of 1925 for Tatem of Cardiff.   (E. Johnson & F.W. Hawks)

they were towed under the Transporter Bridge of 1911 to conduct builders trials and speed trials over the measured mile, before departing for American and Caribbean waters.

The keel was laid in September,1929 of the first of a trio of twin-screw, twin-funnelled and engines-aft whale factory ships. She was launched on 30th April,1930 as *Sir James Clark Ross* 14362/30 for C.A. Larsen of Sandefjord and was completed in August,1930 in time to sail south for the Antarctic whaling season. She was to a new design on dimensions of length 540 feet and 74 feet beam and 34 feet depth to the upper whale gutting deck, and she returned to the yard for modifications on 4th June,1932. Two sisters were completed for Hvalf. Sydhavet and Hvalf. Vestfold of Johan Rasmussen of Sandefjord as *Svend Foyn* 14543/31 and *Vestfold* 14547/31.

The Depression years 1932 to 1935 saw many of the eight berths at the yard idle. Three small tankers were delivered to the British American Oil Co. Ltd, *Britamlube, Britamolene* and *Britamoco* during 1932, as well as a pair of general cargo ships for Cie des Bateaux a Vapeur du Nord,Dunkirk as *Amienmois* and *Remois*, both 3713/32. The yard then built a caisson for the Southern Railway Company dock at Southampton which left the Tees during June,1933. Three tramp keels were laid between March and May,1933 and were delivered as *Devon City* 4928/33, *Houston City* 4935/34 for Reardon Smith of Cardiff and *Arctees* 3953/34. This latter tramp was of 7068 dwt and had been designed by Sir Joseph Isherwood as an 'Arcform' tramp with an unusual hull form. Her cross-section was shaped like a wine cask standing on end, her widest beam being just below the waterline and some 10% greater than a normal tramp. She was launched on 21st January,1934 and completed in March of that year and her fuel consumption in service was lower but she rolled badly in heavy weather with her hatches awash, and the design was only used for a few tramps and tankers. The twin-screw motor coaster *Fauvette* 618/34 was completed for the General Steam Navigation Co. Ltd,London, and there were only two completions during 1935, the coaster *Cragside* 495/35 for the Tyne-Tees Steamship Co. Ltd and the tanker *San Adolfo* 7364/35 for Eagle Oil.

The upturn in trade in 1936 saw the yard complete eleven ships during that year, eight of these being Russian timber ships of 2900 grt. They were of engines-amidships design with a goalpost mast in front of the bridge, and their steam reciprocating engines gave a service speed of 12 knots. Three tramp keels had been laid at the end of 1935 for Reardon Smith of Cardiff and were completed as *Bradford City, Dallas City* and *Cornish City*, all 4952/36. The first of a pair of Mediterranean cargo-liners for Prince Line was delivered in December,1936 as *Syrian Prince* 1988/36, and her sister *Cyprian Prince* was completed in the following month. Three shallow-draft 'mosquito' tankers were delivered during 1937 to the Lago Shipping Co. Ltd, subsidiary of Standard Oil of the United States for use on Lake Maracaibo. Three West African steam traders of 8260 dwt were delivered to the United Africa Co. Ltd (later Palm Line) as *Conakrian* 4876/37, *Lafian* 4876/37 and *Zarian* 4871/38.

A 4000-ton lift floating dock was then built for the South African Railways & Harbour Board with dimensions 380 feet length and 88 feet width, and left the Tees in tow during September,1938 and arrived at Durban on 1st December,1938. Two shallow-draft 'mosquito' tankers were built for Shell, *Rosalia* and *Rebeca*, and three deep-sea tankers of 12000 dwt, *San Delfino*, *San Ernesto* and *British Liberty*, completed the yard production before the outbreak of World War II. The 9000 dwt cargo-liner *African Prince* was completed for the U.S.A. - South Africa service of Prince Line a few days after the outbreak of war, and then the yard was switched to the production of tankers.

During the war years 1939/46 the yard launched a total of 26 deep-sea tankers, sixteen coastal 'Chant' tankers, six tramps and three whale factory ships. The deep-sea tankers comprised ten of the 12000 dwt 'Ocean' type, six of the 14700 dwt 'Norwegian' type, eight of the 12000 dwt 'Standard Fast' type as well as two to private order, *British Vigour* 5844/43 and *British Purpose* 5845/43. The tramps were two standard 'Empire' 'B' types, two for Reardon Smith of Cardiff, *Madras City* 5092/40 and *Orient City* 5095/40, and two ships for United Africa Co. Ltd (later Palm Line) *Kumasian* 7221/43 and *Lafian* 7221/43. The whale factory ships were to the same design and dimensions as the earlier trio built in 1930/31 for Norwegian owners, and completed as *Southern Venturer* 14066/45 and *Southern Harvester* 15088/46 for Chr. Salvesen of Leith, and *Norvhal* 13830/45 for Melsom & Melsom of Larvik in Norway. All three had triple expansion steam engines driving twin propellers, and were followed by a larger motor-driven factory ship *Kosmos V* 19000/48 and 26610 dwt for Anders Jahre of Sandefjord. Her Doxford oil engine was built on the Tyne by the North Eastern Marine Eng. Co. Ltd, as had the steam engines for the earlier trio.

An extra four emergency berths had been used at the yard during the war, and the vast war experience of the yard in building tankers was used to good effect during the golden years of Tees shipbuilding up to 1963 :-

BRITISH ADMIRAL	8735/47	British Tanker Co. Ltd
BRITISH EMPRESS	8745/47	"
BRITISH ENSIGN	8738/47	"
BRITISH ISLES	8738/47	"
MARIE MAERSK	10658/48	A.P. Moller,Denmark
ELEONORA MAERSK	10658/49	"

SAN SILVESTRE 2	10953/49	Eagle Oil 3
SAN SALVADOR 2	10802/50	"
C.J. HAMBRO	15773/49	Erling H. Samuelsen,Oslo
FERNCASTLE	15980/49	Fearnley & Eger,Oslo
JANUS	15943/50	A. Jahre,Norway
SOLOR	15775/50	Samuel Ugelstad,Norway
H.M. WRANGELL	16027/50	H. M. Wrangell,Oslo
BRITISH YEOMAN 2	8738/49	British Tanker Co. Ltd 2
BRITISH GENERAL 3	8775/50	"
BRITISH GUIDE	8778/51	"
LONDON PRIDE	10776/50	London & Overseas Freighters Ltd 23
LONDON ENTERPRISE	10776/50	"
MARLENA	15638/50	Gulf Oil 325
SATURNUS	10608/50	Saturnus Rederi A/B,Sweden
CERES	10608/50	"
MAGWA	15746/51	Gulf Oil 325
SUHAIL	15813/52	"
VANJA	15968/51	Halfdan Ditlev-Simonsen,Norway
KNUT KNUTSEN	15935/51	Knut Knutsen A/B,Norway
WHEATFIELD	10646/52	Hunting & Son,Newcastle 56
GRETAFIELD	10646/52	"
SIBELLA	16041/52	Tschudi & Olsen,Oslo
DUCHESS OF ATHENS	11766/52	S.G. Livanos,Greece
ATLANTIC LORD	11648/53	"
MERCHANT BARON	12101/53	Drake Shpg. Co. Ltd,London 263
ANITA	11955/53	F. H. Samuelsen,Oslo
LONDON VICTORY	12132/52	London & Overseas Freighters Ltd 23
LONDON MAJESTY	12132/52	"
LONDON SPLENDOUR	16195/53	"
LONDON LOYALTY	12132/54	"
LONDON PRESTIGE	16195/54	"
CALTEX CANBERRA	11746/53	Overseas Tankship (Texas Oil) 360
CALTEX PERTH	11746/53	"
MELIKA	20551/54	Gulf Oil 325
CYGNUS	10900/54	Soc. Transoceanica Canopus(R+K)
VASSILIKI	10900/54	Nueva Vista Cia Nav SA
CHLOE	16193/54	Cia Armadora SA (Lykiardopulo)
PRESIDENT BRAND	16210/54	Northern Steamships Ltd,S/Africa
SOUTHERN SATELLITE	12480/55	Chr. Salvesen,Leith 334
KARMT	11767/55	H.M. Wrangell,Haugesund
LONDON INTEGRITY	12132/55	London & Overseas Freighters Ltd 23
SAN PATRICIO 2	10711/55	Eagle Oil,London 3
SAN FABIAN	12180/56	"
SAN FELIPE	12180/56	"
VIVIEN LOUISE	16226/56	British Oil Shipping Co. Ltd,London 66
LONDON VALOUR	16268/56	London & Overseas Freighters Ltd 23
SIRIUS	16215/55	Soc. Transoceanica Canopus (R+K)
PANAGHIA	16009/56	Porto Alegre Cia Nav (R+K)
SAMUEL UGELSTAD	21177/56	Samuel Ugelstad Rederi,Norway

ARABIAN GULF	20504/57	Gulf Oil 325
LONDON TRADITION	16275/57	London & Overseas Freighters Ltd 23
LONDON RESOLUTION	16269/58	"
VIRGINIA	11930/57	Mavroleon Bros. 290
VIOLETTA	11642/58	"
BELGULF GLORY	12017/58	Gulf Oil (Belgium)
BELGULF PROGRESS	12017/59	"
TEESFIELD	12145/59	Hunting & Son,Newcastle 56
REGENT FALCON	12353/59	John I. Jacobs,London 252
SAN EDMUNDO	11955/58	Eagle Oil,London 3
SAN ERNESTO 2	12301/59	"
SAN CALISTO 2	21179/59	"
SAN CONRADO 2	21180/60	"
OVERSEAS EXPLORER	16266/59	London & Overseas Freighters Ltd 23
OVERSEAS PIONEER	16266/59	"
LLANGORSE	21846/60	Evan Thomas Radcliffe,Cardiff 70
VOLUTA	24406/62	Shell Tankers Ltd 1
GULF BRITON	26595/61	Gulf Oil 325
GULF SCOT	26652/61	"
GULF DANE	26652/61	"
GULF FINN	26652/63	"

The yard remained Furness family owned with Stephen Furness as Chairman until 1951 when sold to London financier Charles Clore and his Sears Holdings. Stephen Furness then became in 1955 joint Managing Director of the William Gray yards at Hartlepool (q.v.). Before the sale, the yard built six small open shelterdeckers during 1948/49 for Svea of Sweden and fitted with 1350 bhp Fiat diesel engines. Four cargo-liners had also been completed, *Sherbro* and *Sekondi* both 4810/47 for Elder,Dempster, *Nigerian* 5202/48 for United Africa Co. Ltd (renamed Palm Line shortly afterwards), and *City of Philadelphia* 7591/49 for Ellerman Lines. Six tramps were then built for Greek owners:-

NYMPHE	8251/54	Cia Armadora Trans SA (Lykiardopulo)
PEGASUS	10446/57	Soc. Transoceanica Canopus SA (R + K)
PROCYON	10414/58	"
DUKE OF SPARTA	10823/59	Trent Maritime Co. Ltd (Livanos)
DUKE OF MISTRA	10793/59	"
DUKE OF ATHENS	10815/62	"

A floating dock of length 469 feet had been built in 1946 for A/B Finnboda Vaerft, Stockholm and left the Tees in tow on 28th September,1946; and a similar-sized dock left the river in tow in 1961 for Szczecin in Poland. Whereas the yard berths could accomodate the ore-carrier *Sept Iles* of 31100 dwt built in 1955 for the Iron Ore Transport Ltd of Canada and the tankers listed above in the 1950s and the

'Supertankers' PANAGHIA of 1955 (above) and VIVIEN LOUISE of 1956 (below).

Giant ore/bulk/oil FURNESS BRIDGE of 1971.

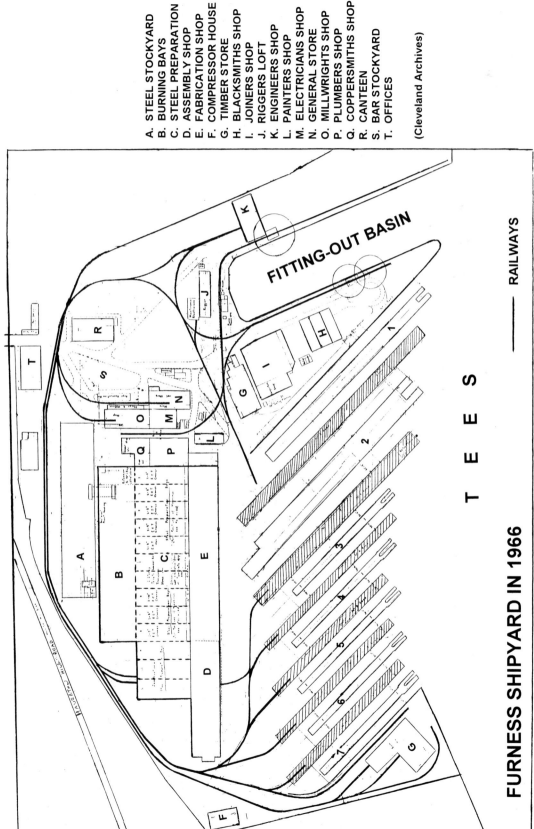

A. STEEL STOCKYARD
B. BURNING BAYS
C. STEEL PREPARATION
D. ASSEMBLY SHOP
E. FABRICATION SHOP
F. COMPRESSOR HOUSE
G. TIMBER STORE
H. BLACKSMITHS SHOP
I. JOINERS SHOP
J. RIGGERS LOFT
K. ENGINEERS SHOP
L. PAINTERS SHOP
M. ELECTRICIANS SHOP
N. GENERAL STORE
O. MILLWRIGHTS SHOP
P. PLUMBERS SHOP
Q. COPPERSMITHS SHOP
R. CANTEEN
S. BAR STOCKYARD
T. OFFICES

(Cleveland Archives)

FITTING-OUT BASIN

T E E S

—————— RAILWAYS

FURNESS SHIPYARD IN 1966

early 1960s, the berths had to be widened and lengthened to build the ever increasing size of supertankers and bulk carriers. Numbers 1 and 2 berths were enlarged to 950 feet length and 150 feet width in 1965/66 with 80-ton and 60-ton berth cranes as shown in the modern shipyard plan, with only four berths then regularly used. Modern prefabrication sheds and cranage were provided to lift large assemblies, with the yard switched to building bulk carriers and giant ore/bulk/oil carriers from 1963, as shown in the following deadweight table :-

DW t

ESSI GINA	53250/63	B.J. Ruud-Petersen,Oslo
NAESS TEXAS	34000/64	Naess Group (sulphur carrier) 319
NAESS LOUISIANA	34000/64	"
SIMONBURN	31410/65	Common Brothers,Newcastle 67
BUCCLEUCH	44000/65	British India/ P & O 42
COTSWOLD	44000/66	"
IRON PARKGATE	72000/66	Turnbull,Scott & Co. Ltd,London 84
HAMLET	51380/66	Brusgaard Kiosterud A/B,Sweden
NORSEMAN	51380/67	Odd Godager A/S, Oslo
POLYFREEDOM	52400/67	Einar Rasmussen A/S, Oslo
THORSDRAKE	52600/67	Thor Dahl A/S, Oslo
HAVERTON	57200/68	Haverton Shipping Co. Ltd 320
HAR SAGGI	77250/68	Transatlantic Trampships Inc. 323
MOUNT KATHERINA	77250/68	"
MOUNT EDEN	77250/68	"
HAR ADDIR	77250/68	El Yam Bulk Carriers Ltd
DUNSTANBURGH CASTLE	102,000/70	Bamburgh Shipping Co. Ltd 255
FURNESS BRIDGE	166,073/71	Furness,Withy & Co. Ltd 19
TYNE BRIDGE	166,753/72	Hunting & Son,Newcastle 56
ENGLISH BRIDGE	166,410/73	Bibby Line,Liverpool 195
SIR JOHN HUNTER	169,080/74	ThornhopeShpg.(Hilmar Reksten)322
SIR ALEXANDER GLEN	169,080/75	"
LIVERPOOL BRIDGE	169,044/76	Bibby Line,Liverpool 195

However it was not all plain sailing, as the launch of the first giant bulker *Essi Gina* in mid-1963 left the yard without work for the first time in thirty years, but orders were then gained from the Naess Group and Common Brothers. In one week in 1965 the yard received orders for the four 77250 dwt bulkers from Israel worth £11M as well as a 52,600 dwt bulker for Norway worth £2M.

The keel of the first of the six giant ore/bulk/oil carriers was laid in October,1969 and she was launched as *Furness Bridge* on 12th October,1970 with her huge bulk sliding down the ways and coming to a halt down-river in the narrow Tees without causing damage. She was fiited out in ten months and was towed stern-first down the Tees for trials in October,1971. Her five sisters took on average just under a year on the berth to build and five or six months to outfit. The last of the six left the river for trials in June,1976 and was renamed *Derbyshire* shortly afterwards. Her loss in a hurricane to the south of Japan in 1980 has received widespread publicity with alleged severe structural problems in some of the six ships. The oil drilling rig *Staflo* was launched at the yard in 1966, and in February,1967 brooke loose from her moorings and drifted one mile downstream to a point just above the Transporter Bridge near the former Dents and Tyne-Tees wharves. No damage was done and she was towed back to the yard for completion.

In October,1968 the Furness yard became part of the massive new Swan Hunter Shipbuilders Ltd consortium that included Smith's Dock Co. Ltd at South Bank. The six ore/bulk/oil carriers were built to a Swan Hunter design, and the yard shared in the building of two tankers of the 'Swan Maritime' deal with partner Maritime Fruit Carriers of Haifa,Israel. These were the 112,000 dwt crude carrier *Interoceanic II* and the 32,000 dwt products tanker *Robkap 6* both launched in February,1977. The yard did complete other ships in the 1970s with the vegetable oil tanker *Matadi Palm* 8870/70 of 13780 dwt being completed for the West African trade of Palm Line, and the bulk carrier *Capulet* 16488/72 of 25000 dwt being completed for world-wide tramping for Bowring of London.

Closer links were forged between the Haverton Hill yard and the South Bank yard of Smith's Dock Co. Ltd in the mid-1970s, with the Drawing Office at Haverton Hill doing technical work for South Bank. At the end of 1976 two orders for container ships for Blue Star Line were transferred to Haverton Hill from South Bank due to a full order book at the latter. The hull of the Blue Star heavy lift ship *Starman Anglia* 2777/77 was also sub-contracted from South Bank to the Neptune Yard of Swan Hunter on the Tyne. She was then towed down for out-fitting at Haverton Hill but just before completion a strike at the yard caused her to be finished off elsewhere. On the nationalisation of British shipbuilding on 1st July,1977 the Haverton Hill yard was transferred to the ownership of Smith's Dock Co. Ltd, a member of British Shipbuilders. The first Blue Star Line refrigerated container ship was named *Australia Star* in January,1978 but could not be launched until April because of a strike at the yard. She was for a new trade between Australia/New Zealand and the Middle East in frozen meat, and her sister was launched as *New Zealand Star* on 20th July,1978 by Mrs. Muldoon, wife of the New Zealand Prime Minister. They could carry 721 refrigerated containers and were of 17082 grt and fitted with 6-cylinder Sulzer oil engines manufactured on the Clyde by Barclay,Curle & Co. Ltd. *Australia Star* was completed in September,1978 and *New Zealand Star* in January,1979, and shortly afterwards the famous Haverton Hill yard closed down and was placed on a 'care and maintenance' basis. The prefabrication sheds and much of the shipyard is still visible today.

Aerial view of the Furness yard in the 1970s (above), and the last ship from the yard, NEW ZEALAND STAR of 1979 pictured as CHURCHILL. (Fotoflite)

SMITH'S DOCK CO. LTD.

This company had been formed in 1899 at North Shields from the shipbuilding and shiprepairing yards of the Smith and Edward families. In 1905 James Edwards took an option on 16 acres of land at South Bank and construction of two dry-docks began in 1907 and was completed at the end of 1908 with the first ships dry-docked in February, 1909. Shipbuilding began in 1910 to the immediate west of the dry-docks, and the first vessel completed was the dredger *Priestman* for C.H. Campbell. She was followed in the same year by twenty small trawlers and drifters, one whaler, two tugs, two barges and three coasters. In 1911 no less than 55 small trawlers, drifters and whalers were completed, and the yard engine works opened with the first engine fitted into the trawler *Lord Percy*. The first of over sixty whalecatchers built to the order of Christian Salvesen of Leith were completed in May and June, 1912 as *Saima, Sedna, Sitka* and *Symra*; and four coasters were built for Spanish, French and Norwegian owners. In 1913 some 27 small ships were built including trawlers, whalers and three Russian minesweepers, and two coasters to the order of subsidiaries of Furness, Withy & Co. Ltd, *Channel Trader* and *London Trader* , both 684/13.

The output during World War I was some 160 small ships including 15 submarine chasers to a yard design, forty minesweepers and 36 'Kil' class patrol boats with the last completing as *Kilmun* in 1920. At the outbreak of war all trawlers then building were requisitioned by the Admiralty, and some 4,000 ships had been repaired by the yard, a further two dry-docks having opened in 1915.

The years 1920/22 saw the introduction of arc-welding into the yard although the majority of the steelwork was still rivetted. Nine colliers were built for export, six for Soc. National d'Affretments, Havre, two for H.M. Wrangell and one for Jacob Olsen of Norway. A further sixteen colliers were built between 1924 and 1930 for British owners such as Witherington & Everett, Sharp Steamship Co. Ltd and Pelton Steamship Co. Ltd. Three small cargo-liners were built for the West African trade of John Holt & Co. Ltd, Liverpool, *Robert L. Holt* 2918/26, *John Holt* 2909/26 and *Jonathan L. Holt* 2909/26. The first tramp was built at the yard in 1924 for the Medomsley Steam Shipping Co. Ltd, Newcastle as *Alistruther* 3811/24, and was followed by two Ropner tramps, *Stonepool* 4803/28 and *Boulderpool* 4803/28. However the main output of the yard between 1927 and 1930 was seventeen Great Lakes grain traders such as *Aycliffe Hall* 1900/28 for the Hall Corporation of Canada with their characteristic bridge-forward engines-aft design.

The onset of the Depression in 1930 saw the yard still with a good order book, enabling the old Ropner shipbuilding yard at Stockton to be reactivated.

Aerial view of Smith's Dock Co. Ltd yard at South Bank in July, 1928, showing two tramps under construction on the berths, three ships in dry-dock, and the whale factory ship SOUTHERN EMPRESS and six whalecatchers alongside. (Smith's Dock Co. Ltd)

Three tramps for Watts,Watts & Co. Ltd were built at Stockton, *Dartford* 4093/30, *Deptford* 4101/31 and *Dulwich* 4102/31 as well as a few coasters and trawlers before the yard closed for ever in June,1931. The South Bank yard launched 25 trawlers and whalers in 1930, and five timber carriers for Scandinavian owners. However restrictions on whaling introduced that year meant that the annual output of the yard was never in large numbers again. Trawlers and a few whalers were the only products of the yard until 1938, with the worst year being 1932 when only the French motor trawler *Fismes* was launched.

In 1938 building of larger vessels resumed with the case-oil carrier *Cerion* 2588/38 completed for the Anglo-Saxon Petroleum Co. Ltd; the shallow-draft 'mosquito' tanker *Avila* 1635/38 for the Lago Shipping Co. Ltd subsidiary of Standard Oil; the collier *Capitaine St. Martin* 3450/38 for Union Industrielle,France; the Russian collier *Kokkinaki* 2019/39; and the good-looking Trinity House lighthouse inspection ship *Patricia* 1116/38.

On the outbreak of war six 560-ton whale catchers building at the yard for Norwegian owners were requisitioned by the Admiralty. In addition it was decided that more escort vessels should be built based on a proven design of the whalecatcher *Southern Pride* completed in 1936 by the yard for Christian Salvesen. This became the 'Flower' class corvette with 19 examples built by the yard and two hundred elsewhere. However the French corvette *La Bastiase* got no further than Tees Bay as she was lost while on sea trials in 1940 and a number of yard employees were killed. Thirteen 'River' class frigates and two 'Castle' class frigates and some armed trawlers were also built. On the merchant side four cargo-liners of 3150 dwt were completed in 1940 for Prince Line - *Norman Prince*, *Lancastrian Prince*, *Tudor Prince* and *Stuart Prince*. At the end of the war the South Bank yard had six building berths and four dry-docks.

The first general cargoship launched after the end of the war was the 4200 dwt *Arakaka* 2814/46 for the West Indian and South American trades of Booker, McConnell for whom a sister *Amakura* 2961/49 was also built. Norwegian owners took nine general cargoships of around 4000 dwt e.g. *Borealis* 2919/48 for the Canary Islands fruit trade of Fred Olsen. Two colliers of 5050 dwt were completed for Union Industrielle, France as *Capitaine Jean Fougere* 3829/47 and *Capitaine Pierre Meric* 3835/47. The last case-oil carrier built for the Shell Group was launched at the yard on 10th November,1946 as the 6100 dwt *Cyrena* 4373/47 and she left the Tees on 27th February,1947 under Capt. J.S.L. Ayre to begin her trading career in the Singapore/Australia area. She had the misfortune to run aground on the delivery voyage to Singapore on the island of Kitava off New Guinea and was off-charter for nine months while being repaired at Singapore. Dutch Shell also had eight shallow-draft twin-screw 'mosquito' tankers built at the yard between 1946 and 1951, which were later used to ship oil from Pladju in Sumatra to Singapore. Shell also had the bitumen tanker *Fragum* 2926/52 of 3416 dwt completed at the yard in April,1952, and later several larger 18000 dwt deep-sea tankers. The yard berths were extended in 1950 especially to build tankers, and the following is a full list :-

GRT

GOULDIA	5437/46	Shell Tankers B.V.
GEOMITRA	5437/46	"
GARI	5437/47	"
GENA	5436/47	"
GLESSULA	5775/49	"
GASTRANA	5437/49	"
GADINIA	5924/50	"
GENOTA	5927/51	"
LIMATULA	6476/50	Anglo-Saxon/Shell
BRITISH LADY	6140/51	British Tanker Co. Ltd
LUMEN	10146/50	H.E. Moss,Liverpool 59
ATHELSULTAN	9149/51	Athel Line 190
ATHELFOAM	7486/51	"
ATLANTIC DUKE	10930/52	Livanos,Greece
LUCERNA	11292/52	H.E. Moss,Liverpool 59
DUFFIELD	10201/52	Hunting & Son,Newcastle 56
FRAGUM	2926/52	Anglo-Saxon/Shell
VALLY	2771/53	Halvorsen,Norway
SILVERBROOK	11276/53	Silver Line 181
BRITISH OAK	11307/53	British Tanker Co. Ltd
LUSTROUS	11301/53	H.E. Moss,Liverpool 59
HADRA	12669/54	Shell Tankers Ltd
HADRIANIA	12160/54	"
NORVEST	3161/54	Bergens Kulkompani A/S
VESTVARD	11916/55	Klosters Rederi A/S, Oslo
FOSNA	10880/55	J. Ludwig Mowinckels,Bergen
HAMINEA	12191/56	Shell Tankers Ltd
SAN FABIAN	12180/56	Eagle Oil
HAMINELLA	12189/57	Shell Tankers Ltd
HANETIA	12189/57	"
AMASTRA	12273/58	"
SAN ERNESTO	12301/58	Eagle Oil
MALOJA	12763/58	British India/ P & O 8
BRITISH KIWI	10957/60	British Tanker Co. Ltd
AMORIA	12324/60	Shell Tankers Ltd
MANTUA	12899/60	British India/ P & O 8
STONEGATE	12270/61	Turnbull,Scott & Co. Ltd 84
ATHELVISCOUNT	12592/61	Athel Line 190
BORDER FALCON	13238/61	Lowland Tanker Co. Ltd 189
BORDER CHIEFTAIN	13238/62	"

LUCIGEN   12800/62   H.E. Moss,Liverpool

Tramps were completed for London owner Fredric Bolton & Co. Ltd as *Ramsay* 6273/52, *Romanic* 6320/54, *Ruysdael* 6452/57 and *Rembrandt* 8104/60 with the latter being gas turbine powered initially. Five Pescara free-piston gasifiers exhausted directly into a gas turbine in a revolutionary all-aft engine room. She sailed on her maiden voyage from the Tees in August,1960 burning cheaper low-grade fuels. However it was impossible to get the fuel injection system correctly adjusted and the gasifiers were not sufficiently robust, and she was re-engined with diesels when sold to Greeks in 1967. The same London tramp owner Bolton also managed two 16000 dwt ore-carriers built at the yard for the North Yorkshire Shipping Co. Ltd, *Redcar* 10746/56 and *Rievaulx* 10974/58. A further ore-carrier was built for R. S. Dalgleish Ltd, Newcastle as *Pennyworth* 10978/58.

The tramp *Tynemouth* 3932/55 for the Burnett Steamship Co. Ltd, Newcastle was the last ship fitted with a steam reciprocating engine built at the yard. Henceforward most oil engines were supplied by Tyneside and Clydeside engine builders.   Sugar Line Ltd, owned by sugar giants Tate & Lyle Ltd and United Molasses, had two sugar carriers of 9800 dwt built at the yard, *Crystal Crown* 8671/57 and *Crystal Jewel* 8671/56. Two cargo-liners were also built at this time, *Araluen* 8485/58 and *Galway* 9539/60, for the Australia/New Zealand trades of the Australind Steam Shipping Co. Ltd and the Avenue Shipping Co. Ltd, both managed by Trinder,Anderson & Co. Ltd,London. The last whalecatcher had been built at the yard for Thor Dahl A/S as *Djerv* in August,1951, and the last trawler was the diesel-electric Hull trawler *Falstaff* for Hellyer Brothers in January,1959.

The yard berths were extended to their maximum size in 1960 for the construction of two Norwegian ore-carriers of 29250 dwt for J.M. Ugland, but it was still a very tight squeeze for *Livanita* 18735/61 and *Senorita* 18556/63. The yard had won orders for five cargo-liners for delivery between 1963 and 1967 for a customer who would come back for more ships later, Manchester Liners Ltd, with *Manchester Commerce, Manchester Renown, Manchester City, Manchester Port* and *Manchester Progress*. Four coastal tankers were built in 1964 for Thailand Petroleum for service on the Mekong river. The yard also won orders for six bulk carriers, constructed from 1964 onwards :-

RILEY	18607/65	Stephens,Sutton Ltd,Newcastle
RIBERA	18088/65	Bolton Shipping Co. Ltd,London
ZIEMIA BYDGOSKA	15732/67	Polish Steamship Company
ZIEMIA MAZOWIECKA	15731/67	"
HEINA	16973/70	J. Ludwig Mowinckels,Bergen
LISTA	16972/70	"

The ill-fated oil exploration rig *Sea Gem* arrived at the yard in early 1965 for modifications, while construction of the semi-submersible oil rig *Ocean Prince* was proceeding at the yard. The latter was launched on 25th July,1965 for O.D.E.C.O. (UK) Ltd and was the first of its type in the world. However in early November of that year it careered down-river for two miles in a zig-zag path in heavy winds, bringing down power lines and colliding with tankers on the way before running aground. Nine tugs controlled the rig and towed her back to the yard for completion, and she became the first rig to strike oil in the North Sea in October,1966. The jack-up oil rig *Transocean II* was also completed in 1966 at the yard for Transworld Drilling Co. Ltd.

Colonel T. Eustace Smith was Chairman and Managing Director of the yard in post-World War II years. He had joined the yard in the 1930s and was moulded in the old style of shipbuilder in ability to find work for his shipyard, each year making a special visit to his Norwegian shipowning and whaling customers from Stavanger round the coast to Oslo to drum up further business. On 5th July,1966 it was announced that the yard was being sold by the Smith and Edwards families to Swan,Hunter & Wigham Richardson Ltd. The yard became a member of the Swan Hunter Group Ltd in November,1966, with Colonel T. Eustace Smith retiring in 1969 and William J. Straker-Smith then sitting on both Boards. However due to distance and pay differentials with the lower paid Tyne workers in the Swan Hunter Group the yard acted independently of the other yards in the Group including the obtaining of orders. The yard had four berths at this time, one of 610 feet in length, two of 565 feet and another of 460 feet in length, as well as four dry-docks.

Five small solvent tankers were completed in 1968/69 for Norwegian owners. The first British cellular container ship was completed in October,1968 for Manchester Liners Ltd as *Manchester Challenge* 12039/68. She had capacity for 500 twenty foot containers and arrived at Montreal in November of that year to inaugurate the first container service to Canada. Five container sisters were also completed at the yard between 1969 and 1974, *Manchester Concorde, Manchester Courage, Manchester Crusade, Manchester Renown* and *Manchester Reward*. In addition the conventional break-bulk *Manchester Miller* of 1959 and *Manchester Progress* of 1967 were converted at the yard into fully cellular container ships.

The yard then made a licensing agreement with Norwegian yards to obtain the design of refrigerated ships for an order for eight ships of 9000 dwt from Island Fruit Reefers Ltd of Haifa, Israel. The Drammen Slip & Verksted provided blueprints for these, and the Akers yard in Oslo the blueprints for five reefers of 11000 dwt for

Blue Star Line. The yard had already built two partly-refrigerated ships for Finland Line, and thus a total of 15 reefers were built in the 1970s :-

AURORA	8854/71	Finland Line
ATLANTA	8854/72	"
EDINBURGH CLIPPER	6680/72	Island Fruit Reefers Ltd
GLASGOW CLIPPER	6680/72	"
TEESSIDE CLIPPER	6680/72	"
LONDON CLIPPER	6680/72	"
NEWCASTLE CLIPPER	6680/72	"
CARDIFF CLIPPER	6680/73	"
BRISTOL CLIPPER	6680/73	"
LIVERPOOL CLIPPER	6680/74	"
AFRIC STAR	9784/74	Blue Star Line
AVELONA STAR	9784/75	"
ANDALUCIA STAR	9784/75	"
ALMEDA STAR	9781/76	"
ALMERIA STAR	9781/76	"

Blue Star Line also ordered two pipe carriers for the North Sea oilfields from the yard and completed as *Star Arcturus* and *Star Canopus* in 1976. Two twenty-knot container ships of 17385 grt and with capacity for 946 containers were then built for Manchester Liners Ltd, with *Manchester Vanguard* completed in May,1977 and *Manchester Venture* being launched on nationalisation day of 1st July,1977 and completing in October,1977.

The yard was now a member of British Shipbuilders, and Managing Director George Parker and Shipbuilding Director Roger Spence had to contend with a series of difficult problems arising from an earlier order for two ro-ro vessels of 7500 dwt from Ellerman Wilson Line. These had been designed by the yard as twin-screw ships with a service speed of 18 knots, but after the late delivery of the first in May,1978 as *Cicero* 5108/78 it was clear the ships would not meet the contract service speed. Not only had the yard incurred late penalty clauses but it had also overrun the contracted price, and it was also left with the second ship *Cavallo* 5108/78 at the yard as the owner refused delivery on unsatisfactory speed grounds and also malfunction of the main internal cargo lift. The legal action took years to settle and *Cavallo* finally left the yard in 1981 after being sold to Federal Navigation of Canada at a very low price.

Two of a large order for 16700 dwt bulk carriers for Poland with British Shipbuilders were completed at South Bank as *Kopalnia Sziombierki* 11922/79 and *Kopalnia Myslowice* 10974/79. An order was then shared with Walker Naval Yard on the Tyne for two partly-refrigerated container ships for a new joint service between Australia/New Zealand and the Gulf of Mexico for Shaw,Savill & Albion/

GEESTBAY on trials in Tees Bay on 16th July, 1981. (Smith's Dock Co. Ltd)

Bank Line. The Chairmen of Furness,Withy & Co. Ltd (parent company of Shaw, Savill & Albion) and Bank Line both wanted their ship to be built at South Bank, and they finally settled the matter by the toss of a coin with Lord Inverforth of Bank Line winning and having *Willowbank* 18236/80 built at the yard !

A pair of handsome four-hold 16 knot banana ships were then completed for the Geest Line service from the West Indies. *Geestbay* 7730/81 and *Geestport* 7730/82 had two sets of twin deck cranes for quick discharge of fruit, and the first of the pair completed visited the Pool of London for promotional purposes. Two large ro-ro vessels were then completed for Brazil as *Jacqueline* 11247/83 and *Karisma* 13683/84, but financial problems caused the former to be laid-up and she did not sail from the Tees until April,1984. The same reason had caused the lay-up of two 'SD14's built at the yard in 1981 for Hong Kong owners, and they were finally sold at the end of 1983 to Empresa Navegacione Mambisa of Havana in Cuba and left the Tees as *Lilac Islands* and *Lotus Islands*. The same shipowner then placed orders for four more 'SD14's with steelwork fabrication starting on the first of these in March,1985, and *South Islands, West Islands* and *East Islands* had left the river by the end of 1986.

The sophisticated oil-rig tender / anchor handling tug / diving support ship *British Argyll* was completed at the yard in 1986 for British Underwater Engineering Ltd, and was the most complex ship ever built at the yard as one of her many features was a moonpool. However machinery difficulties caused her late delivery. The last of the Cuban 'SD14's was launched as *North Islands* on 15th October,1986 and left the Tees during February,1987. The yard closed its gates on 28th February,1987, but has since been partly reopened by companies specialising in North Sea oil work. The dry-docks had ceased shiprepair work in July,1982 but they also have resumed a useful existence under new owners.

ROPNER SHIPBUILDING & REPAIRING CO.

In 1888 the West Hartlepool shipowner Robert Ropner purchased the Stockton yard of Matthew Pearse & Company, which had built the tramp *Preston* 2157/85 for him. Robert Ropner had been born in 1838 as the son of a German Prussian Army officer and emigrated to Britain at the age of 18 years by stowing away in Hamburg, determined on a life in the Merchant Navy. However his ship was only going as far as West Hartlepool and after a rough North Sea passage seasickness changed his mind and he took a job in a Hartlepool bakery. He then worked for a colliery fitting and coal exporting business in Hartlepool. After becoming a naturalised British subject he joined the West Hartlepool shipowner and coal exporter, Thomas Appleby & Company. He was made a partner in 1866 and then devoted most of his time to the shipowning side of the business. In 1874 Ropner decided to branch out for himself as a shipowner and divided the fleet equally with Thomas Appleby, retaining five small steamers for Baltic trading, and by 1888 the Ropner tramp fleet was 25 ships strong.

Ropner saw the Stockton yard as principally the builder of his own tramps, and he had no great ambition to expand the yard. The Pearse yard had been in operation since the 1860s and had latterly been building tramps for customers such as George Pyman of Hartlepool, Christopher Marwood of Whitby, Farrar,Groves & Company,London and H. Cloakes & Son,London. After purchase the yard operated as Ropner & Son and built four tramps for the family fleet in 1889, the first being *Maltby* 2752/89 and of 4350 dwt. During the next six years some 18 tramps were built by the yard for the family fleet, with the yard having the third highest output in Britain in 1895. Between the years 1895 and 1903 inclusive, one hundred tramps were built in nine years or an average of eleven ships/year. This total included fifteen Norwegian ships, three German ships and one Dutch, Spanish, Italian and Russian ship.

His two sons, Robert junior and Leonard, had been placed in charge of the yard almost from the time of purchase, and the family business could hardly fail to make money as new ships were obtained more cheaply than their rivals, and they could also lay keels for their own fleet for later sale 'off the peg' to prospective shipowners at a handsome profit. The Stockton yard built seventy two Ropner family tramps during its thirty six years of ownership by the family, or on average exactly two tramps/year. The yard is best remembered for a standard design known as a 'trunk-decker', the first example being *Trunkby* 2635/96 of 4100 dwt and completed in November,1896. James Laing of Sunderland (q.v.) was also designing very similar 'trunk-deckers' at this time and nearly took Ropner to litigation claiming

The first Ropner 'trunk - decker' TRUNKBY of 1896 (above) with another shown below STAGPOOL of 1905.   (M.R. Dippy)

that Ropner had stolen his designs. In the next 11 years a further 22 'trunk-deckers' were completed by the family shipyard for the family fleet. They had a steel trunk built on the main deck, which in the first examples did not run the full length of the ship but stopped on either side of the 'midships' structure. These 'half trunk-deckers' were later superceded by full 'trunk-deckers' which were very similar to the Doxford-built 'Turrets'. In fact the only differences between the two types was the rounded gunwhale on the harbour deck of the 'Turret', and the almost square stern of the 'trunk-decker'. The final example for the family fleet was *Romanby* of 6100 dwt, completed in 1908, and another 22 examples had been built for other owners with four for Watts,Watts & Co. Ltd,London and four for Evan Thomas Radcliffe of Cardiff during 1896/98.

Robert Ropner Snr. encouraged other local Hartlepool shipowners such as George Pyman, J. F. Wilson, J. S. Allison, Thomas Appleby, J .A. Wood and the West Hartlepool Steam Navigation Co. Ltd, to place orders with the yard by offering to buy large blocks of shares in the ships on condition that he undertook the chartering of the vessels. Cardiff tramp owners were also good customers of the yard with Capt. William Reardon Smith placing the order for his first owned ship of 5500 dwt in 1905 at the fixed price of £32,500. This was completed as *City of Cardiff* 3089/06 and was followed by the 'trunk-decker' *Leeds City* 4298/08 and a dozen more tramps with *'City'* names. Evan Thomas Radcliffe of Cardiff had nine tramps built by the yard, and other Cardiff tramp customers included William Seager, William J. Tatem, and Richard Chellew. The local shipowner Constantine & Pickering Steamship Co. Ltd,Middlesbrough had 14 tramps and coasters built by the yard, and Chapman of Newcastle took ten big tramps from the yard. Robert Ropner Senior represented Stockton as Member of Parliament between 1900 and 1910 and was knighted in 1902.

World War I output consisted of a dozen tramps and one coaster built to private order for customers such as H. Harrowing of Whitby; Constantine & Pickering S.S. Co. Ltd,Middlesbrough; Steel,Young & Company,London; Turnbull Brothers, Cardiff; William J. Tatem, Cardiff and The Clan Line Steamers Ltd, Glasgow. Two sloops, *Viola* and *Snapdragon*, and six 'X' barges were completed for the Admiralty, and the Shipping Controller ordered one tanker *Ashleaf* 5768/17 and ten standard *WAR* 'A and 'C' types. Most of the latter were still completing in 1919 for private owners such as Elder,Dempster; Chapman of Newcastle while the last two 'C' class were purchased by William J. Tatem from lay-up at the yard and renamed as *Molton* 3091/19 and *Monkton* 3088/20.

The yard went into voluntary liquidation in 1919 and re-emerged as Ropner Shipbuilding & Repairing Co.(Stockton) Ltd, but with the scarcity of orders in the subsequent freight rate slump the yard was liquidated again and financially reconstructed in 1922. Nevertheless, the following tramps were completed:-

H.H. ASQUITH	5626/20	Williams & Mordey,Cardiff 3 17
INDIAN CITY 2	6221/20	Reardon Smith,Cardiff 177
ATLANTIC CITY	6236/20	"
ALNESS	3683/20	"
WELSH CITY	6303/22	"
ALU-MENDI	3260/20	Sota y Aznar,Bilbao
ARINDA-MENDI	3282/21	"
AXPE-MENDI	3258/21	"
AIZKARAI-MENDI	3278/22	"
ROXBY	4252/23	Ropner 29
BRIDGEPOOL	4845/24	"
REEDPOOL	4838/24	"
DRAKEPOOL	4838/24	"
AMBASSADOR	4449/25	Hall Bros.,Newcastle 302
BEATUS	4885/25	W. Seager,Cardiff 225
WILLOWPOOL	4815/25	Ropner 29

In addition two hoppers were completed in July,1924 for the Tees Conservancy Commissioners in an effort to keep the yard going. The last two tramps were launched in January and March,1925 with the last completing for the family fleet as *Willowpool* in May,1925. The yard had five berths for ships up to 500 feet in length, and the Chairman at this time was Sir William Seager, a good Cardiff customer and shareholder. The yard was then closed but not demolished and it was resurrected by Smith's Dock Co. Ltd (q.v.) in 1930/31 to complete three tramps and a few coasters and trawlers before closing for good in June,1931.

RICHARDSON,DUCK & CO. LTD.

This yard was a prolific builder of tramps and was established at Thornaby on the south bank of the Tees at Stockton in 1854 as the South Stockton Iron Shipbuilding Company to construct the first iron ship built on the Tees, *Advance*. However the company did not prove to be very successful, and it was purchased by Joseph Richardson (born 1830) and George Nixon Duck, who were Quakers, and they built fifty iron steamers, a paddle steamer, ten sailing ships and 29 barges in the next ten years. Among early iron ships from the Stockton yard were the cable ship *International* 1381/70, *Madura* 2324/73 for the Java Stoom Maats,Holland, *George Fisher* 1231/77 for Edward H. Capper, *Sunbeam* 1784/78 for Woolf &

Haigh,Hull and *Southwood* 1249/80 for D. Wilson,Hull. Morel Brothers of Cardiff took two tramps in 1880, *Beignon* 1332/80 and *Forest* 1167/80, and the local shipowner F. Binnington of Stockton ordered *Elmfield* 1705/83, and Hunting & Pattison of Newcastle ordered the larger iron tramp *Lisnacrieve* 2791/83. Tramps were built 'on-spec' from time to time, and the first steel tramps were completed at the yard in 1886.

    The majority of the steel tramps from the yard were also engined locally by the engine works of Blair & Co. Ltd, Stockton with triple expansion steam reciprocating machinery. One of the most important customers of Stockton-built and engined tramps was William J. Tatem of Cardiff with 17 tramps from this yard starting with *Lady Lewis* 2950/97 and ending with *Braunton* 4575/11. This shipowner also had three tramps built by the neighbouring Craig,Taylor yard and two from the Ropner yard. Evan Thomas Radcliffe of Cardiff ordered 11 tramps from the yard starting with *Wimborne* 3466/98 and ending with *Washington* 5079/05 and including five with the *'Llan'* prefix peculiar to this shipowner. Other Cardiff owners to patronise the yard were Anning Brothers with *Starcross* 2823/94 and James C. Gould with *Grelisle* 5280/18, and Owen and Watkin Williams with *Arvonian* 2794/05, *Snowdonian* 3870/07 and *Tavian* 4567/12.

    A dozen ships were built for Liverpool shipowner William Johnston for his services to the Mediterranean and the Black Sea, all with names ending with *'More'*. Other important customers were Farrar,Groves & Company with offices in Leadenhall Street,London and who named their ships after lighthouses, and twelve tramps were built for them starting with *Lundy* 1828/89 and ending with *Caldy* 4221/13. Hall Brothers of Newcastle named their ships after royal regalia e.g. *Peerless* 3112/98, *Therapia* 3123/00, *Trident* 3129/02 and *Diadem* 3752/06. London owners Court Line took *Cressington Court* 4396/08, and Bucknall,Nephews[331] ordered *Etona* 2495/03 and H. Sammam of Hull ordered *Clinton* 3381/99, while Bristol shipowner Lucas & Company ordered two, *Scarsdale* 2079/03 and *Sterndale* 2925/10 for their Dale Steamship Co. Ltd.

    Stockton also had shipowners at this time and the Field Steamship Co. Ltd managed by E. Aston ordered four tramps from the local yard, *Castlefield* 2190/90, *Holmfield* 2321/95, *Kingfield* 3122/02 and *Glofield* 4395/06. Overseas shipowners were important too, with many ships built for Scandinavian owners, and for German owner de Freitas of Hamburg for whom six steamers of around 2730 grt were built between 1894 and 1896, *Athens, Hellas, Troja, Parthia, Lydia* and *Sparta*. By the turn of the century the yard had built five hundred tramps, cargo-liners, tankers, self-trimming colliers, steel lighters, and later became licensees for the Isherwood system of longitudinal framing and were put on the Admiralty list. The yard became a limited liability company in 1912 while the following ships were being built :-

JESSMORE	3911/11	W. Johnston, Liverpool
BARROWMORE	3832/11	"
BRAUNTON	4575/11	W.J. Tatem, Cardiff
CLOUGHTON	4221/11	Pyman, Hartlepool
NANTWEN	4773/12	W. & C.T. Jones, Cardiff
TONWEN	4567/12	"
EDDYSTONE	4214/12	Farrar, Groves & Co., London
CHANTALA	4949/12	British India Line
KENMORE	3919/12	W. Johnston, Liverpool
DROMORE	4450/13	"
DALEHAM	4809/13	Pyman, Hartlepool
CALDY	4221/13	Farrar, Groves & Co., London

World War I output included a dozen tramps built to private order such as *Beachy Head* 4274/15 for Farrar, Groves & Co., London and *Bryntawe* 3364/17 for H. & B. Goldberg, Swansea, as well as eight standard *WAR* 'A' tramps completed for Chapman and R.S. Dalgleish and Sutherland of Newcastle, Reardon Smith of Cardiff and the Buenos Aires Great Southern Railway Co. Ltd. A standard 'AO' tanker was completed as *War Anglian*, and a number of sloops were also built for the Admiralty.

Another standard 'A' tramp was completed at the yard as *Grelisle* 5208/18 for Cardiff tramp shipowner James C. Goulds and his Dulcia Steamship Co. Ltd. James C. Gould and his cousin Walter T. Gould then acquired a controlling interest in 1920 in the yard, which had become a public company in 1919, along with the Stockton engine works of Blair & Co. Ltd. Later their shipowning, shipbuilding and engineering empire was renamed Goulds Steamships and Industrials Ltd. Several of their tramps with names prefixed *'Grel'* had been built by the yard and had been purchased second-hand and included *Grelhead* 4274/15 ex *Beachy Head; Grelcaldy* 4221/13 ex *Caldy; Grelstone* 4214/12 ex *Eddystone; Grelwen* 4567/12 ex *Tonwen.* Unfortunately protracted industrial disputes in the shipyard in 1922 coupled with the scarcity of orders brought the whole Gould Group down, and on 5th May, 1925 a receiver was appointed and the Gould shipbuilding and maritime empire folded. Some of the last tramps built at the Stockton yard were :-

INKUM	4504/21	J.H. Welsford & Co., Liverpool
ILLINGWORTH	6067/22	R.S. Dalgleish, Newcastle
SILKSWORTH	4921/22	"
RADNOR	4576/23	Cardigan Shipping Co. Ltd, Cardiff

CONISTONE	6097/24	Charles Radcliffe, Cardiff 224
AMBLESTONE	6095/24	"
ROCHDALE	6098/24	"
SOUTHBOROUGH	4542/24	Humphries (Cardiff) Ltd 337

The yard at this time had four berths for vessels up to 420 feet in length, and a receiver was appointed and the yard closed in 1925, the company was wound up and the yard was demolished in 1933.

CRAIG,TAYLOR & CO. LTD.

This Thornaby yard was also a major builder of tramps and colliers, having been established in 1884 and registered as a limited liability company in 1905. Among the early customers of the yard were D. H. Morgan & Company of Newport who ordered *Rosecliffe* 2298/88 and *Wyndcliffe* 1940/89; R.P. Triplett & Company of Plymouth with *Sir Walter Raleigh* 1870/89; and German shipowner De Freitas with *Ithaka* 2269/94; J.E. Guthe of Hartlepool with *Whitehall* 2068/97; R. Stewart & Company of Liverpool with *Puritan* 4042/97; Sir Christopher Furness with *Sylviana* 4187/98 and Edward Haslehurst of London with *Claverdale* 3307/99.

The yard built four ships in 1900 including *Lochwood* 2042/00 for local owners Constantine & Pickering of Middlesbrough. The yard then became heavily involved in building for Cardiff tramp shipowners such as Evan Thomas Radcliffe who had 11 tramps built starting with *Wimborne* 6078/11 and ending with *Catherine Radcliffe* 5585/25; William Seager with four tramps *Tempus* 2981/04, *Amicus* 3695/11, *Fiscus* 4782/17 and *Promus* 4816/18; William J. Tatem with three tramps *Bideford* 3562/10, *Eggesford* 3566/10 and *Exford* 4542/11; Reardon Smith with three tramps *Bradford City* 5261/19, *Cornish City* 5269/19 and *Paris City* 6343/20; Williams & Mordey with *David Lloyd George* 4107/17; Charles Clay with *Daybreak* 3102/20; Walter E. Hinde with *Portcawl* 2406/15; and Owen & Watkin Williams with *Edernian* 2588/06.

North East Coast tramp customers included Albyn Line managed by Allan,Black of Sunderland with *Thistlemor* 4008/06, *Thistleban* 4117/10 and *Thistleard* 4136/12; with Blair,Moffet of Newcastle taking *Kildare* 2340/03. Colliers were built for J. Ridley,Son & Tully of Newcastle e.g. *Whitewood* 1230/07 and for the Pelton Steamship Co. Ltd,Newcastle e.g. *Primo* 1372/18. Scandinavian and

German and Dutch customers were important as well e.g. *Luise Horn* 3412/12 for H. C. Horn of Hamburg, and *Jenny* 1868/04 for Van Ysselsteyn & Company, Terneuzen.

During World War I tramps were built to private order for the Cardiff shipowners mentioned above as well as the cargo-liner *Clan Malcolm* 5994/17 for The Clan Line Steamers Ltd, Glasgow. Eight standard *WAR* 'A' tramps were completed with the last two leaving the yard for British India Line as *Gandara* and *Gazana* in late 1919 and early 1920. Two *WAR* 'C' standard tramps were ordered by the Shipping Controller, with the last completing as *Cosmos Volga* for Watkin J. Williams of Cardiff.

The yard suffered from long periods of idleness in the 1920s especially in 1923 and 1926, but managed to complete the following ships :-

ETHEL RADCLIFFE	5673/20	Evan Thomas Radcliffe,Cardiff
CITY OF TOKIO	6993/21	Ellerman Lines
HADA	4853/21	J. Ludwig Mowinckels,Bergen
HELENA	3112/22	A.C. Lensen,Holland
MAGDALENA	3117/23	"
SEATON	1530/24	H.Harrison(Shpg.) Ltd,London
TAUNTON	1551/24	"
ASHTREE	1561/24	Tree S.S. Co. Ltd (Howard Jones)
VERA RADCLIFFE	5587/25	Evan Thomas Radcliffe,Cardiff
CATHERINE RADCLIFFE	5590/25	"
GLOCLIFFE	4601/27	Globe Shpg. Co. Ltd,Cardiff
NIEMEN	3350/28	Zegluga Polska,Poland
WISLA	3350/28	"
GLOFIELD	4576/29	Globe Shpg. Co. Ltd,Cardiff
PORTFIELD	4425/29	Portfield S.S. Co. Ltd,Cardiff
PORTREGIS	4409/30	"

George B. Craig and Herbert Taylor were the owners of the yard at this time, which had six berths for ships up to 450 feet in length at closure. The yard had launched 227 ships during 45 years of existence, and after the completion of the last tramp *Portregis* in February,1930 the yard was purchased by National Shipbuilders Security Ltd and demolished during 1931.

SIR RAYLTON DIXON & CO. LTD.

50

Rake, Kimber & Company laid out a yard in 1858 on ground where the Transporter bridge now stands and launched the first iron ship *De Brus* built at Middlesbrough on 1st March, 1858. Two other ships were built on sub-contract from Richardson, Duck & Company and after completion of a fourth vessel the yard closed down later in 1858 due to lack of orders. In 1859 Richardson, Duck & Company purchased the yard and put in a young manager from Newcastle, Raylton Dixon. The yard was taken over in 1862 by Thomas Backhouse & Raylton Dixon together with several small adjacent yards. In 1873 Raylton Dixon became sole proprietor and he renamed the yard Raylton Dixon & Co. Ltd, and built a large iron steamer *Torrington* of 2099 grt in September, 1874 for the Commercial Steam Shipping Co. Ltd, London. She was followed by *Tourmaline* of 1875 and *Dolphin* and *Wanderer* of 1882 for the Admiralty.

The yard was more commonly known as the Cleveland Dockyard, and *Strathmore* 2138/78 was built for James Watson & Company, Glasgow and was later used in the Far Eastern trades by Burrell & Son of Glasgow. Six more steamers of over 2000 grt had been completed by 1881, including *Juliet* 2090/81 and *Titania* 1961/80 for C.T. Bowring of Liverpool for Tyne to New York services. E. Arbib of London ordered two tramps completed as *Joseph Arbib* 2071/82 and *Cousins Arbib* 2147/82; and the Gulf Line Association of Greenock ordered five steamers, *Gulf of Mexico* 3172/83, *Gulf of Akaba* 2041/83, *Gulf of Papua* 2042/83, *Gulf of Aden* 2470/87 and *Gulf of Trinidad* 2362/87, the last pair being built of steel. The first steel steamer had been completed as the aptly-named *Transition* of 1729 grt in 1885 for J. M. Lennard of Middlesbrough. Iron steamers had also been built for Scandinavian and European shipowners e.g. *Raylton Dixon* 1817/83 for Harloff & Boe, Norway and *Macassar* 2274/83 and *Jacata* 2423/83 for the Insulinde Steamship Company, Amsterdam.

Steel tramps for the newly formed English & American Shipping Co. Ltd of C.T. Bowring were then built by the yard, *Guy Colin* 2234/88, *Bona* 2477/90 and *Justin* 2206/91. The yard soon acquired a good reputation for building large cargo-liners and built for all the major lines of the day e.g. *Aden* 3925/92 for P & O, and *Santiago* 4188/86 for Wilson Line of Hull, *Dictator* 4116/91 and *Barrister* 4750/93 and four other ships for T. & J. Harrison of Liverpool. The twin-funnelled refrigerated steamer *Ovingdean Grange* 2413/90 and a sister built on the Tyne were the first owned ships of Houlder Line for their meat trade from the Plate and Australia. She cost £40,000 to build and could carry 70,000 cu.ft. of refrigerated cargo with her triple expansion engines supplied by Thomas Richardson & Company of Hartlepool.

Some 16 ships were completed in 1889 including *Echuca* 2826/89 for the Australian services of W. Lund of London, and some 20 ships during 1890 including *Mayumba* 2516/90 for Elder,Dempster by Sir Raylton Dixon & Co. Ltd, the ship-builder having been knighted during that year. Nine steamers of around 3000 grt including *Kintuck* 3596/91 for the China Mutual Steam Navigation Co. Ltd, London and a dozen trawlers and barges were built in 1891. Lamport & Holt of Liverpool then ordered seven passenger/cargo-liners from the yard, starting with *Cavour* 4870/95, their largest ship at that time, and including *Romney* 4501/99 and *Thespis* 4343/01 and the beautiful passenger liners *Velasquez* 7542/06 and *Vasari* 10177/09. *Velasquez* was the first of four 'V' class liners built in British yards during 1906/07 for the new Lamport & Holt service from New York to South America. They had tall masts and funnels and were the best liners in service at that time to South America and were equipped with refrigerated capacity. Lamport & Holt sold *Vasari* in 1928 to Hellyer Brothers of Hull for conversion into a fish factory ship, and she then survived under the Russian flag until broken up in Kaohsiung in 1979 - a great testimony to the strength of construction of the Tees yard.

Overseas liner companies were also prominent e.g. Hansa Line of Hamburg ordered three cargo-liners, *Rothenfels* 2951/93, *Lindenfels* 2969/93 and *Ockenfels* 3589/95; and Cie Maritime Belge ordered four passenger/cargo-liners for their Antwerp to West and Central Africa services, *Albertville* 3953/96, *Leopoldville* 3761/97, *Bruxellesville* 3908/98 and *Philippeville* 4091/99. The Deutsch-Australian Line of Hamburg ordered the crago-liner *Bergedorf* 5125/00, and she was one of eight big steamers completed in 1900 of 31,600 tons, which also included the British India Line pair *Islanda* 5237/00 and *Ismaila* 5265/00. The Konink Java-China Paket Maats of Holland then ordered *Tjilatjap* 3859/03 for Far Eastern service, while Bergen Line ordered the smaller liner *Irma* 1297/05 for local Newcastle to Bergen service. Elder,Dempster of Liverpool were also good customers ordering many ships including *Eboe* 3805/98, *Port Antonio* 4458/01 , *Port Royal* 4455/01 and *Kaduna* 4455/10 and *Kwarra* 4441/11. The yard was by now the builder of the biggest ships on the Tees with four berths for ships up to 550 feet in length and a dry-dock of length 576 feet. The following is a list of dry-cargo ships of around 5000 grt and over built by the yard :-

MONTROSE	5195/97	Elder,Dempster	39
MANCHESTER CITY	5833/98	Manchester Liners Ltd	88
ISLANDA	5237/00	British India Line	42
ISMAILA	5265/00	"	

BERGEDORF	5125/00	Deutsche-Australien Line,Hamburg
VEGA	5766/04	Empresa Nacional,Lisbon
AFRICA	5340/05	"
LUSITANIA	5557/06	"
VELASQUEZ	6988/06	Lamport & Holt, Liverpool 4-7
ATHINAI	6742/08	D.G. Moraitis, Greece
FIONA	5012/08	Colonial Sugar Refining,Sydney
VASARI	10117/09	Lamport & Holt, Liverpool 4-7
BERWINDMOOR	5238/10	J. Esplen,Liverpool 344
LINGAN	4677/11	Furness,Withy & Co. Ltd 19
HOCHELAGA	4681/12	"
BERWINDVALE	6123/11	J. Esplen,Liverpool 344 shell.
KINKASAN MARU	5631/11	Mitsui Busen Kaisha,Japan
WAGAMA	4969/13	Asker A/S, Oslo
WASCANA	4969/13	"

The twin-funnelled twin-screw Greek liner *Athinai* was completed in October,1908 for the emigrant trade from Greece to New York, and had a near sister from the Priestman yard at Sunderland, *Moraitis* 6045/07. Several tramps were also built fitted with the patented Dixon-Harroway water ballast tanks at the side of the hull. The engines-aft colliers *Berwindmoor* and *Berwindvale* were converted to tankers during World War I by inserting cylindrical tanks in their holds, but the yard also built three bulk-oil tankers at this time for the Tank Storage & Carriage Co. Ltd (W.J. Smith),Middlesbrough, *Tuscalusa* 6499/13, *Tamaha* 6496/14 and *Tachee* 6508/14. *Lingan* and *Hochelaga* were ordered by Furness,Withy & Co. Ltd for the coal trade along the St. Lawrence river from Nova Scotia, and also ordered the first ever British motor ship from the yard for their subsidiary Norfolk & North American Steamship Co. Ltd. She was launched by Lady Furness as *Eavestone* 1858/12 and completed in August of that year equipped with a 4-cylinder two-stroke single-acting oil engine from the nearby Furness-owned engine works of Richardsons,Westgarth & Co. Ltd,Middlesbrough. She had a loaded service speed of ten knots for the Pomaron river iron ore trade from Spain, and was fitted with a stove pipe instead of a funnel behind the bridge to vent the exhaust gases. A conventional triple expansion powered steamer *Saltburn* 1777/12 was completed by the yard at the same time for fuel cost evaluation purposes, but after three years service the oil engines of *Eavestone* became too unreliable and she was converted into a steamer in 1915.

World War I output included the important liner *Leitrim* 9700/15 for the Union Steamship Co. Ltd, New Zealand, the refrigerated meat carrier *Baronesa* 8663/18 for Houlder Brothers, the Booth liner *Oswald* 5185/15 for South American service, and the Furness,Withy cargo-liners *Dominion Miller* 6572/16 and *Valemore* 6629/18. *Rona* 6205/18 was completed for the Colonial Sugar Refining Co.

LONDON CITIZEN was built by Sir Raylton Dixon & Co. Ltd as VALEMORE in 1918 (above), Robert Craggs built WELSH PRINCE in 1903 for Prince Line (below).   (J.G. Callis)

Ltd,Sydney, and the Scottish-named *Robert Bruce* 4207/17 and *William Wallace* 4215/17 as well as two coasters. The tankers *Roseleaf* 6572/16 and *Persol* 5896/17 and ten small monitors of 600 tons displacement were delivered to the Admiralty. Some nine *'WAR'* standard tramps were ordered by the Shipping Controller, the last of which was completed in December,1919, with the 'A' type completing as *Binfield* in 1919 and the 'AO' tanker as *War Spartan*.

The yard then found difficulty in obtaining orders in the bad trading conditions of 1920, but completed *Hurunui* 9243/20 for the New Zealand Shipping Co. Ltd, and the dry-cargo *Mont Viso* 4531/21 for Soc. Generale de Transports Maritime a Vapeur,Marseilles, and the coaster *Princess Olga* 1104/20 which became *Lancashire Coast* of Coast Lines soon after completion. The last ships built by the yard were eight colliers for Soc. National d'Affretments, France and delivered throughout 1921 up to July,1922 as *P.L.M. 20* to *P.L.M. 27*. The Chairman of the yard at this time was Harald Raylton Dixon, and he sold it later in 1922 to the Cleveland Shipbuilding Co. Ltd, a subsidiary of the Parsons Marine Turbine Co. Ltd of Wallsend, but the yard closed for good in the following year of 1923 having built over 600 ships.

ROBERT CRAGGS & SONS LTD.

This yard built tramps, coasters and tugs on the south bank of the Tees at Middlesbrough opposite Port Clarence and adjacent to the Raylton Dixon yard. The first iron ship was completed as *Celeste* of 678 tons in January,1875 for J. Manners of West Hartlepool, and only two ships were built in the following year and then only three more up to 1882, when *Alhassanee* of 1579 tons was built for the Emperor of Morocco. The yard was closed in July,1885 to modify it for steel shipbuilding of tankers and tramps, the first steel ship built being the tanker *Attila* 2141/88 for J. M. Lennard & Sons, Middlesbrough, who also had the tanker *Henri Rieth* 2265/93 built at the yard. While the yard was being altered, a dry-cargo ship *Fergusons* was converted to a tanker by fitting tanks into the holds. The tanks were built on the shipyard berths, launched and towed to the sheerlegs for lifting aboard, and the ship could then carry 2,000 tons of oil. The banana carriers *Barnstaple* and *Brookline,* both 1356/94, were completed for Northern Transport Ltd, Newcastle; and typical tramps from the yard were *Portugalete* 2023/97 for Ramon de la Sota, Bilbao and *Harperley* 2368/97 for J. & C. Harrison of London.

At the turn of the century ships of over 7000 dwt were being completed including *Pilgrim* 4295/98 for R. Stewart & Company, Liverpool; *Willowdene* 4709/01 for John T. Lunn, Newcastle; the Russian *Krasny Profintern* 4648/02 and *Alexei Trapani* 4530/02; and *Fitzclarence* 4407/07 and *Fitzpatrick* 4416/07 for William Burrell of Glasgow. Output in 1900 was four ships of 15,360 tons and included sister tramps *Askehall* 4231/00 and *Birkhall* 4202/00 for the West Hartlepool Steam Navigation Co. Ltd. Other local customers included the Constantine & Pickering Steamship Co. Ltd, Middlesbrough with four tramps, *Earlswood* 2353/98, *Homewood* 2024/98, *Kirnwood* 3049/05 and *Toftwood* 3082/06. After the Turnbull shipyard had closed at Whitby in 1902 due to the width restrictions of Whitby harbour bridge, Turnbull had their next two tramps built at the yard, *Helredale* 3567/06 for the Whitby fleet and *Parkgate* 3232/06 for the London fleet of Turnbull,Scott. Cardiff tramp owners Morel Brothers had *Cyfartha* 3014/04 and *Dowlais* 3016/04 built at the yard; James Knott took *Welsh Prince* 4934/03 for his Prince Line; Greek owners ordered *Vasilefs Georgios* 3651/04, *Panaghi Vagliano* 3010/04 and *Eleni Stathatos* 3016/07; Van Ommeren of Holland ordered *Sliedrecht* 3100/05; and the Hungarian Levant Line had *Kossuth* 3602/06 built by the yard.

Sir Joseph Isherwood was a director of the yard, and the first vessel built to his longitudinal framing system was built by the yard and launched as the tanker *Paul Paix* in August,1908. She was followed by the dry-cargo *Gascony* and the Norwegian tanker *Conrad Mohr* both built to the Isherwood system. Eleven ships were built during 1907/08 but the yard then became a casualty of the freight slump of that time with the tanker *Conrad Mohr* 4012/09 the last ship completed in July,1909. These last ships were :-

FITZCLARENCE	4407/07	W. Burrell, Glasgow
FITZPATRICK	4416/07	"
ELENI STATHATOS	3016/07	Stathatos Bros.,Greece
TRANSPORT	3619/07	London Traders Shipping Co. Ltd
LYNROWAN	3384/07	Johnston,Sproule & Co. Ltd,Liverpool
TURUL	3530/07	Hungarian Levant Line
ORSOVA	3549/07	"
BRIKA	3549/08	C.T. Bowring, London
DACRE CASTLE	4261/08	James Chambers & Co. Ltd,Liverpool
PAUL PAIX	4196/08	J.M. Lennard & Sons,Middlesbrough
GASCONY	3133/08	D. MacIver,Sons & Co.,Liverpool
CONRAD MOHR	4012/09	Chr. Michelsen A/S, Bergen

The yard was then demolished but the sheerlegs crane on the fitting-out quay remained in existence until the 1950s.

W. HARKESS & SON LTD.

The East yard at Dock Point, Middlesbrough near the entrance to Middlesbrough Dock was established in 1853 by William Harkess for the building of coasters, trawlers and small colliers. The adjoining yard to the West was that of Robert Craggs & Sons (q.v.). Six small tramps were built at the turn of the century for Owen & Watkin Williams of Cardiff, the largest being *Coranian* 1223/01. One small ship *Jamaica* 1138/08 was completed for West Indian service, and many coasters were launched for Onesimus Dorey & Sons of Guernsey, Thomas Rose of Sunderland, and the local Joseph Constantine of Middlesbrough with seven coasters launched for his Meteor Steamship Co. Ltd, the biggest being *Teeswood* and *Avonwood,* both 864/15. Minesweepers and patrol boats for the Admiralty, and the Trinity House pilot tender *Patrol* 261/14 and some standard 'WAR' coasters were built during World War I. The two largest ships from the yard were then built, *Flaminian* 2866/20 for Ellerman Lines and *Pedrosa* 2662/21 for Compania Vasco Cantabrica,Lisbon (U. de la Torre). The yard had three berths for ships up to 318 feet in length, a dry-dock of length 520 feet and a floating-dock of length 130 feet. The last coaster completed by the yard was *Enid Dunford* 869/22 for E.S. Dunford of Newcastle, and the yard then became another casualty of the early 1920s.

THOMAS TURNBULL & SON, Whitby

The Whitehall Dockyard was capable of building steel tramps up to 5000 dwt with a maximum beam of 44 feet due to a width restriction on Whitby bridge. The shipyard commenced building wooden sailing ships in 1840 and switched to the construction of iron tramps in 1871 with *Whitehall* 763/71. Some 113 tramps were then built between 1871 and 1902 of which 60 were for the Turnbull family fleets at Whitby, Cardiff and London. Twenty six were built for the Whitby fleet by 1882, with the first for the London fleet being *Highgate* 1451/82 and for the Cardiff fleet *Everilda* 1455/82. The first steel tramp was *Dora* 2376/87 for the Whitby fleet and most were towed round to the Tees for the installation of engines and were then fitted out at Whitby. The penultimate ship was launched on 3rd August,1901 as the German *Theodor Wille* 3667/01 and the last tramp *Broomfield* 2386/02 was launched for the Whitby fleet on 10th April,1902, and the yard closed shortly afterwards after 62 years of shipbuilding.

BIBLIOGRAPHY AND FURTHER READING

HISTORY OF NORTH-EAST SHIPBUILDING by David Dougan published by George Allen & Unwin Ltd in 1968.

WHERE SHIPS ARE BORN by J.W. Smith and T.S. Holden published by Reed of Sunderland in 1953.

SUNDERLAND: RIVER, TOWN AND PEOPLE edited by G. Milburn & S. Miller, published in 1988.

SWAN,HUNTER & WIGHAM RICHARDSON LTD, ENGINEERS & SHIPBUILDERS, published by the company in 1906.

LAUNCHING WAYS - HISTORY OF SWAN,HUNTER & WIGHAM RICHARDSON LTD published by the company in 1953.

MEMOIRS OF WIGHAM RICHARDSON 1837 - 1908 published in 1911.

WALLSEND SLIPWAY & ENGINEERING CO. LTD. 1871 - 1929 published by the company.

POWER ON LAND & SEA - HISTORY OF HAWTHORN,LESLIE & CO. LTD by J.F. Clarke published by the company in 1977.

HISTORY OF R. & W. HAWTHORN by B.C. Browne published in 1914.

READHEADS 1865 - 1965 published by the company in 1966.

ARMSTRONG OF ELSWICK by Kenneth Warren published by Macmillan in 1989.

BIOGRAPHY OF W.G. ARMSTRONG by Peter McKenzie published by Longhirst Press in 1983.

FROM COLLIER TO BATTLESHIP, PALMERS OF JARROW 1852 - 1933 published in Durham in 1946.

AUSTIN & PICKERSGILL LTD, 150 YEARS published by the company in 1976.

WILLIAM DOXFORD & CO. LTD published by the company in 1921.

SHORT BROTHERS - MOWBRAY QUAY TO PALLION 1850 - 1950 published by the company.

SHIPBUILDERS OF THE HARTLEPOOLS by Bert Spaldin published by Hartlepool Borough Council in 1985.

SMITH'S DOCK by Ian Macdonald and Len Tabner published by Seaworks in 1988.

TYNE & WEAR AT WORK by Peter Hepplewhite published by Newcastle City Libraries and Tyne & Wear Archives.

TYNESIDE CUNARDERS by Roger Woodcock published by Newcastle City Libraries in 1990.

TYNESIDE SHIPBUILDING 1920 - 1960 by Peter Elson published by Newcastle City Libraries.

TYNE LINERS by Roger Woodcock published by Newcastle City Libraries.

TRANSACTIONS OF THE NORTH EAST COAST INSTITUTION OF ENGINERS & SHIPBUILDERS.

THE SHIPBUILDING INDUSTRY - A GUIDE TO HISTORICAL RECORDS edited by L.A. Ritchie published by Manchester University Press in 1992.

SHIPBUILDING IN BRITAIN by Leslie Jones published by University of Wales Press in 1957.

THE BRITISH SHIPBUILDING INDUSTRY 1870 - 1914 by S. Pollard & P.L. Robertson published in Cambridge,Mass. in 1979.

AT THE SHARP END by George H. Parker published by Brown, Son & Ferguson Ltd in 1992.